MW00444971

Simple Faith

How every person can experience intimacy with God

Eddie Snipes

A book by:
Exchanged Life Discipleship

Published by GES Book Publishing
Carollton, GA

Copyright © 2011 by Eddie Snipes, Exchanged Life
Discipleship, and GES Book Publishing

http://www.exchangedlife.com

ISBN: 978-0-9832247-3-0

Table of Contents

Introducing the Christian Journey

Get ready to blow it. No matter how hard you try, there will be times when you'll fall flat on your face. This book will challenge you with the call to live holy, but keep in mind – this is our goal. There will be times when you feel like you're on top of the world and untouchable by temptation. Then the next thing you know, you're asking yourself how you could be so foolish.

Jesus picked the least qualified men to become the apostles by which He laid the foundation of the church. God's entire plan rested on men who blew it. During the greatest need of Jesus' ministry, He took His strongest leaders to pray with Him, but they kept falling asleep. And then everyone abandoned Him and fled when Jesus was arrested. The odd thing is, Jesus foretold that they would all flee and leave Him alone. The Lord built His plan around men He knew would fail.

God took these imperfect and ill-equipped men and turned the world upside down. This is your life and God's calling for you. It's God's good pleasure to take you – the one who knows to do good but keeps doing what you know you shouldn't do, and fails to do what you should do – and places you into His perfect plan to do His perfect will. And then rewards you for what He does in your life.

What kind of a gospel message is this?

God does not expect perfection from you. He expects you to reflect His perfection – even when you're in the midst of your own failures. Because it isn't about you. It's about God. The power of the Lord is revealed when ill-equipped people submit themselves – failure and all, to Him. For when you are weak, He shows Himself strong on your behalf.

When you blow it, don't think God's anger seethes against you, but recognize your human weakness and His ability to lift you up beyond your limited capabilities. And this all centers around your relationship with Him. Your spiritual condition is not dependent upon your ability to be good, but your intimacy with Christ.

Becoming a good person is not the call of Christianity. Learning how to abide in fellowship with God is the call. And through the relationship, you become more like Christ and He transforms you, one day at a time, into the person He is making you to be. It isn't about your ability to be righteous, but your walk with God who is the author of faith and righteousness.

In this book, my goal is to do two things. Change the way you look at the Christian faith, and help you gain a deeper understanding of what it means to walk with God.

Most people approach Christianity as though they are trying to appease an angry God. The truth is that Christianity is God reaching out to us with the goal of restoring mankind to perfect fellowship with Him. Scripture focuses on showing us how we can conform our lives to an unchanging, eternal God who desires for us to experience perfect fellowship and inherit eternal promises.

We are called joint heirs with Christ. The kingdom is our inheritance. Not earned, but given to all who are sons and daughters of the Lord.

Christianity is so much more than just making sure of heaven. Many evangelistic methods present themselves as a ticket to heaven, or some type of fire insurance to escape hell. I once approached the gospel this way, but I've discovered these approaches miss the mark. Since Jesus said, "The greatest commandment is to love God," a relationship centered upon love should be the starting point of everything we do.

The Christian life is more than waiting for heaven. It's about the journey – your walk with God and fellowship with God's children. Without understanding what it means to walk by faith and experience living in the Spirit, we are shortchanging our lives and missing the great walk of intimacy the Lord has prepared for each believer.

Humans are complex creatures. Sometimes we have the tendency to turn simple tasks into complicated feats. When we expect something to be difficult, we often set out to find a complex solution. This can blind us to the simple things standing before us. Let me give an example.

Two guys dropped by a house to run a quick errand. When they returned to the car, the doors were locked. The driver, a friend of mine, had a bad habit of leaving his keys in the ignition, so they were locked out. They borrowed a coat hanger, shoved it through a crack in the window, and began digging for the door lock. The little boy next door watched with interest.

Minutes rolled by and frustration set in. Both guys took turns poking and prodding until one made a desperate suggestion. "We might as well just break the window." Not wanting to pay for a window, the driver took another try with the coat hanger.

To his surprise, the door popped open. Stunned, he stepped back. Two little feet emerged and there stood the neighbor's kid. "How did you get in there?" my friend asked. A few moments ago he was standing outside the car.

"The back door was unlocked," he said.

While they were digging on one side, the kid decided to try the doors, and found one open. It was a simple solution, but no one thought about trying the back doors.

Faith is often like this. People search for complicated formulas, rules, and lists of to-do's. But the truth is, faith is so simple, a child can understand. Look at **2 Corinthians 11:3**

But I fear, lest somehow, as the serpent deceived Eve by his craftiness, so your minds may be corrupted from the simplicity that is in Christ.

Did you catch the main point? Simplicity that is in Christ.

Years ago I discovered an amazing truth. The more I learned the scriptures, the more I discovered how simple God's truth really is. For most of my life, I approach the Bible as a mysterious book, filled with complicated theological laws. For many, this is how the Bible appears. Once I asked a group of men and women to explain what doctrine meant. The answers varied in their wording, but the most common consensus was something like: *Arguing about theology and complicated biblical philosophies.*

When I pressed for a definition of theology, the idea was professors and theologians disputing over words and meanings.

Nothing could be farther from the truth. This may be what our modern era has made theology and doctrine into, but as the Apostle

Paul stated above, the goal of scripture is to maintain the simplicity that is in Christ. The Bible only becomes complicated when we bring in outside influences, and lose sight of the intention of the word. In fact, the word 'doctrine' simply means, 'The teachings of scripture.'

The Bible is written on the sixth or seventh grade level. Few of the scholarly terms we see thrown around are actually in the scriptures. The Bible isn't complicated and is written for the benefit of all. God's intention is to communicate to you all things that pertain to your life and godliness. In the scriptures we first see the revelation of God to us, and then the reconciliation of our lives to Him. From this gift of the revelation of God's love, all things flow.

Jesus also affirmed the simplicity of the gospel when he said, "The greatest commandment is to love God with all your heart. The second command comes out of the first, to love your neighbor as yourself. On these two commandments hang all the law and the prophets."

Could it be any simpler than this? Through two commandments everything else is fulfilled. This book will begin with what it means to love, and then we'll examine the simple truths that guide our spiritual understanding-which springs from a loving relationship with our God.

Truly, the Christian life is simple to understand. The challenge is that we naturally want to make things complicated.

There is a story in the Old Testament about a ruler named Naaman who visited Israel because he heard a prophet could heal him. Elijah the prophet didn't do as Naaman expected. Instead of visiting the sick man and making a big show, he sent a messenger with a simple instruction, "Go and wash in the Jordan River."

Naaman stormed away in a fury. In essence, he complained that he expected the prophet to come and do something grand, do something ceremonial, and give him some great instruction. As he journeyed to his home country, a servant came to him and said, "If the prophet had asked you to do something great, would you not have done it? How much more should you obey when he says, 'Wash and be clean?'"

Naaman's response is typical human nature. The simplicity in Christ is just to wash and be clean, but we want to create a complicated system where we feel as though we are accomplishing something. Yet, like Naaman, we need to stop and realize the simplicity of truth, and take it to heart. When Naaman agreed to obey, his life changed. The same is true for the Christian life.

To walk in victory, there are only a few basic keys to understand – and none are complicated. As we move forward, keep one thing in mind. This book cannot change your life. In fact, no book can change your life. This book seeks to give you the tools so that you can apply yourself to the truth of scripture. The Bible says we must be doers of the word and not hearers only. Hearing (or reading) can give you the information, but it only profits those who are willing to apply themselves to the truths they learn. As the Lord said, "My ways are not your ways." The challenge of faith is to believe the simple truth of God, even when it contradicts our personal feelings or ideas of how things should be.

Each step into faith reveals the truth of God's plan and reveals the next nugget of truth that had once been out of view. The word is called a lamp unto our feet. A lamp gives enough light to see the next step. Though we are told where the path is leading, we are also stepping out of the comfort zone of human nature and into the uncharted territory of walking in the Spirit.

Even if we know and believe the Bible, it isn't faith until we step onto the path of belief. Without stepping out, knowledge doesn't benefit us and we cannot move forward. Understanding truth is only profitable when we believe to the point of faith.

With that in mind, let us explore the life giving truth – the simplicity of the faith.

Simple Love

For God so loved the world that he gave[1]...if God so loved us, we ought to love one another.[2]

We have already looked at how Jesus explained that God's commandments are fulfilled in love. It's not the other way around. Love fulfills the law, but the law cannot produce love. We'll look at how the law is fulfilled through Christ in another chapter. This chapter will explain the love of God since it is the foundation everything is built upon. The Bible says that if we gave everything we possess to the poor and even if we give our own bodies as a burnt offering, without love it means nothing, and profits nothing.[3]

The Bible uses this extreme example to show Israel that the process of fulfilling the law cannot win God's favor. In the Old Testament, God established a Law of Atonement where an animal would be sacrificed in their place as an offering for sin. This atonement was not what fulfilled the law of righteousness. Not only that, if they went beyond the law and offered themselves in sacrifice to God, it still would not be sufficient.

To understand the love of God we must first realize how it compares to human love. The New Testament scriptures were written in Greek. The Greek language has three words we translate into the word love.

Philia is a brotherly kindness type of love. It means to love with warm affection or friendship.

Eros means passion and is often referred to as a sexual type of love. The Bible never uses Eros as a word for love, but the Greeks used this word in much the way we hear it used today. People associate physical passion with love.

The last word is **Agape**. Agape is self-giving, self-sacrificing, outward focused love. It is the type of love that focuses on another

---

[1] John 3:16
[2] 1 John 4:10-11
[3] 1 Corinthians 13:3

without regard to self. The love of God is always referred to as Agape.

Philia and Eros are normal parts of human nature, but Agape is not. When I love another in my own human nature, it is always in light of how my life is fulfilled. I may give because it makes me feel good to sacrifice, or I may love my friends of whom I expect a returned friendship. Ultimately, I am seeking my own fulfillment through my love for others. While that isn't necessarily wrong, it falls short of Agape.

Agape is the love of God. It is first given to us, and then we use it to express the love of God to others. Consider **Romans 5:5**

Now hope does not disappoint, because the *love of God has been poured out in our hearts by the Holy Spirit* who was given to us. (Emphasis added)

This is why Jesus said the first commandment is the love of God and the second commandment comes out of the first. We must first experience the love of God and then we'll have the power to love others because the Holy Spirit has placed God's Agape love into our hearts.

To put human love into perspective, consider a rich young ruler who approached Jesus to ask how he could obtain eternal life. He begins with the wrong perspective and Jesus lets him know immediately. The man starts by calling Jesus a good rabbi (or as some translations word it, Good Teacher). Jesus responds by rebuking him for calling anyone good except for God.

In the religious culture of that day, people often put their Rabbis on a pedestal, and even called themselves after their teacher's name. Jesus taught his disciples to not allow anyone to call them rabbi, father, teacher, or master. The reason is the same as Jesus explained to the ruler in this account – with only one exception - Himself. In this account, Jesus told the ruler not to look to him as a good rabbi, but to put his focus on God. When instructing His disciples, Jesus commanded them *not* to allow others to call them rabbi, and then he pointed to Himself as the only example of a rabbi or teacher.[4]

Jesus rebuked the young man for calling Him good, but then called Himself good when teaching about His own authority. Why the contradiction?

There is no contradiction. In both cases, Jesus is taking the focus off the flesh and pointing toward the spiritual. The young ruler wasn't looking at Jesus as the Messiah, but as a human rabbi. He was not to be imitating the role of a teacher, but imitating God alone. Take a few minutes to read the story of the rich ruler in Matthew 19:16-26. From the beginning, the ruler was focused on his own human efforts. Whether looking at a teacher or at the rules of religion, the young man was focused solely on human abilities. His trust was also in his own ability to keep the law. As Jesus listed the commandments, the man declared his ability to keep them as though it were a checklist. Then Jesus gave the final test, "You shall love your neighbor as yourself."

The young ruler said, "I have kept all these commandments from my youth up." It's interesting that this man declared his own perfection, yet deep down he knew something was missing. The man was blind to his own inability to fulfill the requirements of the law. Therefore, Jesus pulled back the veil by saying, "If you will be perfect, go and sell all you have, give to the poor, and then come and follow me."

Notice, even with this statement, Jesus was not declaring that giving up all his worldly goods would save him. The real solution was in following Christ, for as we shall see, salvation is found in Jesus alone. Yet, his requirement unveiled the problem. The man was not able to keep the law. If he truly loved his neighbor as himself, he would not have balked at giving his possessions to the poor. The requirement Jesus gave was intended to reveal the man's inability to keep the commandments he claimed to have fulfilled.

Jesus met many rich men during his life, yet this is the only time we see Him asking someone to sell all their possessions. The truth is, money was this man's god and his own works were his plan

---

[4] Matthew 23:8

of salvation. Jesus dismantled his personal religion with one statement.

The same is true for you and me. If you are trying to love God by your own strength, you are the rich young ruler who comes to Christ wondering why you feel like you've done all the right things, yet something is still missing. Like the rich young ruler, God calls us to lay down our own efforts so we can receive the true riches- salvation and the love of God.

God so loved.

Look at a passage most people are familiar with, **John 3:16** "For God so loved the world that He gave His only begotten Son, that whoever believes in Him should not perish but have everlasting life.

Stop for a moment and think upon the first part of this passage, "God so loved...that He gave." This is what agape is all about. This is spelled out for us in **Romans 5:7-8**
7 For scarcely for a righteous man will one die; yet perhaps for a good man someone would even dare to die.
8 But God demonstrates His own love toward us, in that while we were still sinners, Christ died for us.

A good man is not a sinner. To sin is to commit a violation against another. Would we die for those who violate us? It's not likely.

Who would die for their friend? Most of us would like to think we would, but it's not until someone is in a life or death situation that they discover the answer to this question. Several years back I went through a layoff at work. Each person was called into a room and told their fate. I remember the mixed feelings I had when I walked out of the meeting. I had survived, but several of my peers did not.

Though it hurt to see their lives shaken, there was also a sense of relief knowing my financial life would remain unscathed. This example shows our human limitations. Though there are times when we might be willing to sacrifice ourselves for the good of those we think deserve it, in everyday life we rarely are willing to sacrifice for our peers, and even less likely for those we feel are less deserving.

Our human nature doesn't fully grasp the concept of sacrificing everything for someone who deserves punishment. The heroes of our movies don't sacrifice their lives to rescue the enemy they are trying to stop. Yet, this is what it means to be a sinner. The Bible says that before someone is redeemed, they are at enmity with God. The word enmity means to show hostility toward someone out of hatred. It's a declaration of war by our actions, against another person. Yet the picture is that while our actions were a direct affront against God, He loved us enough to sacrifice on our behalf – and to do so while we were still showing hostility toward Him and His word.

This is the picture of love / agape. It is a self-giving love that sacrifices for the good of someone completely hostile toward God. While God is demonstrating love, our sinful human nature is casting that love aside to pursue the sins that are an affront to God's own nature. Yet while we were in this state of rebellion, God demonstrated more love by bearing the penalty of our sins and then calling us out of rebellion and into fellowship with Him.

Most of us don't like to think of ourselves as hostile toward God, so let's put this into perspective. What happens when someone tries to tell us what to do? The natural reaction is to resent it. Have you ever had someone try to impose their will upon you when you didn't believe they had the right to do so? It brings up feelings of hostility. People react differently outwardly, but inward, we all have similar feelings.

I had a friend who worked for a large corporation. A new VP took over his group and paid a surprise visit. When the stranger walked in and started barking orders, several members of his group rebelled at the idea. Someone asked, "Who does this guy think he is?" In their ignorance, they rebelled against authority. Once they realized he was a high ranking VP over their group, their attitudes made a quick turnaround.

Through our ignorance, we have all also rebelled against God. When God reveals Himself to us, we then either repent and receive His favor, or continue in rebellion and choose consequences over mercy. In a later chapter, we'll look at this in more detail, but first let's explore the love of God given to us.

The Treasure of God's Love.

The Bible says that we love God because he first loved us[5]. In fact, according to Romans, it's the goodness of God that leads us to repentance. This is contrary to most people's idea of repentance. Sometimes people have to see the futility of this temporary life before they can see the joy of eternal life, but ultimately, it's God's love that draws each person near.

It's time to recognize the goodness of God. Why do people stray? Often times it's the false belief that something better is out there somewhere. Everyday life testifies to this. We've all heard the saying, "The grass always looks greener on the other side of the fence." When we get on the other side, we find the benefits we expected aren't there. We must recognize that God desires what is good for us. Only then will we understand the value of trusting Him. The Lord understands our human perspective and gave us His promise to look out for our good. Consider this passage from **Jeremiah 29:11**

For I know the thoughts that I think toward you, says the LORD, thoughts of peace and not of evil, to give you a future and a hope.

This passage was given to Israel before they were taken captive by Babylon when the Lord's people chose to follow other gods instead of Him. When they chose to follow pagan gods, the Lord allowed the pagan nations to rule over His people. Even in the midst of their judgment, God made it clear that His thoughts were for their prosperity and good. The Old Testament is written in

---

[5] 1 John 4:19

Hebrew, and the original Hebrew word means, thoughts, plans, or purpose. God's plan is to bless and pour His love into their lives, and the same is true for any who will trust Him today. Look at the wonderful promises of **Psalm 36:7-9**

7 How precious *is* Your loving kindness, O God! Therefore the children of men put their trust under the shadow of Your wings.

8 They are abundantly satisfied with the fullness of Your house, And You give them drink from the river of Your pleasures.

9 For with You *is* the fountain of life; In Your light we see light.

Follow the flow of thought in this amazing passage. It begins with trust. Those who trust God draw near and rest under the shadow of His wings. The picture is a mother hen protecting her brood. Jesus used this illustration when He wept over Jerusalem and cried, "How often I desired to gather you as a hen gathers her brood, but you would not come." God still gives the same cry over his people today. It is His desire to gather us near Him, show us what it means to have true intimacy with God, and give us the plans He intends for us. But this is only found under the shadow of His wings – and only those who trust Him will come.

Look at the promise given to those who will come. They are abundantly satisfied with the fullness of His house. What does it mean to be abundantly satisfied? The picture is to overflow with abundance. It's to have more than enough to satisfy our hearts. Does God want you to be deprived? No. God wants you to drink from His river of pleasures. His river is a fountain of life. The love of God reveals His plan to abundantly satisfy our lives, but it requires trust, and answering His call to come.

The world has a river, but it's polluted with corruption and sin. It seems good, but only because we have never tasted the fresh waters of God's river. Proverbs 10:22 says that the blessing of the Lord adds no sorrow with it. The same cannot be said for sin. On one side, we are trusting in our own actions to satisfy our desires. On the other side, God is calling us to leave our ways behind, trust Him, receive his love, and experience what it means to have fullness of joy. Until you believe the promise, you won't trust God enough to leave the world behind.

The first step is to see the love of God, then receive that love. Once the love of God is poured out in our hearts, we will then have the power to love others. I cannot love the people I'm convinced don't deserve it. Or perhaps the better way of putting it is that I can't love those I feel deserve judgment. Yet, this is exactly what God commands me to do.

The Bible doesn't command us to love with philia (friendship) love. This is because we naturally love those who return our love. I always feel love toward my friends. God doesn't need to command us to love with eros, or affection. Think about marriage. When my spouse is affectionate, I don't need to be commanded to return that affection.

The Bible repeatedly commands us to love with agape love. Since God has poured His agape love into our hearts by the Holy Spirit, He has also empowered us to show that same love to others. By nature, agape is to love those who don't deserve it. I am commanded to take the love God has given me, and pass it on to others. I'm called to take God's undeserved love toward me, and love others without measuring their worthiness to be loved.

This is why Jesus said the second command comes from the first. I love God by establishing myself in the love He has given me (remember, we love God because he first loved us), and then I am loving my neighbor with the same love God has given me. In my human nature I cannot love my neighbor as myself. I will never take food off my table and feed a stranger while I starve. In truth, my natural reaction is to hoard extra while my neighbor is in need.

Like the rich young ruler, I cannot philia love my neighbor as myself because human nature lacks that capacity. I can, however, agape love my neighbor as myself. Philia love is natural to man and is given in response to what has been received or expected to be received. Agape love comes from the Holy Spirit within us and is not dependent upon our needs or self-centered desires.

Because of God's love shown to me, I can take my underserved agape – given to me by the Spirit – and give it to my neighbor without measuring their worthiness. To understand this fully, take a look at **1 Corinthians 13:4-7**

> 4 Love suffers long *and* is kind; love does not envy; love does not parade itself, is not puffed up;
> 5 does not behave rudely, does not seek its own, is not provoked, thinks no evil;
> 6 does not rejoice in iniquity, but rejoices in the truth;
> 7 bears all things, believes all things, hopes all things, endures all things.

When the love of God is poured out in our hearts, it flows outward. Our self-will is the only thing that stands between the love of God in us and the love of God shown to others. When I'm acting according to selfish human nature, I see the need of others and the Spirit within me calls me to reach out. When I'm acting selfishly, I may resist the call of God and withhold love. Anger, disappointment, and other human emotions can rise up and tempt us to withhold God's love. When we submit to human nature and resist the love of God, we are acting in the flesh and pushing against the love of God.

We all do this from time to time, but as we mature in the faith, we begin recognizing the value of allowing God to reign freely and discover a world of agape love that flows through us and toward others. Often we mistake philia love as agape, but it is not. Agape calls us to love even when we don't feel like it. When it flows unhindered, the Spirit within us becomes a fountain of life. When agape love is hindered, life begins to stagnate.

Consider the attributes of agape love:
Agape / Love is patient
Does not envy
Does not lift itself up
Isn't puffed up – or selfish
Isn't rude
Isn't self-seeking

Is not provoked
Doesn't think evil
Endures all things
Hopes in all things

With these things in mind, we can identify the source of our love. If I require something in return before I can love, it isn't agape. If I must be praised in order to stay motivated to show love, it isn't agape. If being provoked or wronged causes me to cut off my love, it isn't agape. Agape keeps giving without expectation – other than the hope of God being glorified through the love He has given me.

When we are provoked, human nature attempts to arise and take over our hearts. However, when we understand the command of God to love without condition, I can choose to resist human nature and submit to the love of God. It is not me producing agape. It is me submitting myself to God's agape love so the Spirit flows outward from my life to others.

This is why understanding love is easy; but keeping the command to love is difficult. If it came natural, it wouldn't require a command. Loving the loveable is easy; therefore we are not commanded to love with philia love. Loving with agape is difficult. By its nature, agape is not self-seeking; therefore, we must abide in the love of God and not allow our human nature to rule our hearts. As we move forward we'll discuss how to put these things into practice. For now, we must understand that we keep ourselves in God's love so we can remain empowered to love others. Consider this passage from **Jude 1:20-21**

20 But you, beloved, building yourselves up on your most holy faith, praying in the Holy Spirit,
21 keep yourselves in the love of God, looking for the mercy of our Lord Jesus Christ unto eternal life.

The next chapter will discuss faith in detail, but keep this passage in mind. As we build our lives upon our faith, we keep ourselves in the love of God and by this, we are able to love each other. Faith is important in this discussion. When I trust God, I believe in the command to love my neighbor. Though living out the love of God may cost me, I also have the assurance that God will fulfill His promise, and I will be abundantly satisfied in Him.

I am not looking to people as my source of fulfillment. God alone holds this role. I love because I am first loved, then because I have been commanded. I keep myself in his love knowing God will more than make up for anything I sacrifice. I can't out love God. Nor can I sacrifice more than God will give. If I truly believe God, I can love when I don't feel appreciated and give to those who are unworthy – just as God also gave to me when I was unworthy.

Love Your Enemies

There was a man who was very rich. His house was filled with luxury and he wanted for nothing. At least nothing in the material sense. The heart of this man was empty, thus he began a quest for fulfillment. Before we look at his journey, let's look at how he became wealthy.

The lucrative career he chose was collecting taxes. When we think of taxes, we all have negative feelings. In his era, tax collectors were the lowest form of human existence. He worked for the Roman government. When Rome conquered a nation, they allowed the people a few unique freedoms. They were allowed to keep their culture, language, and rulers. However, Rome also set up their own rulers who held a higher position of authority. They also required every citizen to be bilingual and learn a simplified version of Greek. Each nation would also be put under tribute. In other words, they had to pay taxes to Rome.

As long as rulers behaved under the Roman governors, people learned the national language, and taxes were paid, subcultures were acceptable in this form of government. This method of compromise helped maintain stability in one of the world's longest lasting empires.

It's not hard to imagine that paying taxes to a foreign government wasn't a popular idea. I say foreign because Rome wasn't native to their culture. To simplify tax collecting, Rome would hire locals to collect the tribute money. A local understood the town's economy and knew who had money, and had a good idea of how much.

A tax collector had the backing of the Roman government, so resisters could be arrested or have their property seized. Rome also turned a blind eye to the amount of money collected. Collectors only had to meet their quotas. Anything collected above this amount was bonus money for the collector. In the eyes of the community, tax collectors were legalized thieves.

This rich man was despised by his neighbors. He was a traitor because he joined with the oppressive government against his own people. He was a thief because he raised extra taxes against his neighbors so he could pad his own pockets. When the townspeople refused to pay the inflated tax prices, the soldiers came in to take it by force. When a man complained that his taxes were higher than he knew Rome required, the soldiers showed no concern. The commander had no interest in even making sure the money collected made it to the government.

"That's on him. Tax collectors know the amount due. I'm a soldier, not an auditor," would have been his answer to the locals.

The commander knew it was a rip off, but did not care. This created hatred against this tax collector, and all others like him. In fact, all tax collectors were like him. The free money is what lured these worthless and greedy fellows into this despicable profession.

This man grew wealthy beyond his wildest dreams. He had the biggest house, best food, servants, and great possessions. Though his financial goals were coming to pass, he felt empty. Having all this wealth didn't fill the void of loss of friendships and self-respect. One day he heard about Jesus coming to town. Hope rose in his heart and he sought the one people claimed to be a Savior.

The town's people pushed him away and kept him far back from the one he wanted to see. At this point, many will recognize the story. He saw where Jesus was walking, ran ahead, and climbed a tree where he could see Jesus and get his attention. The man's name was Zacchaeus.

Jesus called him down, came to his house, and Zacchaeus gladly gave up his wealth for the new life Jesus offered. He gave the substance of his house to repay those he robbed with the sword of the Romans.

The Apostle Matthew was in the exact same position. He was probably a miserable man, sitting among the money he collected at the receipt of customs. Jesus walked by and said, "Matthew, come and follow Me." Matthew left his position and it's wealth behind without a second thought, followed Jesus, and became an apostle and the author of the Gospel of Matthew.

At this point you may be wondering what this has to do with loving your enemies. It has a lot to do with it. Jesus used tax collectors as an example of loving your enemies. In our culture, we read this and it doesn't evoke the same feelings as it did to the culture of His day. A tax collector was the most despised group of people in the Jewish culture. They were manipulators, thieves, traitors, and bullies. They had the power to accuse their enemies of crimes, and bring the judgment of the government upon the people.

Everyone feared and hated tax collectors. It was the profession of ill repute. No one was considered more corrupt and more worthless as a human being than a collector in that era. They were the enemy. Jesus even used them as illustrations in many of His teachings.

Now let's look at what it means to love our enemies. Loving those who hate us and cause harm, goes against everything engrained into our nature. Yet this is exactly what Jesus commands. It's perhaps one of the most difficult parts of the Christian life because it goes against everything our human nature is founded upon. Humanly speaking, it's not possible to love someone who is actively trying to harm us. Love in the Christian life is not based upon human love or our abilities at all.

Keep in mind, the love of God is poured out into our hearts by the Holy Spirit once we receive Christ. God is not asking you to give your love to those who don't deserve it. God is asking you to take the love He has poured into your heart, and give His love to those around you. This applies to friends, neighbors, family, and even enemies. This love is what reflects true Christianity to the world around us. Until we have the opportunity to love those who show hate, little distinguishes us from the world. Look at **Matthew 5:44-48**

> ⁴⁴ "But I say to you, love your enemies, bless those who curse you, do good to those who hate you, and pray for those who spitefully use you and persecute you,
> ⁴⁵ "that you may be sons of your Father in heaven; for He makes His sun rise on the evil and on the good, and sends rain on the just and on the unjust.
> ⁴⁶ "For if you love those who love you, what reward have you? Do not even the tax collectors do the same?
> ⁴⁷ "And if you greet your brethren only, what do you do more *than others?* Do not even the tax collectors do so?
> ⁴⁸ "Therefore you shall be perfect, just as your Father in heaven is perfect.

It's hard to look at this and not scratch our heads and say, "How?" During our casual reading this may not seem that difficult, but let the opportunity come to put it into practice, and you'll see how hard it is to love.

If someone gets in our face, yelling and screaming curses, it's not our natural reaction to say, "I bless you." There are people in this world filled with hatred and destructive behaviors. Some people are just mean. They think nothing of harming another – whether it be by words or actions.

What if someone uses us? There are those who manipulate others by preying upon their trust, only to use them for personal gain. Swindlers think nothing of leaving families destitute while they make off with their money. They will even use Christianity as a means to personal gain, building trust only to create an opportunity to prey on others.

Do we bless them? Can we bless? It isn't our natural reaction. Yet Jesus made it clear that unless we are able to practice this type of love, we are no different than those we consider to be ungodly among us. The Bible requires a hard thing. "Bless and do not curse."[6] This is only possible when we are abiding in the love of God. Both the command and the promise is found in **Proverbs 25:21-22**

> [21] If your enemy is hungry, give him bread to eat; And if he is thirsty, give him water to drink;
> [22] For *so* you will heap coals of fire on his head, And the LORD will reward you.

The opposite is also true. We are commanded not to seek revenge, for vengeance belongs to the Lord alone.[7] When we take vengeance into our own hands, we put ourselves in God's place. Our enemy escapes consequences from God and we bring that upon ourselves for our disobedience. However, if we do good, pray *for* (not against) those who harm us, the Lord rewards us and then takes action on our enemies.

His first goal is mercy, just as the Lord showed us mercy while we were enemies of God. How God chooses to deal with those who wrong us is not our concern. In fact, when we rejoice over our enemies in their struggles, it displeases God and according to the Bible, His wrath is turned away from our enemies[8].

The reward is not in seeing someone suffer, but in the blessings of the Lord. If we obey, the Lord rewards us and instead of increased bitterness, we find freedom.

By nature, you cannot love those who hate you, but when you abide in the agape love of God, you will find the power to love those who seek your harm, and you will be rewarded with God's blessing when you show love to others, whether they be enemies or friends. This is simple to understand, but difficult to live out. Often we must pray for strength. When you pray for enemies, you will find a love you didn't know existed.

Let me reiterate this principle again. Abide in the love of God. The Lord's love (agape) is outward focused. That means it is seeking a way out of our hearts and into the lives of those around us.

---

[6] Romans 12:14
[7] Deuteronomy 32:35, Romans 12:19 and Hebrews 10:30
[8] Proverbs 24:17-18

Resisting the outward expression of God's love through us creates a calloused heart. However, to surrender to the love that transformed our heart will become a wellspring of life to us as it passes God's life changing love to others.

Either way, our life will be affected by God's love. A resistant heart becomes calloused and bitter, cutting off God's love through us and preventing us from experiencing this life giving power. However, when we allow it to flow, our lives will be constantly transformed.

I've never met a bitter person that had life. I've also never met a loving person that lacked life. Love creates life. Life is fulfilled in us as agape reaches outward to others.

Simple Faith

The Apostle Paul wrote to the Corinthian church and expressed his fear that they might be drifting away from the simplicity of their faith in Christ. The same threat faces you, your church, and every Christian on a daily basis. If we allow human philosophy to muddy the waters of truth, nothing will be clear.

I once had a discussion with someone about faith. In our talk, it was stated that faith was too complicated to understand. Books on theology and Christian philosophy clouded the issue and made things seem too hard to grasp by anyone other than learned scholars. Once again, I pointed back to the simplicity of the gospel. The Bible says, "Abraham believed God, and his faith was accounted to him for righteousness."

Faith = believing God.

Could it be any simpler than this? What was the evidence that Abraham believed God? When God commanded, Abraham believed the promise and then obeyed the command. I can't say, "I believe God," and then act in disobedience. If I truly believe, my life will show it. Disobedience is rooted in unbelief, but obedience is born from faith. Let's look at an example.

Look back in history to the time of Jacob and Esau in the Old Testament. Esau was the firstborn son. In that culture, the firstborn received a double portion of the family inheritance and received the family blessing. What's more, these were descendants of Abraham; therefore, the one who held the birthright was rightfully the carrier of the promise that would ultimately be fulfilled in Christ. As we read through the New Testament, we see that God's promise to Abraham that all nations would be blessed through his descendants was the promise of our redeemer – Jesus Christ.

Esau despised his birthright and willingly forfeited his right to the promise by trading it to Jacob for a pot of stew. He considered satisfying the cravings of his flesh as more valuable than the promise of God. For this reason, he sold his birthright to Jacob for food. When he rejected the promise given through his birthright as the firstborn son, God rejected Esau from the future blessing that carried the promises of God.

In the course of time, Jacob's mother came up with a plan to obtain the blessing for her son. Jacob and Esau's father was the son of Abraham, and God established him as a prophet. His blessing was the promise of God. Isaac planned to bless his firstborn, Esau. Knowing the end of his life was near, Isaac called Esau and sent him into the field to hunt for venison. He loved the venison stew Esau made, so the plan was to have a nice meal and then bless his son.

When Jacob's mother heard the command, she prepared the stew for Isaac while Esau was gone, and sent Jacob into the room to be blessed. Isaac was nearly blind, so he was deceived into believing he was blessing Esau. When Esau returned, he discovered what Jacob had done, and made plans to murder Jacob. To avoid being killed by his brother, Jacob fled the country to live with a relative.

All this background has little direct application to faith, but it sets the stage for one of the best examples of faith in the Bible. God shaped Jacob's life for twenty years, and then sent him back home knowing he would have to face his brother. Just before Jacob encountered his brother, God changed his name from Jacob to Israel.

As is often the case in the Old Testament, God embeds the gospel into the events of scripture. Jacob had once looked for blessings in the efforts of his own hands. He took what he wanted and hoped he could get enough. He supplanted – or chased after things, trying to take what he wanted. Life was fleeting away, and Jacob struggled to fulfill a desire that could not be fulfilled outside of God.

Previously, Jacob's goal had been to get what he wanted and life was nothing more than grappling for things he hoped would make him happy. Then the time came when God redeemed him out of his old life, and gave him the promise. No longer was he called Jacob – which means 'the supplanter', but now he was called Israel – which means 'God prevails'. No longer was he dependent upon his own efforts to find fulfillment, but now he would trust in God, who would prevail and cause him to inherit all that had been promised through is forefather, Abraham.

This is a picture of prevailing through the Christian life. Before coming to Christ, we grapple for satisfaction, and the only fulfillment we find is in what we take by the heel and claim for our own. As satisfaction eludes us, we keep wrestling against God and man, looking for the things we think will make us happy. History proves that the one who possesses the most is rarely happy or satisfied, yet because it's the only way we know, we pursue life just as the rest of the world does. Then the Lord calls us out of that lifestyle, gives us His name, and we become inheritors of the promise.

Now, we too live by the promise that God prevails. Many Christians don't understand this and still grapple for the world, but the truth is, the promise is ours and all we must do is trust in our God who prevails, and go where He leads.

When the nation of Israel turned from the promise and lived like supplanters, God always referred to them as 'the house of Jacob'. Yet when blessing them or revealing the promise, God called the nation, 'the house of Israel.' We, like Israel, either walk in the failing world system and live like those pursuing something that can't be obtained in the flesh, or we live like conquerors and walk in the promise of 'God prevails.' To walk in the promise, we have to step out of human nature and into faith.

This is the trial Jacob / Israel faced. God visited Jacob while he lived with his uncle and commanded him to go back to his homeland – the very place where his brother waited to take vengeance upon him. God said for him to return, and the Lord would be with him, bless him, and make him a great nation. It's the call of faith. Go, and God will bless. Step out in faith, and trust in the promise.

Jacob arose, gathered his family and possessions together, and headed toward home. Not knowing how his brother would respond, Jacob sent a messenger ahead of him to greet his brother. The messenger returned and said, "Your brother gathered together four-hundred men and is coming this way toward you."

That wasn't a good thing to hear. Shouldn't God have given him a sign of peace? No one arms four-hundred men and rushes to meet someone just to say, 'hello'. Clearly, war was in Esau's heart. Jacob had no army, no defense, and no plan of escape. The normal human reaction would be to turn around and run. No one would blame him if he did. This was the moment of truth.

The command of God was, "Go back to your home," which was the Promised Land God gave to Abraham. The promise was, "I will be with you to bless and prosper you." Circumstances seemed to testify against God's promise, but Jacob chose to believe God over his human instinct.

Let me stop for a moment and point out an important truth. Fear and doubt aren't necessarily a lack of faith. It's often said that faith and fear can't coexist, but this is not true. People are made to feel guilty because they feel fear when in danger or facing a circumstance that seems impossible. The truth is that faith is of the Spirit, and fear is of the flesh. The Bible tells us that the flesh and the Spirit of God are at war against each other. We'll explore this in greater detail later on, but keep this truth in mind. Jacob didn't pretend his fear did not exist. Nor did he try to muster up a false faith. He acknowledged his fear before God and prayed for the Lord to guide him.

Jacob divided his family into two groups so one could escape if the other was attacked, and then stopped and took in the dire situation that surrounded him. He had obeyed God, and instead of protection, he was now helpless as an army rushed toward him. He then approached God with a request, and a declaration of obedience. Look at **Genesis 32:9-12**

> 9 Then Jacob said, "O God of my father Abraham and God of my father Isaac, the LORD who said to me, 'Return to your country and to your family, and I will deal well with you':
> 10 "I am not worthy of the least of all the mercies and of all the truth which You have shown Your servant; for I crossed over this Jordan with my staff, and now I have become two companies.

11 "Deliver me, I pray, from the hand of my brother, from the hand of Esau; for I fear him, lest he come and attack me *and* the mother with the children.

12 "For You said, 'I will surely treat you well, and make your descendants as the sand of the sea, which cannot be numbered for multitude.' "

What a wonderful example of prayer founded upon faith! The two companies were his wives and children. They were divided so they could not be attacked together.

Notice, he didn't deny his fears, he confessed them. He didn't bargain with God, he testified that he was acting in obedience. He didn't say, "I obeyed; therefore, you owe me." No, Jacob acknowledged that he was not worthy of any of God's mercies. And then he claimed the promise that God gave him. God wants us to trust in His promises. And live by them.

Jacob did not put himself into this position, God did. It was to test Jacob's faith so he would choose to either trust in God, or turn back to the perceived safety of the old life outside of God's will.

It's equally important that we understand the difference between acting in faith, and tempting God. The Bible forbids us to tempt God – or put God to the test. To put God to the test is to take it upon ourselves to put our lives or safety in a position where God must intervene to save us. God has the right to put Himself to the test so we must choose to trust His word or our fears, but we have no right to manipulate God by our will.

When the word commands us to obey and we must face persecution or suffering in order to obey, that is an act of faith. When we decide to place ourselves into harm's way, that's an act of the flesh. I can't jump in front of a bus and pray, God save me. I can't overspend and then give the last of my money to charity and say that God has to miraculously pay my bills. I've even seen people provoke persecution and then wonder why God allowed them to suffer. There is reward in obedience, but not in foolishness masquerading as faith.

In Jacob's case, he crossed the river separating himself from his brother. He was afraid and was in fear for his life, but his prayer was, "You commanded me to do it. I'm afraid. I know I'm unworthy of your deliverance, but I stand upon your promises."

Then a crazy idea struck Jacob. He made several bands of goats and sheep, then sent them in droves toward his brother. Messengers were sent with each band to tell Esau that these were a present from his servant Jacob.

In my mind's eye, I picture Esau scoffing at the idea. "Does he think a worthless flock of sheep is going to stop my revenge?" Then he encountered another. And another. And another. At some point, Esau probably shook his head at the absurdity, and eventually it struck him as funny. By the time he reached Esau, his anger had been pushed aside and he could do nothing but greet his brother and ask about the droves of sheep he kept passing.

The method God uses isn't relevant. What is relevant is God's faithfulness. He commands our obedience, and then puts us into a position to either believe his promises, or believe our fears. Sometimes Esau comes into our lives as a sinful desire for what opposes God, or as a fear that calls us to flee from God. Neither are sin unless we choose them over believing God. Faith isn't the absence of fear and doubt – faith overcomes fear and doubt. Faith is how we overcome. Look at **1 John 5:**

> 4 For whatever is born of God overcomes the world. And
> this is the victory that has overcome the world -- our faith.

Faith can't be overcome; but it can be neglected. Even in fear, we have the power to believe God. We also have the power to disbelieve God and put our trust in fear.

There will be times when God will put you to the test, for it proves whether you are trusting in Him, or yourself, circumstances, or feelings.

Faith is not complicated, but it is something our lives must be built upon. There are many misconceptions of faith, so in the next chapter, we'll dig deeper into what the Bible teaches about faith and how it applies to our individual lives.

Simple Faith

What is Faith?

Faith isn't a mystical force. As we have seen, faith is believing God and that belief causes us to act in obedience. Faith isn't a substance as some claim by misunderstanding how the Greek is translated. Let's take a moment and look at a passage that is often misunderstood, but is very important in understanding faith. Look at **Hebrews 11:**

1 Now faith is the substance of things hoped for, the evidence of things not seen.

The King James and the New King James Versions use the word 'substance' in this passage. I'm going to use a little Greek here, but don't let it turn you off. Knowing how words are translated can bring life to passages of the Bible. In Hebrews 11, the Greek word is 'hupostasis', which means: to put under, substructure, foundation, steadfastness of mind, confidence, firm trust, assurance, something of substance, or a real being.

While all these words can be used in translation, it should be self-evident that the context in which a word is used must be consistent with how we define the meaning of the word itself. When translating, don't think of these as multiple choices where we just pick one which suits our fancy. Rather we need to understand that the translation is based on a definition. The Greek word is an idea, and the translator must choose an English equivalent which best conveys that idea into words, and do so while being consistent with what was being communicated in the original Greek.

Even if you don't know Greek, you can get an understanding of what the word means by looking at all its possible English translations. Taken together, we can understand what is meant by substance by looking at the overall definition of hupostasis. Substance in this instance does not mean that faith has physical properties, but that it has 'real substance' in what it assures us of.

When someone makes empty promises, we say that their words have no substance. In other words, there is little assurance someone will fulfill their word if their promises were empty in the past. The opposite also is true. If someone is reliable and keeps their promises, we say their word has substance. This also applies to how hupostasis is translated in the above passage.

The Greek word 'hupostasis' is used four other times in the New Testament. Three times it means to boast or have strong confidence, and one refers to the real being of the person of Christ. The English word 'substance' is used two other times in the New Testament. Both are in Luke and both are Greek words that mean possessions or wealth. These examples are physical items, but is not the word 'hupostasis' as used in Hebrews 11:1.

Clearly this passage in Hebrews is referring to faith as being our firm assurance of things hoped for. As was the case in Jacob's life, by faith, we also can have the confidence to hope for what we cannot see, knowing God will stand true to his word even if circumstances seem to indicate otherwise. Only by a firm assurance in God's word can we have hope in the midst of trials and testing.

Building upon faith

Let's take a moment to dispel another misconception of faith. Mark Twain made the following quote famous, "Faith is believing something you know isn't true."

Any Christian would refute this statement; however, many live as though this is their mission in life. They try to make themselves believe, and when doubts creep in, they try to overcome doubt by attempting to muster up more faith. It's purely a human effort – and it's destined to fail. Best case scenario, human faith is unfruitful. Worse case, people give up on believing. They give up because faith has failed them and they get tired of pretending. Manmade faith is often nothing more than self-deception.

Many years ago, my wife began a relationship with a woman who seemed very religious. As with most Christians, my wife had unanswered questions that nagged at her. She confided some of her struggles with her friend and was summarily rejected. The woman she believed to be her friend sent a scathing letter to her saying, "You have a disease called doubt. As with other diseases, doubt can be spread. I can't be friends with you or maintain contact with you because I don't want to catch your disease of doubt and corrupt my faith."

The absurdity of this lady's reaction left me stunned. While the Bible tells us to bear up those who are weak in faith, the human-based faith can only survive in a vacuum, and therefore cannot bear up anyone, for it is dependent upon mankind.

The great irony is that many people are shields to their faith rather than being shielded by faith. The Bible says that faith is the shield that protects the Christian from attack; therefore, if our faith needs to be protected rather than being our protection, it is not a true biblical faith.

The woman who feared doubt did not have true faith. Like so many others, her faith only survives as long as she can protect her beliefs from being questioned. She stands as the shield to her faith and through human will, protects the fragile belief system she has placed her hopes upon. Read the testimonies of Christians-turned-atheist. In almost every case, the testimony is the same. "I got tired of pretending."

Perhaps we aren't supposed to pretend. A Christian should not be afraid of truth – for all truth ultimately points to God. When you look at the arguments against the Bible they are often a woven tale that avoids anything that affirms the Bible and only accepts the things that are in agreement with the presupposed position, or can be twisted to fit the argument.

Another irony is that manmade faith has the same substance, whether someone claims to be an atheist or a Christian. Atheists stand as guards to their faith in humanistic thinking, weeding out and attacking anything that challenges their fragile belief system. They react with the same volatile emotions when something questions their foundation of sand. There is little difference between the counterfeit faith of religion and the counterfeit faith of atheism. And they both create similar reactions from the possessor when challenged with ideas that rattle their foundation of sand.

Many arguments are fashioned this way, and an entire book could be written with examples. Rather than picking out an example from the plethora of arguments against the Bible, let's use the Bible itself as an example. My grandfather often used this as a tease, but it serves as a good example in our discussion. In this case, I can only accept the KJV's wording, and through it, I can prove that women are dangerous drivers. Look at these passages from Acts:

Acts 27:15
we let *her* drive
Acts 27:17
and so were driven.
Acts 27:20
all hope that we should be saved was then taken away.

There you have it. The Bible disapproves of women drivers, right? I used the text exactly as written, without alteration, and I am able to prove my point by scripture. In reality, the only thing I have done is exclude information. What's missing fills in the key to an accurate understanding. By hiding information that doesn't say what I want to be said, I can give the false impression that I've proven something that is actually false.

If we look at Acts 27 in context, we discover that 'her' is a ship that the Apostle Paul and Luke were aboard. It was caught in a violent storm, and they struck the sails and allowed the ship to be driven wherever the storm would take them. In despair, the men felt that all hope was lost.

Excluding key pieces of information can make this text to appear to say something it does not say. The same is true for science, history, archaeology, and any other source of information. A critic can present a persuasive argument by excluding what he or she doesn't want you to know, and presenting what can appear to say what they want you to believe. How do we defend against this? Simply by finding out the whole truth. What is missing is often what dispels doubt. This is why the Bible commands that we study to show ourselves approved.

Sometimes the information we need is not available. Yet if you know what you believe and why you believe it, the missing evidence won't rattle you. It's amazing that we can have a mountain of evidence, but if we have one criticism we can't answer, we'll doubt the mountain and trust the objection.

Rather than covering our eyes and pretending questions don't exist, we need to look at the question and explore the objection in light of what we know is true. Only then can we have confidence. The person who runs from the disease of doubt can never have confidence in the truth. Sometimes the questions aren't answered easily, but honestly seeking for answers will give the Christian confidence. And honestly looking at the mountain of truth will give assurance when the molehill of doubt arises.

In discussions with people who claim to be ex-Christians, I see a pattern. They began by refusing to look at questions honestly and standing as guards to protect their faith. A college environment or another source of influence put them in a position where they couldn't escape criticism. By sheer human will, they fought doubt until it finally overcame them. In frustration, they declared that their faith was a childish fantasy and they gave up the whole thing.

Now they stand and guard to protect their new faith in humanism against the attacks of Christianity. They use the exact same methods; they have just changed sides. They still will not look at the whole truth with honesty. So now they continue to guard half-truths and protect their new faith, only it's easier to stand in the atheist camp since there are more allies.

The truth of the matter is that you don't need to protect God – or your faith. Faith is not forcing yourself to believe something. Faith is being assured of truth so that it becomes your firm foundation. If you can't stand with confidence, you are lacking a foundation and your faith is manmade.

Let's now look at what Jesus said about faith. Look at **Luke 17:5-6**

> 5 And the apostles said to the Lord, "Increase our faith."
> 6 So the Lord said, "If you have faith as a mustard seed, you can say to this mulberry tree, 'Be pulled up by the roots and be planted in the sea,' and it would obey you.

Rarely will you hear this passage looked at in light of what Jesus was communicating to the disciples. Just like the rest of us, the disciples who learned under Jesus struggled with doubt. Daily they witnessed the model of perfection – Jesus Christ. In the light of His life, they recognized something was deficient in their own lives. Throughout His life, Jesus professed absolute trust in the plan of our Heavenly Father. It was a plan that would lead Him to the cross. Yet He never wavered. In the same sense, Jesus constantly challenged his disciples to follow His perfect plan.

Jesus and his disciples knew the religious leaders of the day were seeking to destroy them and several times it looked like they might succeed. Once, they were nearly stoned, and to His disciple's dismay, Jesus went right back to the city where their lives would again be in peril. Jesus said that He couldn't die until His time was fulfilled. How could this man so firmly believe in God's plan that He could walk right into peril without batting an eye? The disciples wanted this confidence, so they said, "Lord, increase our faith."

Did Jesus give them a list of 'faith principles' or 'laws of faith'? No. He made it clear that they already had all the faith they needed. Jesus often used a mustard seed as an illustration. He often called it the least of all seeds. Jesus wasn't saying, no seed is smaller than a mustard seed. It was a word picture that every person in that culture could understand. Mustard was a spice that everyone used and it was likely the smallest ingredient people could identify with. One time Jesus held up the tiny seed and declared it to be a symbol of how the Kingdom of Heaven grows from the smallest source.

In regards to faith, Jesus is again holding up a seed that looked so insignificant. "If your faith is this big, it can move mountains." Jesus used both mountains and trees to illustrate the power of our faith. Both are objects that appear immovable, yet none can stand before faith in the heart of the one doing God's will. So the answer to faith is, "You don't need more."

Jesus again uses this as a teaching opportunity when the disciples failed. In Matthew 7, Jesus gave his disciples power to cast out demons and heal the sick. He sent them out to preach his coming, and they returned in victory, excited that even the demons had no power against His name. Victory was turned into confusion when their faith was challenged.

After returning from a mountain, Jesus saw a commotion around His disciples. When He approached, the people informed Him that His disciples could not cast out a demon from a man bent on destroying himself. This was after the disciples had experienced great victory and rejoiced that demons were subject to them in Christ's name. After Jesus cast out the resistant spirit and healed the man, the disciples came to Him to find out why they couldn't do it. Look at Jesus' answer in **Matthew 17:19-21**

19 Then the disciples came to Jesus privately and said, "Why could we not cast it out?"

20 So Jesus said to them, "Because of your unbelief; for assuredly, I say to you, if you have faith as a mustard seed, you will say to this mountain, 'Move from here to there,' and it will move; and nothing will be impossible for you.

21 "However, this kind does not go out except by prayer and fasting."

The plain meaning is easy to overlook. The reason they failed was because of unbelief. Yet, Jesus made it clear that they indeed had the power, for all they needed was a mustard seed of faith – and then nothing was impossible. Nothing also means this event in which they failed. So we can see that Jesus empowered them to do this very thing. The disciples succeeded in Matthew 7, but here in Matthew 17 they failed. Unbelief caused the failure, and the solution is found in prayer and fasting.

Prayer and fasting does not increase their faith. Jesus made it clear that they already had enough faith. Instead, it was a call to weaken the flesh and build them up in the Spirit. Fasting brings the flesh under subjection while prayer puts their focus on the Spirit.

Unbelief is of the flesh, but faith is of the Spirit. The disciples were so focused on their unbelief that they could not walk by faith. All of their efforts combined could not muster up faith – and indeed it did not need to. They were already given the gift of faith. The problem was that they were walking in the flesh. The flesh verses the Spirit is a topic for another chapter, but keep in mind that Jesus *never* increased their faith. He *always* reminded them that they had what they needed. Unbelief may hinder their faith, but the solution wasn't to gain more faith, but to deal with what was causing their flesh to dominate their lives.

Romans 12:3 tells us that God deals every person the measure of faith. Faith isn't something we build, nor is it something we obtain or increase. Faith is a gift from God. Anytime spiritual matters become man centered or man dependent, we have stepped outside of true faith. The Bible never tells us to build our faith; it tells us to build our lives upon our faith. Look at **Jude 1:20-21**

20 But you, beloved, building yourselves up on your most holy faith, praying in the Holy Spirit,

21 keep yourselves in the love of God, looking for the mercy of our Lord Jesus Christ unto eternal life.

This passage doesn't tell us to build faith. The Bible says that we have a most holy faith that we should build ourselves upon. It's most holy because it comes from the Most Holy God. We keep ourselves in the love of God by keeping his word. This is another avenue we'll explore later. Let's also consider **Romans 10:17**

So then faith *comes* by hearing, and hearing by the word of God.

Why does faith come by hearing the word? It goes back to our examination of Hebrews 11. Faith is a sure foundation. The word is our foundation and as we hear the truth of God, we learn how to build our lives upon it. We hear, believe, and build ourselves upon the most holy faith that is revealed in the word. The word is by the Spirit (see John 6:63) just as faith is of the Spirit. You can know the word and still not have faith, but you can't have faith without the word. The power to believe (or live by faith) has already been given to us by the Holy Spirit. What's lacking is our understanding of God's word and how to live in the Spirit where faith is discovered.

Rather than faith being something we force ourselves to believe, faith is believing God. It is God revealing His word to us in a way that creates such certainty that we build our lives upon that unshakeable foundation. Faith is believing God so that we are accounted as righteous. By faith, we move our foundation from human nature, and build it upon the assurance of God and His promises. A false faith says, "I believe," but then remains on a dead foundation built on the weakness of human nature. Then all spiritual matters are dependent upon man and have no part in the eternal power of God. When faith depends on mankind, it is a weak foundation and will not stand when we need the rock of a firm assurance.

We have a better foundation. When we believe God's word and build ourselves upon that most holy faith, the disease of doubt has no power over us and we need not to convince ourselves to believe anything we aren't sure to be true. We will have the firm assurance of truth and that assurance is the shield and strength of the Christian life.

The Simple Truth about Jesus

One day Jesus asked His disciples, "Who do men say that I am?"

It's a question that each of us must answer, and how we view Jesus is no small matter. In fact, the identity of Christ is the foundation of our faith. Jesus claimed that he was the rock the church is built upon. No structure can be strong unless it's built on a solid foundation. For this reason, we must understand who Christ is, for if our understanding is flawed, the gospel won't truly be understood. If our understanding is flawed, our faith will also be flawed. Let's begin with **Luke 9:18-22**

[18] And it happened, as He was alone praying, *that* His disciples joined Him, and He asked them, saying, "Who do the crowds say that I am?"

[19] So they answered and said, "John the Baptist, but some *say* Elijah; and others *say* that one of the old prophets has risen again."

[20] He said to them, "But who do you say that I am?" Peter answered and said, "The Christ of God."

[21] And He strictly warned and commanded them to tell this to no one,

[22] saying, "The Son of Man must suffer many things, and be rejected by the elders and chief priests and scribes, and be killed, and be raised the third day."

In Matthew's gospel, we are told that Jesus said that Peter was blessed, for flesh and blood didn't reveal this to Peter, but the Father in heaven has done so. The true revelation of Christ comes from above.

Who is Jesus? His identity was in dispute during His lifetime, and it's still in dispute among the world today. I say, in dispute, but the dispute is among those who do not know Him. To those who know Christ, that identity is revealed to us through the Holy Spirit, and through the scriptures (which is also by the Holy Spirit[9]). "Who do you say that I am?" It's a question every person must answer in their heart.

Some are thrown by the fact that Jesus didn't openly proclaim His identity. In John 10:24, the Jews confronted Jesus and said, "If you are the Christ, tell us plainly." Since Jesus didn't come straight out and say, "I am the Christ," critics of Jesus point to this as evidence that Jesus wasn't the Messiah.

Actually, Jesus did make this claim on several occasions,[10] just not before the Pharisees and religious leaders until his trial.

We can see the reasons why He was indirect in His public statements. The religious leaders made it plain that they wanted an opportunity to accuse Him. In fact, even Jesus' indirect answers were close enough to make His identity known. When this was the case, the leaders tried to stone Him for making Himself equal to God.

Jesus veiled His identity to the masses until after He declared, "My hour has come[11]," referring to the crucifixion.

In the passage above, he instructs His disciples not to make Him known, and then gave the reason. Because of His identity, He would be condemned and crucified. This came to fruition when He stood before the Sanhedrin to be tried. The high priest said, "I put you under oath by the living God to tell us if you are the Christ, Son of the living God."

When Jesus answered and said He was, the Sanhedrin declared, "We have heard it ourselves. He has spoken blasphemy and is worthy of death."

His acknowledgment that He was the Christ (or Messiah) was the evidence that convicted Him to die. This is why Jesus didn't openly declare Himself to the world until it was time for Him to fulfill His purpose of dying for man's redemption.

---

[9] 2 Timothy 3:16
[10] Matthew 16:16-17, John 9:35-37, John 4:25-26, Matthew 23:10, Mark 14:61-62
[11] John 12:23

The Simple Truth about Jesus

I say all of this so there is no confusion. Jesus never denied that He was Christ / Messiah, nor did He ever deny that He was God. Quite the opposite, as we shall see. He did veil this truth to the masses and only revealed this to His disciples, but even when He chose to veil His identity, Jesus still didn't deny it.

Is Jesus God?

To the world, the answer is 'no'. But to the disciple of Christ, those who believe the scriptures, the answer must be 'yes'. Before we look into the New Testament, let's go back to the Old Testament and see how Christ was identified. Let's begin with a passage that describes the attributes of Christ. Look at **Isaiah 9:6**

[6] For unto us a Child is born, Unto us a Son is given; And the government will be upon His shoulder. And His name will be called Wonderful, Counselor, Mighty God, Everlasting Father, Prince of Peace.

This is God's proclamation to Israel of their coming Messiah – Christ. The first thing to take note off is how God distinguishes the child from the Son. The child is born, but the Son is given. What does this distinction mean? Hebrews 13:8 says, "Jesus Christ is the same yesterday, today, and forever." He remains unchanged from the past, to the present, to the future. Add to this **Philippians 2:5-8**

[5] Let this mind be in you which was also in Christ Jesus,
[6] who, being in the form of God, did not consider it robbery to be equal with God,
[7] but made Himself of no reputation, taking the form of a bondservant, *and* coming in the likeness of men.
[8] And being found in appearance as a man, He humbled Himself and became obedient to *the point of* death, even the death of the cross.

Though He existed in the form of God, Jesus humbled Himself, took on the likeness of men, and submitted Himself to die on the cross. Notice that it would not have been considered robbery to be equal to God. This next passage is strikingly clear in light of what Jesus explained about Himself. God declares that He alone is our Savior, and there will never be more than one God. **Isaiah 43:10-11**

> [10] "You *are* My witnesses," says the LORD, "And My servant whom I have chosen, That you may know and believe Me, And understand that I *am* He. Before Me there was no God formed, Nor shall there be after Me. [11] I, *even* I, *am* the LORD, And besides Me *there is* no savior.

Not only is there one God, but there will never be another God formed. Add to that, the Lord declares, "Beside me, there is no Savior." This passage foretells of the words that Christ would declare to the leaders of Israel. **John 8:24**

> [24] "Therefore I said to you that you will die in your sins; for if you do not believe that I am *He,* you will die in your sins."

Jesus is quoting God's declaration to the people in Isaiah. They must believe that Jesus is 'He' as foretold in the Old Testament. Let's look at another passage in the Old Testament that testifies to Jesus' divinity. Look at **Isaiah 44:6**

> Thus says the LORD, the King of Israel, And his Redeemer, the LORD of hosts: 'I *am* the First and I *am* the Last; Besides Me *there is* no God.

There is something we must note regarding the English translation of the Old Testament. There are several Hebrew words that are translated into 'lord'. However, when you see the word LORD in all caps, it indicates that this word was translated from the word 'Jehovah'. Jehovah is ONLY used for God. This is true when Jehovah is translated into GOD. All caps means the word is YHWH or Jehovah. Nothing but God, the creator of all things, is called Jehovah/YHWH.

Knowing this is important when looking at the promise of Christ in the Old Testament. In Isaiah 44:6, the LORD / Jehovah refers to himself as the King of Israel. Not only that, He declares that

He and His Redeemer, who is also Jehovah, LORD of hosts are one God and beside Him there is no other God. A similar declaration is made in **Isaiah 48:16-17**

> [16] "Come near to Me, hear this: I have not spoken in secret from the beginning; From the time that it was, I *was* there. And now the Lord GOD and His Spirit Have sent Me."
>
> [17] Thus says the LORD, your Redeemer, The Holy One of Israel: "I *am* the LORD your God, Who teaches you to profit, Who leads you by the way you should go.

This is a prophecy of the coming Christ. As with many prophecies, it is told in real time as though God were declaring it as it unfolded. Another example of this is Psalm 22. This prophecy in Psalms is told from the perspective of Christ on the cross, and is spoken as though it happened during the crucifixion.

In the passage from Isaiah 48, the Redeemer, who is GOD, is sent by the Spirit and the Lord GOD. Then the Redeemer declares, "I am the LORD your God."

In this passage we see that Christ, the Redeemer is being declared as Jehovah, and we also see the future declaration of Jesus when He calls Israel before He is crucified. The Lord GOD (God in all caps, Jehovah) and His Spirit have sent Me (the Redeemer). So Jehovah and His Spirit (the Holy Spirit) are sending Jehovah (the Messiah) to His people to teach them the way they should go.

In Isaiah 7:14, the virgin birth is foretold, and God said that the child shall be called Immanuel. Immanuel simply means, "God with us." That's exactly what Jesus became at birth, God with man.

We can see through the Old Testament that God is sending God to be the Redeemer. He also makes it clear that there is ONLY one God. Confusing? It can be, but hopefully it will be clearer by the time you finish this chapter.

The point you need to understand at this time is that God himself has declared that the Messiah is God, was sent by God, and that God alone is our redeemer.

The New Testament Christ

Let's look at Christ's divinity in the New Testament, beginning at **Colossians 2:8-10**

[8] Beware lest anyone cheat you through philosophy and empty deceit, according to the tradition of men, according to the basic principles of the world, and not according to Christ.
[9] For in Him dwells all the fullness of the Godhead bodily;
[10] and you are complete in Him, who is the head of all principality and power.

The purpose of this passage is to warn God's people not to adopt their view of Christ from the world or human philosophy (including religion), but to understand that in Christ dwells the fullness of the Godhead. What does that mean? The word 'godhead' in this passage is the Greek word 'theotes', which means, the state of being God. We've already examined the Old Testament, where God himself refers to the coming redeemer as Jehovah. The following New Testament passages will continue to affirm this truth.

Before we move ahead, let's first examine a phrase that seems to confuse some people. Look now at **Colossians 1:15-18**

[15] He is the image of the invisible God, the firstborn over all creation.
[16] For by Him all things were created that are in heaven and that are on earth, visible and invisible, whether thrones or dominions or principalities or powers. All things were created through Him and for Him.
[17] And He is before all things, and in Him all things consist.
[18] And He is the head of the body, the church, who is the beginning, the firstborn from the dead, that in all things He may have the preeminence.

When this passage is looked at in its full context, there is little to be confused over, yet that word 'firstborn' causes some to get caught up into a human way of thinking. We have already seen that God foretold that the child would be born, but the Son would be given. He existed before the world began. Look at the words of Jesus just before his crucifixion in **John 17:5**

> [5] "And now, O Father, glorify Me together with Yourself, with the glory which I had with You before the world was.

We'll dig into this a bit later, but first let's understand the word firstborn. Normally, the firstborn son was just that – firstborn. By birth right, the firstborn son had honor over his brothers. The firstborn received a double inheritance, carried the family blessing, and took the spiritual leadership over the family. As in the days of the patriarchs, the firstborn became the prophet whom God revealed Himself through, and even foretold what would occur in the later years of Israel.

There were times when the honor of the firstborn was given to someone who wasn't first. We've already looked at one example in the previous chapter. Esau was the firstborn, but the honor of that birth right was given to the second, Jacob. Esau sold his birthright (firstborn position) to Jacob, and then God gave the blessing of the firstborn to Jacob as well. Then the promise came through the second son as though he were the firstborn.

Another example comes from Jacob's children. At the end of Jacob's life, he adopted two of his grandchildren to be named among his inheritance. An interesting thing happened. Manasseh was the older child, yet Jacob blessed Ephraim and declared him as the firstborn. Not only was he exalted over his older brother, but he was exalted over his uncles as well. He was named among them as if he were a brother, and declared to be the firstborn. In Jeremiah 31:9, God called Ephraim the firstborn tribe in Israel. In special circumstances, the firstborn was given to someone outside of the physical birth order.

I say all of this to point out one important truth. Firstborn is used to identify honor, and not always the order of birth. Therefore, calling Jesus the firstborn over all creation does not mean Jesus is a created being. It simply means that He has preeminence over all creation. In fact, the passage in Colossians explains that Jesus is declared as the firstborn for this very reason – that he might have the preeminence.

Also note the rest of the information in these passages. "He was before all things." "In Him all things consist." Though he was born in a manger two-thousand years ago, He existed before the world began. The Bible also makes it clear that Jesus is the creator of the world. We'll look at this further in a moment. Before moving on, notice that Jesus is called the firstborn over all creation, and then called the firstborn from the dead. Not only does He reign over all creation, but He is the first to rise in a glorified body.

The Bible says that all who are in Christ will be raised like Him – in a glorified body. Though Jesus raised two people from the dead during his ministry, both remained in a corrupt body, still under the curse of sin. When Jesus died, He was raised incorruptible, and He gave this as an example of what we hope for and the promise of things to come. He is the firstborn from the dead, and we will be raised in that same eternal life when all things are fulfilled and we enter the Kingdom of Heaven.

Creator of the Heavens and Earth

Jesus is called the Creator of all things. Some have taught that Jesus was first created, and then created all other things, but this contradicts the scriptures. God created all things. Look at **Genesis 1:**
[1] In the beginning God created the heavens and the earth.

Each step in Creation is performed by God. God said, "Let there be light." "Let there be land in the midst of water." He then called plants, animals, and all other areas of creation into existence. Throughout the Bible, God attributes everything created to the work of His own doing. Look at **Isaiah 45:18**
[18] For thus says the LORD, Who created the heavens, Who is God, Who formed the earth and made it, Who has established it, Who did not create it in vain, Who formed it to be inhabited: "I *am* the LORD, and *there is* no other.

Who created all that we see? According to the Bible, God created the heavens and the earth. The earth was formed by God – the LORD – Jehovah. Then God needed to make sure we understood that He alone is God and there is no other. Jesus is not a god, the Father a god, and the Spirit a god. There is only one God. Remember the passages in the Old Testament we looked at earlier? When Jehovah declared that he was sending Jehovah to be our Redeemer, He affirmed that even though Jehovah was sending Jehovah, there was still only one Jehovah.

This can be confusing. The problem is that we serve an infinite God. The Bible contains all that God has revealed about Himself, but not all that God is. A limited mind can't grasp an unlimited God. To put this into perspective, think about numbers. Can you picture the highest number possible? Of course not. Pick any number, and you can always add more to it. Divide any number, and you can always divide it more. Eventually, any avenue of numbers becomes incomprehensible. If we can't comprehend something like the infinity of numbers that we use in everyday life, why are we surprised that we can't comprehend an infinite God?

Some things have to be taken by faith. I can look at known evidence and reasonably conclude that something is true without having to see all the evidence. Science does this all the time. It's called 'theory'. In scientific theory, nothing is proven. We prove certain attributes true or false. In reality, little in science can be proven true. When something doesn't fail, science draws conclusions based on the assumption that what wasn't proven false will continue to pass future experiments. Yet even those logical assumptions are often proven false as knowledge increases and then the theory is updated with a new assumption.

With God, we have certain truths he has revealed about Himself. These show us what we need to know in order to trust his word and walk by faith, but it never will fully reveal the infinite God to the human mind. It may not make sense to my mind for God and His Spirit to send God as my redeemer, but that is something God has declared about Himself. I can see the Father as he has been revealed in scripture. I can see the Son. And I can see the Holy Spirit.

These all reveal something about God, but they don't reveal all that God is.

I know this is a bit wordy, but it's important for you to understand this, for there are people who deny the divinity of Christ based solely on the fact that they can't understand how He can be God, and the Father be God. It doesn't matter if I understand. It matters that God has declared this to be true. Look now at **John 1:1-14**

> [1] In the beginning was the Word, and the Word was with God, and the Word was God.
> [2] He was in the beginning with God.
> [3] All things were made through Him, and without Him nothing was made that was made.
> [4] In Him was life, and the life was the light of men.
> [5] And the light shines in the darkness, and the darkness did not comprehend it.
>
> ...
> [10] He was in the world, and the world was made through Him, and the world did not know Him.
> [11] He came to His own, and His own did not receive Him.
> [12] But as many as received Him, to them He gave the right to become children of God, to those who believe in His name:
> [13] who were born, not of blood, nor of the will of the flesh, nor of the will of man, but of God.
> [14] And the Word became flesh and dwelt among us, and we beheld His glory, the glory as of the only begotten of the Father, full of grace and truth.

In the Old Testament, God declared that He, Jehovah, created the heavens and the earth and that there is none beside Him. He alone did this. Now we see that Jesus is that creator. Colossians declared this truth, and now we see the book of John making the same declaration. God entered the world He created, and the world did not receive Him. Just as the people of Jesus' day did not recognize Him, people in this era also do not. But if you receive Him,

God gives you the right to be called by His name and adopted as a son.

There are so many scriptures that identify Christ, that we would need a separate book to explore this topic more fully. For the sake of time, I'll wrap up this subject with the words of Christ as He equates Himself with God. Read through the book of John and notice how many times the religious leadership called Jesus a blasphemer for making Himself equal to God. On one occasion, Jesus introduced Himself as the Son of God. The Pharisees were outraged because they said this was to claim equality with God. Jesus did not refute their interpretation. In fact, He repeatedly affirmed it.

Christians are called 'children by adoption', but Jesus is called the only begotten Son of God. As the Bible states, He is the word made flesh; He was in the beginning with God, and He is God[12]. On one occasion, Jesus is explaining how the Old Testament pointed to Him.

As the Pharisees disputed with Jesus, He made the claim that Abraham rejoiced to see His day. The people scoffed at such an idea that a man who was not even fifty could claim to have seen Abraham, who had been dead for thousands of years. Jesus then made a statement that was unquestionably a claim that He was the God of the Old Testament. **John 8:57-59**

> [57] Then the Jews said to Him, "You are not yet fifty years old, and have You seen Abraham?"
> [58] Jesus said to them, "Most assuredly, I say to you, before Abraham was, I AM."
> [59] Then they took up stones to throw at Him; but Jesus hid Himself and went out of the temple, going through the midst of them, and so passed by.

Without knowing the Old Testament, it's easy to miss the significance of Jesus' statement. The significance was not lost on the Jewish leaders, for they immediately rushed to get stones with the intent of executing Jesus for claiming to be God.

---

[12] John 1:1

To understand what Jesus was saying, we need to go back to the second book of the Old Testament, Exodus. Israel was in bondage and God called Moses to go into Egypt and declare their coming deliverance. Now let's look at **Exodus 3:13-15**

> [13] Then Moses said to God, "Indeed, *when* I come to the children of Israel and say to them, 'The God of your fathers has sent me to you,' and they say to me, 'What *is* His name?' what shall I say to them?"
> [14] And God said to Moses, "I AM WHO I AM." And He said, "Thus you shall say to the children of Israel, 'I AM has sent me to you.' "
> [15] Moreover God said to Moses, "Thus you shall say to the children of Israel: 'The LORD God of your fathers, the God of Abraham, the God of Isaac, and the God of Jacob, has sent me to you. This *is* My name forever, and this *is* My memorial to all generations.'

This is what Jesus is referring to, and the Jews fully understood this. There is no other way to interpret the phrase, "Before Abraham was, I AM," other than that Jesus was claiming to have existed before Abraham, and to have done so in the form of God.

There is much more that could be said about this topic, but it's sufficient to say that the scriptures affirm that Jesus is Jehovah, creator of all things, and God of the universe. The Old Testament identified the coming Messiah (or Christ) by declaring God / Jehovah would visit his people as their Redeemer. Jesus identified Himself as God. The apostles called Jesus God and the creator of all things. In the Old Testament, God calls Himself the First and the Last, the only God and declares that there is no other God beside Him, nor will there be any afterward. In Revelation – which by the way is actually called the Revelation of Jesus Christ – Jesus calls Himself the First and the Last. His glory was veiled on earth, but the Book of Revelation gives a glimpse of Christ in His revealed glory.

In the revealing of the glory of Christ in Revelation, God identifies Himself as the beginning and the end, first and the last, the one who was dead, and behold is alive forevermore[13].

As stated at the beginning of this chapter, a false Jesus cannot save. If Jesus was a glorified man, He still cannot save.

The message of the gospel is this: God is just, but redeemed mankind by paying our penalty in His own body so we could be reconciled to Him, righteous and pure because He died for us. This is the miracle of love. A passage that adds to this is **Acts 20:28**

"Therefore take heed to yourselves and to all the flock, among which the Holy Spirit has made you overseers, to shepherd the church of God which He purchased with His own blood.

It is God who purchased our redemption with His own blood. This is yet another testimony that God was in the form of Christ, redeeming us by shedding His own blood on the cross.

In the next chapter, we'll examine the amazing gift of being transformed from corruption into a new incorruptible spiritual nature. It's all because of grace – the unmerited favor of God – and was given to us through Christ by His sacrifice on the cross, where He bore the penalty of sin in His own body.

As you can see, there is no shortage of information on this topic. The Bible says that God establishes His word by two or three witnesses. God fulfills this requirement for the testimony concerning the divinity of Christ. Jehovah in the Old Testament declared that the coming Messiah would be Jehovah. Jesus declared Himself as the Messiah and the I AM of the Old Testament. The writers of the New Testament also declare that Jesus is God, the creator of all things.

Jesus is Immanuel, God with us[14] and He is God, who purchased our redemption with His own blood to reconcile us to Himself. Jesus is the embodiment of God's love and grace toward you.

---

[13] Revelation 1:11, 1:17, 2:8, and 22:13
[14] Isaiah 7:14, Isaiah 8:8, Matthew 1:23

The Simplicity of Salvation

It is often said that all roads lead to God and that we worship the same God by different methods. Is this true? The answer to this question is of vital importance, for each of us will stand before Him. Can we be confident in any one way to God? Can we be confident in the idea that all worship God in different ways?

It was Jesus who said, "I am the way, the truth, and the life. No one comes to the Father except by Me." He also said He was the door to salvation and any who try to enter another way is a thief and a robber.[15] Jesus is very exclusionary. He went as far as to say that the world only loves those who are part of its system, but will hate the ones who follow Him.[16] The reason is that Jesus calls us out of the world, its religions, and its ways of thinking. He then calls us to live as pilgrims journeying through a country that is not our own.

From the beginning of our discussion, we see that Jesus pitted Christianity against the world. It's not possible to accept the words of Jesus and the world religions at the same time. Nor is it possible to accept other religions without rebuffing Jesus. This truth is being challenged every day and in many creative ways. An example is this Hindu proverb. There are variations, but the proverb goes something like this:

A student approached a guru and asked, "Why do men argue about religion and how do we know what God is like?"

The guru explained how philosophers and theologians are like blind men around an elephant. Each one was asked to feel of the elephant and describe it. The blind men began arguing among themselves. The one who felt the leg said, "An elephant is like a mighty tree."

One who felt the ear said, "You're wrong. An elephant is like a large fan in your hand."

---

[15] John 10:1
[16] John 15:18-19, 2 Peter 2:10-11, Psalm 84:5

The Simplicity of Salvation

"You're both wrong," said the one who felt its side. "An elephant is like a great wall."

Each man described different parts of the elephant, arguing that what they experienced was what the elephant is like. The guru turned to the young man and said, "This is what the religions are doing. Each one is right and no one is wrong, except those who dispute the others."

This proverb sounds good on the surface, and indeed there is one clear truth in this Hindu proverb – though it isn't quite what the originator intended. In fact, this proverb proves the truth of scripture. While the guru claimed that no one was wrong, the truth is that they all were wrong. The elephant wasn't a great wall, nor a fan, nor a tree, nor any of the attributes these men said.

The truth in this proverb is that all these men were blind and all were wrong.

Isn't this exactly what Jesus said in the Bible? Men are blind until God makes them see. Until God opens our eyes, we are lost in darkness and all our views on salvation are wrong. Even the nation of Israel, from whom God raised the prophets to pen the scriptures, were lost in their blindness and wrong in their views of salvation. Jesus said that He came to make the blind see, and those who claim to see would continue in blindness, and remain in their sins.[17] In John 8:24, the religious leaders debated with Jesus. He didn't tell them that we all must find God in our own ways. Instead, He said, "Unless you believe that I am He, you will die in your sins."

What does Jesus mean, "I am He?" This goes back to who Jesus is as we explored in the previous chapter. He must open our eyes to see, and only then do we discover who the true God is. Indeed we are like blind men, unable to discern who God is. It is not mankind discovering God. Instead, it is God opening our eyes as He reveals Himself to us. Not man finding God, but God finding man. It's not merely a discovery of enlightenment; it's a power outside of our own abilities creating life within us.

---

[17] John 9:39-41

Spiritually, the Bible says we are dead, but in Christ we are made alive. The dead cannot raise himself, nor can we who have no eternal life create that life by our own efforts. We'll look at this in more detail shortly, but first, let's look at some common questions Christians will likely face.

Why do Christians believe Jesus is the only way of salvation? You've likely heard someone ask this. Perhaps you've asked this yourself. Other similar questions often asked are:

Why doesn't God just forget about sin and take us all to heaven?

Why would a loving God condemn someone to hell just because they don't believe in him?

These are important questions and hopefully this chapter will be a tool in helping you answer these in either your life, or in discussing this with others who ask.

Why would a loving God condemn someone just because they don't believe?

This is a common question and fully deserves an honest answer. The first step in answering this question is to recognize that there is an error in perspective. The question is flawed. God is *not* condemning those who don't believe. He's redeeming those who *do* believe. Consider **John 3:17-20**

[17] "For God did not send His Son into the world to condemn the world, but that the world through Him might be saved.
[18] "He who believes in Him is not condemned; but he who does not believe is condemned already, because he has not believed in the name of the only begotten Son of God.
[19] "And this is the condemnation, that the light has come into the world, and men loved darkness rather than light, because their deeds were evil.
[20] "For everyone practicing evil hates the light and does not come to the light, lest his deeds should be exposed.

Let's think for a moment on the weight of this verse. "God did not send His Son into the world to condemn the world...he who does not believe is condemned already."

The message of the gospel is not, believe in Jesus or God will condemn you. The message of the gospel is that you are already under condemnation; therefore, Jesus has come to redeem you and take you out of that condemnation. This is why Jesus said, "You are not of the world, but I have called you out of the world."

Just as with the blind men and the elephant, mankind is already groping in the darkness, and human nature is corrupt in its ideas. We have formed our philosophies out of our own assumptions, while in blindness and confusion. A blind man may be able to persuade other blind men that an elephant is a tree. He may also be able to persuade others who are blind that he knows the truth about God. Yet he remains groping in the darkness alongside others who are also groping.

To the blind, a false description may appear to be true, but to those who have seen the elephant, his words appear foolish. Those who can't see the elephant think it's absurd when someone claims to have actually seen it, but those who can see it understand. When it comes to faith in Christ, those whose eyes have been opened see the world's religions as foolish as calling an elephant a tree. People groping blindly in the darkness embrace any plausible religion, and often think it's absurd that anyone could actually claim to know truth.

So we can see that God did not send us the Messiah to condemn the world and cast them into darkness. Man is already in darkness and is already under condemnation. Only those who refuse to receive their sight will remain in darkness, and those who refuse to be pulled out of the pit of blindness will remain under condemnation.

Why is man blind and already under condemnation? The Bible says that all men are under condemnation through Adam, but are given life through Christ. Look at **1 Corinthians 15:21-22**

[21] For since by man *came* death, by Man also *came* the resurrection of the dead.
[22] For as in Adam all die, even so in Christ all shall be made alive.

Does this mean we are being judged for Adam's sin? Yes and no. We inherit our human nature through Adam, but we are held accountable for our own actions. In a discussion a man once scoffed at the idea that people are born with a sinful nature. To answer his objection, I pointed to the nature of a child. I didn't have to teach my kids to be selfish. They were born with the ability to take toys from other children. Even though they have never seen anyone hit, they hit their siblings. They knew how to throw tantrums without having any examples to imitate. Every misbehavior they practice came natural, without any training or guidance. In fact, as a parent, my responsibility is to use instruction and consequences to guide their behavior toward an acceptable standard. My training can alter outward actions, but it does not change the heart.

Where do children learn selfishness? It is part of their nature. And it remains part of our nature as adults. Why are we selfish by nature? It's just that – nature. Human nature.

I was born with a selfish, sinful nature, and something needs to be changed within me. Though I was born with my natural tendency toward sin, I am still the one who chooses to sin. As a child, I knew the rules laid down by my parents, yet I willfully disobeyed when the rules didn't fulfill the desires of my selfish nature. Why do people steal, cheat, manipulate, lie, lust, or act out on negative behaviors?

An American politician fell into scandal for his infidelity a few years back. When caught, he began with denial but eventually had to admit it in the face of evidence. He even redefined words to both hide and justify his actions. Like a child, he followed the selfish desires of his heart and even tried to manipulate to get his way. At some point he made the statement, "I'm just wired this way." It was meant to justify his actions, but he hit on the heart of the problem. We are all 'just wired this way'. He got caught and made into a public spectacle, but we all struggle with our fallen human nature.

The Simplicity of Salvation

It's easy to point to someone caught with their hand in the cookie jar, but we've all struggled with various failures and temptations. Our struggles may differ in some areas, but we all have a bent toward sin.

It is for this reason that we are all under condemnation. I was born into blindness, corruption, and my own fallen nature guides me in my decision making, morality, and world view. Since we are drawing our internal standard from selfish human nature, we choose to sin when we value temptation over a contradicting moral standard. We are making foolish choices because we have no ability to see the value behind God's moral requirements. It is spiritual blindness – for man cannot see into the spiritual world God desires for him until after he receives sight from the Lord. Look at **1 Corinthians 2:14**

> [14] But the natural man does not receive the things of the Spirit of God, for they are foolishness to him; nor can he know *them,* because they are spiritually discerned.

Why don't other religions understand the things of God? They can only discern with blind eyes and misinformed ideas. Therefore, the ways of God are foolishness. Until you have eyes to see what's beyond human perception, little makes sense. Consider this illustration.

In the past, the oceans were considered the silent deep. Nothing could be heard in the water that couldn't be heard on land. Go below the surface of the water and what do you hear? You might hear a skewed sound of water lapping on the shore or a passing motor boat, but the sounds of the ocean were imperceptible. An uninformed man may stick his head under water, not hear anything, and conclude that nothing is down there based on the silence.

Today we have sonar and sensitive instruments that can detect sounds the human ear cannot. We have discovered that the ocean is filled with sounds man cannot hear on his own. We now know that whales can speak to each other across hundreds and even thousands of miles of ocean. And that they have a language by which they can communicate with specific messages to each other.

What had been the silent deep is now understood to be active and alive. The human ear still cannot perceive, but sounds are everywhere. The ancient man who said, "Nothing is down there," made a logical assumption based on his limited understanding, but he was blind to the truth. Toying with religion is very much like this. Sometimes people make statements like, "Try Jesus. If you don't like Christianity, you can go back to your life." This is like asking someone to stick their head in the ocean and try to perceive what they cannot see or understand.

There must be spiritual eyes in order to see spiritual things, and this is a gift of God that is promised to those who believe upon Christ. In a few minutes, we'll explore the new life and the transformation of the believer, but first, let's answer our other introductory question.

Why doesn't God just eliminate all sin and take us to heaven?

To understand this question, we should first look at what makes something a sin. Did God arbitrarily conjure up a list of rules for man to abide by? The Bible gives us the answer. Take a moment and look at these two passages:

Genesis 1:27
So God created man in His *own* image; in the image of God He created him; male and female He created them.
Romans 3:23
For all have sinned and fall short of the glory of God.

Man's behavior is measured against the image of God. We are created in God's image for the sake of reflecting God's glory. According to Romans, all sin is the result of man falling short of the glory we were created to reflect. Therefore, we know that sin is anything that contradicts the nature and glory of God. Why is that important? My hope is that you will understand the answer to this question by the end of this section.

It's important to understand that morality finds its roots in God's own character. The Bible says that everything was created by God for His pleasure.[18] Man was created for the purpose of having fellowship with God and reflecting God's glory. When we deviate from God's design by taking part in behaviors that are contradictory to His character, we have departed from the standard of God. Mankind gets his goodness from the Lord, and through that goodness we have fellowship with God.

Sin is stepping away from God's character and choosing a contrary way. Righteousness is found by abiding in God's standard and enjoying fellowship with our Creator.

The Bible says that sin cannot abide in God's presence. Anything contradictory to God's character cannot abide with God. When Israel strayed from God, He declared that two cannot walk together unless they are in agreement. Therefore, God cast the idolatrous nation away and they were destroyed by the nations around them – though He preserved a remnant that would one day recognize the worthlessness of idolatry and return to the Lord.

This is a historical example that explains our relationship with God. When man sins, his character is no longer in agreement with God's character, and fellowship is no longer possible. Sin, or the things that oppose God's character, have no effect on God; however, God has a great effect on sin. Sin also has a great effect on us as individuals. According to God's own declaration, everything that exalts itself in opposition to God will be cast down. After all, this is His creation and He is worthy to set the standard and remove anything that opposes His nature.

An atheist once stated that this was evidence that God was selfish. To this I asked, "Do you have fellowship with people that do the things you hate? Or provoke you with inappropriate actions? Or challenge your personality and demand you change to conform to their ideas?"

Fellowship abides among those who have a common interest. When we seek fellowship with our Creator, He gives us the power to conform to His nature and character. When we demand that God

---

[18] Revelation 4:11

become like us, fellowship is not possible. And yes, demanding that God accept the things that contradict His nature is equivalent to demanding that God change to fit our character. God cannot change. We can. As we'll explore later, this is the purpose of the Holy Spirit in our lives.

Every sin will be judged by God and given the wages of sin. The Bible says that the wages of sin is death[19]. Death came by sin and sin came through Adam[20]. This was made evident when Adam first sinned. Fellowship with God was broken and Adam could no longer abide in God's presence. In fact, Adam hid with his wife to avoid God.

God judged man by cursing everything around him. This is known as the fall. Scripture teaches that all of creation groans with the burden of sin as it awaits the final redemption when God will restore all things to their intended purposes.

After the fall, Adam recognized his own nakedness and was ashamed. The Lord took an animal, slew it, and used the skins to cover the nakedness of Adam and Eve.

This is the gospel story tucked away in Genesis. Without the shedding of blood, there is no remission of sins[21]. Why? Because the wages of sin is death. Before man chose to sin, God warned that in the day he disobeyed, he would die. Physical death began as a slow process, but spiritual death was immediate. Through Adam, we also are spiritually dead and will remain that way, unless we are given a new spirit that has life, as God intended before the fall.

We are dead until raised into life.

The Bible has much to say on this topic, but we are going to look primarily at two passages. As we discussed earlier, we were born into sin and though our sin nature is inherited, the penalty of sin – spiritual death – spreads to all because all sin and fall short of

---

[19] Romans 6:23
[20] Romans 5:12
[21] Hebrews 9:22

The Simplicity of Salvation

God's glory[22]. Eternal life comes through the Spirit, but all are dead and unable to obtain that life. A dead man cannot raise himself. This is why works cannot obtain salvation. You can throw flowers on a corpse, but it's still dead. Decorating a corpse doesn't improve its condition – or its eventual destination – to decay.

Something that has the power to give life must intervene to raise the dead. Having said this, let's look at **Colossians 2:11-14**

> [11] In [Christ] you were also circumcised with the circumcision made without hands, by putting off the body of the sins of the flesh, by the circumcision of Christ,
> [12] buried with Him in baptism, in which you also were raised with *Him* through faith in the working of God, who raised Him from the dead.
> [13] And you, being dead in your trespasses and the uncircumcision of your flesh, He has made alive together with Him, having forgiven you all trespasses,
> [14] having wiped out the handwriting of requirements that was against us, which was contrary to us. And He has taken it out of the way, having nailed it to the cross.

This passage has a lot of great information for us to harvest, so let's examine it a little closer. First, let's look at the concept of circumcision. In both the Old and New Testaments, God said that true circumcision is within the heart[23].

Whether we look at the Old or New Testament, the gospel is clearly seen in the ordinance of circumcision. Circumcision was when the foreskin of a male child was cut away. It was the sign of the covenant. The flesh would be cut away, and God would declare the child to be part of His covenant. It was the removal of the flesh for the purpose of partaking in a spiritual promise.

In Colossians above, the scriptures are declaring that while we were outside of God's covenant, the Lord circumcised our hearts by taking away the flesh and joining us to His promise. Once again we can see that the Old Testament pointed directly to what God was

---

[22] Romans 5:12
[23] Jeremiah 4:4, Romans 2:29

about to do. Circumcision serves as an illustration for God's people to see the promise unfolding before their eyes.

In Jewish custom, a child was eight days old when circumcised. It wasn't the child performing the work. He merely laid there while circumcision was performed. In the same way, we are circumcised in our hearts by Christ. It isn't the works we have done – it is God's work done on our behalf when we receive it by faith. God declares His salvation, and we either believe it by faith (which is a gift of God), or disbelieve through the flesh (which is the rebellion of man).

Notice also, we are buried in the flesh, and then raised from our spiritual death into eternal life. It is putting the flesh in the grave of baptism so God can raise us in the Spirit of eternal life. Look at **2 Corinthians 5:17**

> [17] Therefore, if anyone *is* in Christ, *he is* a new creation; old things have passed away; behold, all things have become new.

Throughout the New Testament we see this explained in various ways. Before Christ transforms us, we are spiritually dead. When we respond by faith to God's call, something happens. We don't just add religion to our lives. Our old life is buried with Christ. This is the purpose of baptism. Scripture teaches that we are baptized to wash away our sins, while calling on the name of the Lord. Getting dunked only makes a person wet. It is an act of obedience by faith and we call upon the Lord to wash away our sins.

We don't call upon the physical water. Baptism represents the death and burial of our old life in the flesh, then we are raised in newness of life. We are transformed into a new creation by the power of God. Now we live according to the Spirit because we are a new person. The old things are passed away – in the grave of baptism – and now everything is new. We are not calling upon the water for salvation. Nor are we putting our trust in an ordinance. Salvation is putting our trust in Christ, calling upon Him to circumcise the flesh (or remove the fleshly nature from our hearts) and give us new life in the Spirit.

When a man named Nathaniel came to Jesus, he wanted to understand the Kingdom of God. Jesus said that he must be born again. In our culture, born again means different things to different people, but scripturally, it means that we have died to our old life and are born into a new life by the Spirit. Jesus explains this further in **John 5:21-25**

> [21] "For as the Father raises the dead and gives life to *them,* even so the Son gives life to whom He will.
> [22] "For the Father judges no one, but has committed all judgment to the Son,
> [23] "that all should honor the Son just as they honor the Father. He who does not honor the Son does not honor the Father who sent Him.
> [24] " Most assuredly, I say to you, he who hears My word and believes in Him who sent Me has everlasting life, and shall not come into judgment, but has passed from death into life.
> [25] "Most assuredly, I say to you, the hour is coming, and now is, when the dead will hear the voice of the Son of God; and those who hear will live.

Faith comes by hearing the word of God.[24] Jesus affirms this as he makes it clear that we must believe his word and allow him, the Son of God, to give us passage from death to life.

Simply die to find life

How great is that promise we just read from Jesus! Those who believe shall not come into judgment, for they have passed from death to life. The new life of the believer is not destined for judgment. The judgment of condemnation only applies to the dead. That doesn't mean we aren't accountable for our actions, but it does mean we are on a different road that leads away from death.

---

[24] Romans 10:17

As with all things spiritual, the opposite of human nature is usually the truth of God. Human nature grapples for the gusto of life by grasping for more and more. Living it up is thought to be the meaning of life. The world grapples for life, doesn't find it, and hopes the solution is to grapple for more. With God, however, life is found through death. Not physical death, but death to our life rooted in the flesh. Let's look at the words of Jesus to understand this better. **John 12:23-26**

> [23] But Jesus answered them, saying, "The hour has come that the Son of Man should be glorified.
> [24] "Most assuredly, I say to you, unless a grain of wheat falls into the ground and dies, it remains alone; but if it dies, it produces much grain.
> [25] "He who loves his life will lose it, and he who hates his life in this world will keep it for eternal life.
> [26] "If anyone serves Me, let him follow Me; and where I am, there My servant will be also. If anyone serves Me, him *My* Father will honor.

In this passage, Jesus is foretelling of His coming death on the cross, but He also informs his disciples that this principle applies to them as well. We follow Christ in death – not by being crucified physically, but by being crucified with Him through repentance – turning from our ways – and surrendering our lives to Him. Baptism is the burial of our old life. It is an outward testimony of laying down our lives.

Let me stop for a moment and point out an important truth about repentance. The word means to turn around or have a change of mind, but this definition must be applied in light of the rest of what we know about how God works in our lives. It is not merely you and I deciding to change. It is the work of God who grants repentance to us (See 2 Timothy 2:25). It is the work of God in our hearts, changing our perception on life, and then empowering us to turn from the life of the flesh and toward the life of the Spirit.

Repentance is not you and I deciding to change. Turning over a new leaf may make a temporary change. Deciding to stop a certain behavior may indeed have a limited benefit. While these are noble human efforts, repentance is much more than this. It is God pulling the veil from our heart so we can understand His voice spoken into our spirit. We hear His call to stop going in the direction of our own ways, and to take His hand that He may lead us into the way of the Spirit – the way of eternal life. God's drawing in our heart is the way of repentance.

With that understanding, let's go back to the illustration Jesus gave in the book of John. The picture is a seed. Let's consider the grain of wheat Jesus used as an illustration. A grain of wheat is dry and lifeless. To see this truth, pick any seed. Corn is shriveled, hard, and dry. Nothing in it shows any signs of life. Someone who didn't understand the science behind it would think there was no way to get life out of this dead kernel.

Something strange happens when you bury a seed. Water soaks into the hard shell, something deep within comes alive, and the dead outer shell breaks open and a new plant emerges. The plant looks nothing like the seed. The seed itself dies when the plant emerges. As the plant grows, the dry remains of the old seed fall away and are forgotten.

This is the picture Jesus is painting. When we die to ourselves, our old life is buried with Christ, and a new life emerges. I say 'old life' but a better way may be to say 'our old ways of living for the flesh'. Spiritually, our old life is dead. The miracle of life from the seed is a visual image, but nothing compares to the new birth within us by the Spirit. We are buried with Christ, following him to the cross, and then God raises us up as a new creation with life that doesn't compare to the flesh we are leaving behind. Look at **Colossians 2:11-14**. We've already looked at this passage, but I want to read it again in the context of our current topic.

> [11] In Him you were also circumcised with the circumcision made without hands, by putting off the body of the sins of the flesh, by the circumcision of Christ,
> [12] buried with Him in baptism, in which you also were raised with *Him* through faith in the working of God, who raised Him from the dead.

[13] And you, being dead in your trespasses and the uncircumcision of your flesh, He has made alive together with Him, having forgiven you all trespasses,
[14] having wiped out the handwriting of requirements that was against us, which was contrary to us. And He has taken it out of the way, having nailed it to the cross.

Notice the word pictures given to us in this passage. We were uncircumcised. The flesh of human nature surrounded us like the hard shell of that seed. We were dead, unable to even comprehend life. Yet, while we were still dead in our old ways that were contrary to God, He made us alive. He forgave us of all our sins by nailing it to the cross so that He could make us alive with His Spirit. The lifeless shell was taken out of the way, and we have emerged as a new creation. Christ bore the penalty of our sins in His death, and rose from the grave to lead us into life.

The message of the cross is not, you're going to hell if you don't believe. The message of the cross is that you were already dead in your sins, and Jesus provided life to you and anyone else who receives His words and the gift of salvation.

The Law – Simply a Tutor

There was a man who dedicated himself to being blameless under the law. He sat under the most respected tutors, lawyers, and priests. The excitement and dedication he had drew the attention of his elders, and he excelled above his peers and became a powerful force in the religion of his day. A religion that found its roots in the Old Testament Law that God established to guide His people.

The Old Testament law was so integrated into the Jewish culture that it united the religious and political systems of its day. This man protected the law with all his might and was determined to do the will of God by enforcing it to the letter.

You may have already identified this man – Saul the Pharisee. Later he would abandon his religious profession and would make his living building tents. His tent making funded a lifetime of missionary work. God would soon change his name to Paul, and he would become the apostle responsible for penning two-thirds of the New Testament.

Before Paul understood the purpose of the law, the law was his life, and all he held dear. After his encounter with Christ, he declared that all he once held dear was nothing more than trash. The law itself wasn't the trash, but it became trash when it was mixed with human effort. Religion that is dependent upon man is flawed to the core. Yet the law served an important role. Look at **Galatians 3:22-27**

[22] But the Scripture has confined all under sin, that the promise by faith in Jesus Christ might be given to those who believe.

[23] But before faith came, we were kept under guard by the law, kept for the faith which would afterward be revealed.

[24] Therefore the law was our tutor *to bring us* to Christ, that we might be justified by faith.

[25] But after faith has come, we are no longer under a tutor.

[26] For you are all sons of God through faith in Christ Jesus.

[27] For as many of you as were baptized into Christ have put on Christ.

The passage above was written by the very man who once made it his mission to stamp out faith in Christ because he thought it was a threat to the law. Then he understood that Christ didn't destroy the Old Testament Law, but fulfilled it. It's important to understand that God didn't try one thing, fail, and then try something new. The Old Testament wasn't a failure that led to the New Testament. The Old Testament and the law that undergirded it serves the New Testament and was instrumental in guiding man to God's unfolding plan. Let's look at the three things God ordained the law to accomplish through the Old Testament, and how it applies to our faith in this age.

The Law Condemns

At first glance, this seems like an odd purpose. We think of the law as a means to accomplish good works. Not so. It serves to open our eyes to something greater than human effort – the unmerited and undeserved favor of God. How does condemnation point us to favor? To understand this, let's first look at what the law is doing.
Romans 3:19-21

[19] Now we know that whatever the law says, it says to those who are under the law, that every mouth may be stopped, and all the world may become guilty before God.
[20] Therefore by the deeds of the law no flesh will be justified in His sight, for by the law *is* the knowledge of sin.

Once again, we see the odd purpose the law is serving. Notice that keeping the law and doing the deeds of the law do not justify us before God. It is impossible for man to fully keep the law for we cannot overcome our own human nature through human effort.

Remember our discussion about the rich young ruler? He claimed to be keeping all the commandments including to love his neighbor as himself. While that is something we strive for, ultimately we love ourselves over our neighbors. We may give a hungry man the food or change we can spare, but we don't take food off our own table and give it to someone else while we have needs or wants.

The purpose of the law is to show me that I cannot measure up to the standard of perfection required for holiness. I can boast about my charity, good works, and noble efforts – until I look at my reflection in the mirror of the law. It is then that I see my inability to act without selfish motives. The deeper I look into the law, the more I realize how much I fall short of the glory of God. The law reveals to me my sinful human nature and condemns me for falling short in any area.

Just as with our legal system, keeping ninety-nine percent of our laws do not justify us when we break the law in one area. Showing a judge all the laws you have kept doesn't inspire mercy. The law only focuses on where we break its commandments. In the case of the Bible, failure to keep the law in every point shows my need for God's mercy. The law has no mercy; therefore, we need something greater than the law to redeem us.

Condemnation points me to the cross. When I recognize my inability to raise my dead life from the grave of human nature, I then have the knowledge of sin so that I look outside myself for answers. At this point I must look to the cross where the burden was lifted and life is given. There are many religions, but none raise the dead and bear the penalty for our sins so that we are declared as being just and worthy of life, when we should have been condemned.

The Law Constrains

Why did God give the Ten Commandments? Why am I warned not to covet anything that belongs to my neighbor? Why did the Old Testament issue such harsh penalties for lawbreakers? It is to constrain man's behavior.

Without the fear of consequences, lawlessness abounds. This can easily be seen just by looking around. Consider the countries that lack the ability to enforce the law. South of our border there are drug cartels ruling cities. Murder is a daily occurrence and justice is rarely enforced. Across the ocean war lords reign unchecked. They rampage through towns, murder, take people hostage, and terrorize without discretion. People flee these crimes and look in vain for refuge, but weak governments cannot enforce laws to protect citizens.

The law keeps man in check. Without accountability, man tends toward corruption. There must be either an internal or external restraint. The law is an external restraint.

The Bible refers to the fear of the Lord as the beginning of wisdom. Wisdom is simply the ability to make a wise choice based on the word of God. It isn't a choice for the moment out of a desire for instant gratification. Wisdom counts the cost, looks ahead to the benefit, and directs us to make a choice that is good. Or causes us to resist a choice that is not good, and has negative consequences.

The reason the fear of the Lord is the beginning of wisdom is because we fear the consequences we see our choice will bring. Knowing with certainty that we will be held accountable is a strong deterrent. Why does someone with an out of control temper at home suddenly find control in public? Or at work? When the consequences are real, restraint follows. This is what the law does.

The fear of the Lord is the beginning of wisdom, but the disciple of Christ has the ability to grow into mature wisdom. Wisdom based on fear is to do what is right or not do what is wrong because we fear consequences. Mature wisdom is to do what is right because we see the value of what is right.

Children learn to obey out of a fear of consequences for their actions. If someone matures correctly, as they grow into adulthood, they learn to recognize the value of doing what is right, and no longer need to be kept in check by threats of punishment. The same is true for the Christian. The fear of the Lord recedes as wisdom matures and we see the value of doing what is right simply because we recognize it is good.

The Law Teaches

The law is our tutor (or schoolmaster) that brings us to Christ. We hit on this a bit earlier. It is the law that took mankind by the hand and led him to the cross. The law showed us what is right. It showed us how we ought to live. The law revealed the character of God and what we must be in order to walk with Him. Then it showed us the inability of man to live by that standard without the Spirit of God empowering us to do so. Like a merciless schoolmaster, it deals decisive penalties for failures.

The Bible explains the reason for this – "So that no flesh should glory in His presence."[25] The law teaches that God is perfect, requires perfection, and then condescended to man's level in order to reconcile us to Himself. Just as my children cannot boast that they did something to make themselves worthy to be my children and to be in my house, we cannot think we have done anything to deserve to be God's children. There is nothing we can do to make God accept us. Nor can the law accomplish this. The law simply teaches us to look toward our Redeemer and accept His gift of adoption into His kingdom.

These are the things God teaches about the law as it pertains to us. To understand the law more clearly, let's look at what the law teaches about Christ.

The Sacrifice

From the beginning, the law pointed to Christ. Often people think that God provided one way of salvation in the Old Testament, and a new way of salvation through Christ in the New Testament. This is not the case at all. The Old Testament law was the tutor that prepared mankind for the coming of Christ and according to the Bible, the Old Testament saints are saved through Christ just as we are.[26]

---

[25] 1 Corinthians 1:29
[26] Hebrews 11:24-26, 1 Corinthians 10:2-4, John 8:56

Moses is the prophet that wrote down the first five books of the Old Testament. That's why the law is often called, The Law of Moses. The beginning of God's revelation in word began while Israel was enslaved to Pharaoh and the Egyptians. God showed his power by breaking the will of Pharaoh through the ten plagues. These plagues came to their conclusion when God struck the firstborn of every house in the land. Every house lost their firstborn – except the ones that had the blood on the doorpost.

God instructed his people to sacrifice a lamb, take the blood and strike the door posts and the mantle. When you think of this, what symbol comes to mind? First, Jesus is called the Lamb of God, signifying that He was the sacrifice for sins. The blood on the door is the image of the cross, and striking it symbolizes Christ being nailed for our sins. When judgment came, everyone was already under condemnation. Death did not pass over those who did good deeds or kept strict religious practices. The only deliverance from judgment was the blood on the door posts.

In other words, Jesus did not come to condemn the world, but that the world might be saved through Him. He who does not believe is condemned already. In Exodus, the gospel we now read in John 3 was already being preached. These sacrifices pointed to Christ and though it was called the sacrifice of atonement, it was an act of faith in God's symbolic ordinance. The sacrificed did not pay for sins, it was merely an act of faith given for the Old Testament saints, who were waiting for God's redemption. The sacrifices practiced in Israel for thousands of years did not pay for sin. Let **Hebrews 10:1-10** explain:

[1] For the law, having a shadow of the good things to come, *and* not the very image of the things, can never with these same sacrifices, which they offer continually year by year, make those who approach perfect.

[2] For then would they not have ceased to be offered? For the worshipers, once purified, would have had no more consciousness of sins.

[3] But in those *sacrifices there is* a reminder of sins every year.

[4] For *it is* not possible that the blood of bulls and goats could take away sins.

[5] Therefore, when He came into the world, He said: "Sacrifice and offering You did not desire, But a body You have prepared for Me.

[6] In burnt offerings and *sacrifices* for sin You had no pleasure.

...

[9] then He said, "Behold, I have come to do Your will, O God." He takes away the first that He may establish the second.

[10] By that will we have been sanctified through the offering of the body of Jesus Christ once *for all.*

Just as God slew an animal in the Garden of Eden to cover the nakedness of His people, the animal sacrifice of the law served no other purpose than to remind man that the wages of sin is death, and to ease his conscience with the yearly reminder.

Faith is not a New Testament concept. Abraham believed God, and his faith was accounted to him for righteousness. In the book of Habakkuk in the Old Testament, we are told, "The just shall live by faith."[27] Many wicked men made sacrifices, but God was not pleased. For those who did not obey in faith, God declared that their sacrifices were not acceptable.[28] At one point, God calls the sacrifices an abomination to Him[29]. These people were performing things God required through the law, but the Lord used words like 'it is an abomination', 'things I hate', and 'I abhor', to describe their works. Though it was required by the law, these works did not put the religious seeker in a loving relationship with God. That is accomplished and has always been accomplished by faith in God's plan of redemption.

The Apostle Paul made an interesting statement about the religious followers of his day. "For they are ignorant of God's

---

[27] Habakkuk 2:4
[28] Jeremiah 6:20
[29] Isaiah 1:11 - 14

righteousness, and seek to establish their own righteousness." They were very zealous over the scriptures, but they missed the key to understanding – all things point to Christ and are fulfilled through Christ.

Without Jesus Christ, the law is dependent on sinful human nature. Then it becomes religion plus man's effort. When mankind, who has fallen short of God's glory, becomes the foundation of religion – even religion that believes the scriptures – that religion also falls short of God's glory. It becomes man's effort to raise himself to God – a goal that cannot be obtained.

The Old Testament saints kept the sacrifices by faith, looking ahead to the salvation yet to be revealed. This is why Jesus said, "Abraham rejoiced to see my day,[30]" and "Moses considered being reproached for Christ to be more valuable than the riches of being Pharaoh's grandson.[31]" We live by faith, looking back to the salvation that has been revealed through Christ. The only difference between our salvation and theirs is that they trusted God without seeing what was to be revealed, but we trust God through what *has* now been revealed.

When the Bible explains New Testament faith, it points back to Abraham and even calls him the father of faith. He is how God revealed faith and righteousness. Abraham did many works, but the Bible doesn't credit righteousness to anything he did. He believed God and was credited with righteousness. In the same way, we believe God and are credited with righteousness.

God declared that salvation is in Christ, and when we believe, we find the righteousness of God. No human effort. No good works. God simply reveals salvation to us in the cross, and we believe or reject it.

---

[30] John 8:56
[31] Hebrews 11:26

The Law – Simply a Tutor

Clarifying the Covenants

As you may know, the Bible is divided into the Old and New Testaments. The Old Testament is divided into 39 books, and the New Testament contains 27 books. Generally speaking, the books of the Bible are divided by author or time period. For example, the Apostle Paul wrote two letters to the Corinthian church. Each of those letters stands alone as a book of the Bible.

While the books are divided by author or time period, there is an undergirding foundation to each of the Testaments. The first covenant is the underpinning of the Old Testament. Just before Jesus was crucified, He proclaimed that he was bringing in a new covenant.

The word 'covenant' simply means: an agreement made between two people. It is like a binding contract.

On the surface, these terms may sound like theological jargon, but there is an exciting truth unveiled through these covenants that point directly to how God relates to you and I as individuals. I want to show you how the Old Covenant unveils the love of God for mankind that wasn't fully realized until the New Covenant was confirmed through Christ.

God's Covenant with Abraham

When the Bible teaches the Christian what it means to have faith, Abraham is the example. Yes, the Old Testament patriarch is the model for New Testament faith. Abraham was before the law. This is significant because the Bible makes it clear that the covenant with Abraham came by faith through the promise, and not by the works of keeping the Old Testament law. We'll look at this shortly, but let's first take a look at the covenant of faith given to Abraham.

Genesis chapter fifteen is an amazing passage. The chapter begins by God declaring, "I am your exceedingly great reward." The New Testament points back to God's relationship with Abraham as an example of how God relates to us as believers. We think of rewards as things, but the true reward is God. If we have intimacy with God, we have everything. If we lack that relationship with God, we have nothing of lasting significance.

The Bible calls Abraham the friend of God[32]. Jesus declared to his disciples, "I no longer call you servants...I call you friends.[33]" In both the Old and New Testaments, the joy of faith is friendship with God. It's the goal behind redemption.

The faith of Abraham and the relationship he had with God is the same as God offers to the Christian today. God spoke to Abraham and revealed the promise of his inheritance. Then the Bible says that Abraham believed God, and it was credited to him for righteousness[34]. This is how the Christian believes today. God reveals the promise of our new life through Christ, and by faith we believe God and we are credited with the righteousness of Christ[35].

Hopefully you will begin to see the harmony of the Old Testament and the New Testament. What God did in ancient times was a foreshadowing of what God was about to do through Christ. All the Old Testament points to the coming Christ, and all the New Testament points back to our redemption through Christ.

The same is true for the covenant of Abraham. After Abraham's justification by faith, God introduced the covenant. If you aren't familiar with the word 'justification', it simply means to be justified – or to be declared just. Those who were once under the accusation of sin are declared just through Christ, and no longer are accounted as sinners. This is a topic we'll go into later. For now, be aware that Abraham was justified by faith when he believed God, prior to any covenant.

After being declared righteous, God offered the covenant – or a binding agreement with Abraham. The Lord pointed to the land surrounding Abraham and declared, "I will give you this land for an inheritance, and to your descendants."

At this time, the land had inhabitants who already possessed it. Knowing this, Abraham asked a natural question – how? God not

---

[32] James 2:23
[33] John 15:15
[34] Genesis 15:6
[35] 2 Corinthians 5:17-21

Clarifying the Covenants

only reveals the how, but takes it a step further. God explains that the current inhabitants will be deposed once they become morally bankrupt[36], but then God seals the promise with a covenant.

In the ancient times, when two parties entered into a binding agreement, they would take an animal – usually a ram or a cow, slay it, and lay half the animal on the side where one party sat, and half where the other party sat. They would then swear an oath to each other, and both parties would walk between the pieces. The meaning of the ritual was that each person agreed that what was done to this animal would be done to them if they broke their part of the agreement. In other words, the covenant could not be broken without a death penalty. Keep this in your mental cache. It will be significant when we see how God brings in the New Covenant.

Something interesting happens as God prepares to make the covenant for Abraham. He asks Abraham to prepare the sacrifice[37], but does not allow Abraham to participate in the confirmation. Look now at **Genesis 15:9-12, 17-18a**

[9] So [God] said to him, "Bring Me a three-year-old heifer, a three-year-old female goat, a three-year-old ram, a turtledove, and a young pigeon."

[10] Then he brought all these to Him and cut them in two, down the middle, and placed each piece opposite the other; but he did not cut the birds in two.

[11] And when the vultures came down on the carcasses, Abram drove them away.

[12] Now when the sun was going down, a deep sleep fell upon Abram; and behold, horror *and* great darkness fell upon him.

...

[17] And it came to pass, when the sun went down and it was dark, that behold, there appeared a smoking oven and a burning torch that passed between those pieces.

[18] On the same day the LORD made a covenant with Abram, saying: "To your descendants I have given this land...

---

[36] Genesis 15:16
[37] Genesis 15:9-10

At this point, Abraham's name has not yet been changed, so he is still being called Abram. For the sake of clarity, I will continue to refer to him as Abraham.

Notice that God had Abraham prepare the sacrifice, but did not allow him to walk between the pieces. This is significant. The covenant was with Abraham and his descendants after him. If Abraham had been the confirming party, and either he or his descendants failed to uphold their part of the agreement, the covenant would be broken and judgment would fall. Sin has consequences. Israel (the nation that inherited the promise) sinned and turned their back on God repeatedly. According to the rules of the covenant, the violating party would be slain for breaking the covenant.

To protect Abraham and his descendants, God made the covenant with Himself, but Abraham was the beneficiary. This event was used to show the certainty of God's promises in **Hebrews 6:13-18**

> [13] For when God made a promise to Abraham, because He could swear by no one greater, He swore by Himself,
> [14] saying, "Surely blessing I will bless you, and multiplying I will multiply you."
> [15] And so, after he had patiently endured, he obtained the promise.
> [16] For men indeed swear by the greater, and an oath for confirmation *is* for them an end of all dispute.
> [17] Thus God, determining to show more abundantly to the heirs of promise the immutability of His counsel, confirmed *it* by an oath,
> [18] that by two immutable things, in which it *is* impossible for God to lie, we might have strong consolation, who have fled for refuge to lay hold of the hope set before *us*.

In other words, to give God's people confidence in the certainty of God's promise, He swore the oath against His life, not against the life of any fallible man. Once again, we see the Old

Testament revealing the truth of our promise. To make the promise sure, God swore the oath by Himself. Therefore, even in judgment when Israel abandoned God, the people had the promise of returning to the land and obtaining the promise by simply repenting and reconciling with the Lord.

When the people failed, the covenant remained, for God was the guarantee of the covenant. The oath was between God and Himself, not God and Abraham. However, through that covenant, God blessed Abraham and his descendants with the benefit of the promise.

The law that came through Moses is not how God's people obtained the promise. The promise has always been by faith, and even when the people fell short on keeping the law, the promise wasn't nullified. Look at **Galatians 3:17**

And this I say, *that* the law, which was four hundred and thirty years later, cannot annul the covenant that was confirmed before by God in Christ, that it should make the promise of no effect.

Who was the covenant made through? God in Christ. God swore the oath to Abraham through Christ, and the covenant wasn't dependent upon the law. When the people fell short, they could not nullify the promise of the covenant. Man cannot break a covenant made between God and Himself. Both the Father and the Son were present at the confirmation of Abraham's covenant, and are symbolized through the smoking oven of judgment and the light of the gospel torch.

The law cannot nullify the promise. The success of the law was dependent upon man, so it failed. But the promise cannot be annulled by the failure of man, because it was confirmed by God in Christ. So even in the Old Testament, we see Christ being the covenant maker, though he was not fully revealed until his human birth.

The Bible says that the weakness of the law was man[38], and that the purpose of the law was to restrain man[39], show man his

---

[38] Romans 8:3

inability to justify himself, and therefore turn to Christ[40], to teach man about Christ[41], and to foreshadow Christ[42]. These are all roles of the law. One thing strangely absent is justification. The role of the law was not to justify man. Justification by faith was presented as God's plan more than four-hundred years before the law was given.

Since man *is* the weakness of the law, it also stands true that any promises that are dependent upon man are at risk of failure. Any covenants dependent upon man are destined for judgment. Therefore, God swore a covenant by Himself with Abraham and his descendants as beneficiaries of the promise. God's New Testament plan is no different.

The New Covenant

The New Testament and all of Christianity is founded upon the new covenant. A bit of study reveals the new covenant clearly foretold and foreordained in the rituals and practices of the Old Testament. A testament founded upon God's first covenant. In fact, covenant and testament are interchangeable in their meaning, but for the sake of clarity I'll use testament to refer to the division between the Old Testament times and the New Testament times.

The problem with bringing in a new covenant is that something must be done about the old covenant. The Bible says that it is to be done away with in order to unveil the full plan of God. The old covenant foreshadowed what God was going to do through the new covenant, but the new can't be ushered in until the previous one passes away.

Remember when I said to keep the meaning of the covenant ritual in your mental cache? This is where it becomes significant. God swore by Himself as a guarantee for the covenant with Abraham. In order to break the old covenant, it must be done to Him as was done to the sacrifice. The person breaking a blood oath

---

[39] Galatians 3:23
[40] Romans 3:19-20
[41] Galatians 3:24-25
[42] Hebrews 9:19-28

Clarifying the Covenants

must be slain. And yes, this was part of God's plan from the beginning.

God did not arrive at the New Testament era and say, "Oops." The Lord foretold of how He would break the old covenant. The Bible says that the old covenant was confirmed by God in Christ[43]; therefore, since Christ is the guarantee of the old covenant, He must lay down His life to break it. And this is exactly what Jesus foretells of Himself in the Old Testament. Look at **Zechariah 11:10-14**

> [10] And I took my staff, Beauty, and cut it in two, that I might break the covenant which I had made with all the peoples.
>
> [11] So it was broken on that day. Thus the poor of the flock, who were watching me, knew that it *was* the word of the LORD.
>
> [12] Then I said to them, "If it is agreeable to you, give *me* my wages; and if not, refrain." So they weighed out for my wages thirty *pieces* of silver.
>
> [13] And the LORD said to me, "Throw it to the potter" -- that princely price they set on me. So I took the thirty *pieces* of silver and threw them into the house of the LORD for the potter.
>
> [14] Then I cut in two my other staff, Bonds, that I might break the brotherhood between Judah and Israel.

So much is said in this passage. Let's begin at the end. In the Old Testament times, in order to enter God's covenant with Abraham, one had to be a Jew. Either they had to have been born a Jew, or they had to convert to Judaism. This is why there was so much confusion in the book of Acts in the New Testament. Jesus was a Jew, and so were his disciples. When God poured out His Spirit upon all people, treating the Jews and the Gentiles alike, Jewish believers had a hard time accepting this.

The word 'Gentile' simply means anyone who is not a Jew. For thousands of years, God centered His covenant upon Israel. Now that covenant was broken, and the Jewish Christians had a hard time understanding the significance of this.

---

[43] Galatians 3:17

This is why Zechariah's prophecy is so important. The Old Covenant was based on the physical descendants of Abraham, but the New Covenant brings everyone into the covenant through a new spiritual birth in Christ. In order to open up the world to the promises of God, the Old Covenant that promised it to the bloodline of Abraham had to be broken.

Jesus alluded to this when he said, "Other sheep I have which are not of this fold; them also I must bring, and they will hear My voice; and there will be one flock and one shepherd.[44]"

The Jewish nation looked upon themselves as the sheep of God. God cared for them, nurtured them, and protected them as the fold of His sheep. Now Jesus is saying that another fold will be brought in, and they will be united as one people along with the Jews. This is the gentiles. This is part of the New Covenant. Look at **Matthew 26:27-28**

[27] Then He took the cup, and gave thanks, and gave *it* to them, saying, "Drink from it, all of you.

[28] "For this is My blood of the new covenant, which is shed for many for the remission of sins.

Even Jesus' disciples didn't understand this until God revealed his plan to the New Testament church. The cross is where the Old Covenant was broken, and the New Covenant was born. Jesus took the staff of His protection over the flock of Israel, broke it in two, allowed himself to be nailed to it in the form of a cross, and redeemed all people through the New Covenant.

Think back to the first covenant. Who prepared the sacrifice, and who confirmed the covenant? Man prepared the sacrifice. Abraham prepared it, but God confirmed it by swearing by Himself while making Abraham and his descendants the beneficiaries of the promise. The covenant was between God and God, symbolized in the burning furnace of judgment and the torch of light.

In the same way, man prepared the sacrifice of Jesus, but the covenant was between God and Himself, with us as the beneficiaries of the promise. In the first covenant, only Abraham, the father of

---

[44] John 10:16

Clarifying the Covenants

the Jews was called upon to prepare the sacrifice. In the New Covenant, God called upon the Romans (gentiles) and the Jews to jointly prepare the sacrifice.

The Jews prepared the sacrifice through the trial that provided false testimony and then condemned Jesus with an illegal court. The gentiles prepared the sacrifice through the Romans who knowingly condemned an innocent man under Governor Pilot, and then executed Jesus on the cross.

Man prepared the sacrifice, but the covenant was between God as the Heavenly Father and Jesus the Son. Isaiah 53 says that it pleased the LORD (the Father) to bruise Him (the Son), and make his soul an offering for our sin.

So we can see that the covenant was between God the judge of sin (burning oven) and the Son who is the light of the world (the flaming torch), with us as the beneficiary to the promise. The promise is our redemption from judgment against sin, and becoming joint heirs, who are now welcomed into the fold of God.

How can we not rejoice in the amazing work of God? And how can we not stand in awe of the foreknowledge of God? He revealed these things from the beginning. The Old Testament saints could not understand these things because Christ had not yet been revealed. We, on the other hand, can see clearly through the lens of the cross and see how God has been working out his plan for thousands of years.

Dare to be Disciplined

In 2005, a college player was taken in the first round of the NFL draft. This man had everything going for him – speed, talent, instincts. He had everything he needed to be an NFL star. He was so good at defense that he took down everyone in his path. He lacked one thing – discipline.

Unable to control his own behavior, legal troubles began to mount. He was finally suspended for an entire season and cut from the team that once had faith in his abilities. Another team took a big gamble and signed him in the midst of his suspension.

The skilled player once again had the opportunity most athletes only dream of. A new series of legal troubles led to another suspension. By the time the season ended, a player considered to be one of the most talented in the NFL had been suspended twenty-two out of twenty-eight games. Not one of his suspensions were related to his on-field performance. The lack of discipline caused this man to become his own worst enemy.

You have probably heard the word 'discipline' used in regards to the Christian walk. If not, you certainly have heard it used in other contexts. Athletes discipline themselves to train, eat right, and stay on course to reach their goal. A student must discipline themselves to study to make the grade. A soldier is disciplined to learn the art of war. Someone who is well disciplined is considered a high achiever.

In our spiritual lives, discipline plays a vital role just as it does in many other areas of life. Before we discuss what discipline is, let's look at what it is not as it pertains to our walk of faith.

What Discipline is Not.

Discipline is *not* what makes the Christian righteous. Nor is discipline equivalent to spiritual maturity. Nor is discipline the thing that produces faith in our lives – though many people treat it as such. Discipline also should not become a legalistic set of rules.

Legalism is to try to live by a set of rules in order to become righteous or to attempt to merit God's favor. One danger of any discipline is the risk of the process becoming the focus. I'll explain. As is evidenced by the book you are reading, I'm a writer. Being a writer, I'm involved in several writing groups and organizations. One thing I've discovered is that bad advice abounds. There is much good advice, and what I draw from other writers far outweighs the crumbs of bad advice that falls onto my plate. Yet, I have to learn how to discern between the good and the bad. One person's suggestion becomes another person's guideline. Like a game of whisper, the more people it passes through, the more it mutates.

Let me give an example. The word 'was' is highly frowned upon in modern writing circles. Since many passive sentences use the word was, writers are encouraged to search for that word and then examine the sentence for passiveness. The next person who passes on this tidbit of information gives their version of helpful advice, "Cut down on the 'was' words."

The next person passes it along by saying, "Don't use the word 'was'."

Recently someone shared with me the advice they received from a professional writing coach. The editor highlighted every 'was' and gave the rule for this writer to abide by. "The word 'was' should be avoided at all cost. It should never be used more than once every ten-thousand words." What was once a guideline has become a concrete rule. Many writing professionals can't enjoy reading because they are looking for rule violations.

I've heard similar statements about using 'that', words ending in 'ly', and many such rules. As rules are spread by word of mouth, they eventually become commandments in the minds of others, even though no such rule actually exists.

Things to be on a 'look out for' become things to be stamped out within a few generations of passing along advice. Guidelines and disciplines have great value, but good advice turns into bad advice when one person's preference becomes a rule for everyone to obey. One of the standard books on writing etiquette began as a college professor's guidelines for his students. He set his preferences for term papers and the book preface even states this, but over time it has become the bible of writing authority. One man's preference became everyone's rule.

This also happens regularly in matters of faith. I grew up in church and witnessed many such examples. One pastor I knew had lived a very rough lifestyle before coming to Christ. His idea of fun had once been to hang out in a pool hall and drink until he couldn't see straight, and then to fight anyone who crossed him.

After coming to faith, he rightly abandoned his old lifestyle and never visited another pool hall. When visiting someone's home, he saw a pool table in their den and was appalled. I listened to the preacher vocalize his shock and ask why anyone claiming to be a Christian family would allow a tool of the devil into their home. In his mind, the pool table represented the life he had escaped from.

I've seen similar comments about a deck of cards. Since some people gamble with cards and gambling addicts drag families down into destitution, they believe cards are evil.

There are many areas of preference that become points of legalism. We all know that God only likes music written between 1830 and 1940, right? That's why we only allow music from the old time hymnals. Of course this isn't true. While there is nothing wrong with a church singing the old time hymns, we also must realize this is a preference issue and not a God ordained commandment.

Legalism arises when we try to merit God's favor by keeping rules, or when we turn preferences into commandments. Often, those preferences are very relevant in our lives and part of our personal disciplines, but they are ways we structure our routines and not what God requires of everyone.

When someone says, "You must have quiet time and Bible study early each morning in order to be spiritual," that is legalism. It may be true that some people need to study early because they are too tired in the evening and can't be consistent without an early routine. That is a discipline. However, some people can't study early because they aren't a morning person, and they get their second wind when the sun goes down and the house grows quiet.

"You must study in the morning to be faithful," is legalism.

"Try studying first thing in the morning. It works for me," is a valid suggestion and is how someone disciplines their own life.

I could go on and on, but hopefully, you get the picture. Personal preference should not become a commandment. There are many voices out there claiming to be the voice of God, but the Bible makes it clear that we have liberty. When the Galatian church was plagued by those who brought in rules that they claimed were necessary in order to be right with God, Paul rebuked them and said, "Oh foolish Galatians, who has bewitched you?"

The Apostle Paul then made two important points to this confused church. First, he asked them how they could think that they began their life of redemption by faith, but now think they must be made perfect by works of the flesh. In other words, if we recognize that we are saved by grace through faith and not by any merit of our own, why would we think we must now earn God's favor after becoming a child of Him? We live the same way we are redeemed, by grace through faith – and that is not of yourselves.

Another important point was made in **Galatians 5:13**
For you, brethren, have been called to liberty; only do not *use* liberty as an opportunity for the flesh, but through love serve one another.

We are given great freedom in the faith. Where God is silent, we must not insert a command. The overarching principle is that we must not use our freedom to serve our sinful flesh. So, if the Bible gives no specific command or instruction, I have the freedom to discern what is best according to my own life. As long as I can walk faithfully with the Lord, and I am not serving the flesh, I have freedom to discern where I need discipline, and which areas I can exercise freedom.

We all have different personalities and weaknesses. Things that draw me into sin may not even be a temptation to someone else. Consider the pool table. Someone who associates a pool table to their old sinful lifestyle may be inclined to cast that out of their lives. For them, their walk of faith is evidenced by their abandonment of their old passion of playing pool while carousing.

Yet for the person who has never been in that lifestyle, a pool table is nothing but a felt table, ten balls, and a stick. It's no more than a game.

This is where you must learn to discern between biblical doctrine and personal preference. How God works in your life is based on your personality, strengths, weaknesses, and God's calling for your life. What creates discipline in your life won't necessarily work in someone else's life. What works in someone else's life may not work in your life.

Don't let the preferences of another become a burden to you. Or a source of guilt. The Bible makes it clear that we cannot let our lives be judged by another person's conscience[45]. That also is a form of legalism.

What Discipline Is.

We've already seen that discipline is not what fulfills our goals or makes us righteous. Discipline *is* a method that keeps us in the state of mind where we can keep moving forward.

Our minds naturally gravitate toward slackness. Discipline guards us from drifting away from what we value. Think about exercise. Why do we do it? Exercise isn't the goal; exercise is how we reach for the goal. Your goal might be to lose weight. It may be that you are lacking energy and need to get your body back into a healthy state. Exercise isn't the achievement – it's the method by which we reach for our goal of becoming fit and healthy.

Academic studying is a discipline. Without studying, a student will not make the grade. The goal is a better education, and the discipline of study is the means by which students reach for that goal.

What happens when study habits slip? The goal of passing the class or making good grades slide out of reach. What happens when you skip exercise for a few days? It's hard to force yourself back into action. It doesn't take long to get into the slack mode and let a

---

[45] 1 Corinthians 10:29

Dare to be Disciplined

discipline slip into the deep waters of apathy. As a writer, I try to write something every day. If not, it takes great effort to stir my lazy mind back into action. Without discipline, I just remember I haven't done something and think, "I really need to do that. Someday."

Discipline keeps us motivated, even when we don't feel like doing anything. It keeps us moving forward and maintaining momentum. Without discipline, everything becomes like our New Year's resolution. Something kick starts us every now and then, but without real discipline, we can't keep the goal in view.

When it comes to spiritual matters, we must have a process in place that works with our personalities *and* overcomes our weaknesses. Unless you find a way to schedule specific, intentional activities, you won't maintain any level of real spiritual growth. Everyone says, "I need to do more Bible study or be more consistent in my prayer life." The truth is, that won't happen unless you structure these things into your daily life. Bible study is a command, but study habits are disciplines.

Discipline is based on value. What you value is what you will pursue. Of course, there must be an evaluation before you recognize value. This is what goal setting is all about. You can't pursue a goal you don't have. Saying, "I need to spend more time in the word," is not a goal. Evaluating your life and determining what character traits you value can become a goal.

Perhaps I want to overcome a character flaw, such as being snappy toward my family. Or maybe I value knowing God intimately and want to see the fruit of the Spirit maturing in my life. The Bible says, "By this all men shall know you are my disciples, your love for one another."

We know that love (agape) is the fruit of the Spirit and comes from God. Maybe I'll make it my goal to know the love of God so I can show that love to others. Or perhaps I see the passage that says, "Walk in the Spirit and you will not fulfill the lust of the flesh." My goal could be to do the things God commands so I can experience what it means to walk in the Spirit.

When I graduated from high school, I had no educational goals. I was undisciplined and unmotivated. I flunked out of college.

No surprise there. I aimed for nothing and I achieved what I aimed for. After spending a few years in the military, I completed my duty and got a job. I worked my way up to a management position and then the war in Iraq began. I was recalled into the army and my career took a blow.

Though legally, companies were required to hold jobs for soldiers, I discovered that my job had been filled when I returned. Now married, I saw the need for marketable job skills. Obtaining a valuable job skill became important to me, so I returned to college with a motivation and a goal. I went from making D's and F's to achieving A's and B's.

Having something important to strive for gave me motivation. Motivation led me to discipline, and through discipline I worked, studied, and endured until the goal was in my hands.

This is where the rubber meets the road. If you sit back and think, "I really should do something," it won't happen. You may get started, but you won't endure. But when you see the goal, and it's something of value, you'll be motivated to persevere. This is where discipline comes into play. Determine what you need to do, and set a plan in motion to accomplish it.

Bible study and quiet time are actions. They are actions that require discipline in order to maintain consistency. At such and such time, I will allocate x number of minutes, and that time isn't available for anything else. Or if you have the type of schedule where a specific block of times may or may not be available, make room in other ways. I won't check my email until I've read and journaled for thirty minutes, or completed a certain number of written pages. Set shallow pleasures aside until after disciplined time has been fulfilled.

For this to work there must be a goal. Most Christians have a theoretical faith. The benefit of spiritual maturity doesn't seem real or attainable. Or the things of this life crowd their lives and appear more valuable than they actually are. We can see the temporal life around us, but we can't see the hidden things of eternity. Perhaps a first goal would be to see the reality of spiritual benefits in the word. Many have begun the journey by wanting to know the truth of scripture.

Be consistent with discipline. Be uncompromising with your goal. But don't become legalistic. If circumstances cause me to miss a day, I won't beat myself up over it. Guilt is not a good motivator. Simply take the next opportunity and get back on track. Do not allow yourself to miss two days if at all possible. The reason is not that you will have failed, but because when you lose momentum, you lose motivation.

Discipline is a tool that keeps you moving forward and in a goal oriented state of mind – even when you feel like being lax.

Don't expect God to sing your praises because you set time out to read your Bible. The reward is not because you were disciplined. The discipline is a tool by which you reach for something you value. What you value is the reward. God doesn't owe me payment for spending time in the scriptures. The scriptures unveil the reward. God told Moses, "I am your exceedingly great reward." This is the reward and from a close relationship with God, everything else flows. Discipline is the path toward the reward – intimacy with God.

Understanding discipline is important, so let's summarize it again. Thinking that what I do is what makes me righteous is a step into legalism. When I think a reward is due because I set time aside for God, I've become legalistic in my thinking. Keep the goal in mind. The work isn't the goal. The work is how we reach for the goal. The goal is what we value. God indeed desires to give us of His kingdom, but faith comes before the promise. We will effectively discipline ourselves when we believe in the value of what God says about Himself and His word.

When hearing the word 'discipline', don't think of do's and don'ts. Think of a means to reach for a goal. Determine what you value in the Christian walk and the promises of God, set a goal, and place checks in balances in your life to keep you focused and motivated in reaching for that goal. That is discipline. It's the vehicle on the road that you drive toward what you value.

The Lord Sings Over You

This is a good time to change gears and evaluate our motivations. Do you view God as someone watching over you with tender care, or someone watching over to strike your backside when you step out of line? Most people struggle with their idea of how God views them. The majority of us have heard the passages where God says, "Be holy, for I am holy[46]," and Jesus' command, "You shall be perfect, even as your heavenly Father is perfect,"[47] but how do we as imperfect people apply these commands to our lives?

When we fall short of perfection – which is often – we know we have failed to measure up to the standard of God's character. Then we acquire the 'Adam and Eve syndrome'. When Adam and Eve sinned, they ran and tried to hide from God. They recognized that they were not worthy to face a holy God, and rightly so. But what was God's response? He covered their shame. Though there were consequences for their actions, the Lord didn't reject them. He showed mercy. God covered their shame and then began revealing a plan for their redemption.

When Asaph (the son of one of King David's chief musicians) thought upon the merciful way God dealt with His people, it gave him a heart of praise. Though Israel entered into God's covenant, they rebelled against their Creator. The people benefited from the Promised Land the Lord gave, but they couldn't keep their heart from wandering away. God could have cast them away each time they fell, but He showed long patience and mercy. Look at how Asaph reflects on this in **Psalm 78:38-39**

[38] But He, *being* full of compassion, forgave *their* iniquity, And did not destroy *them*. Yes, many a time He turned His anger away, And did not stir up all His wrath;

[39] For He remembered that they *were but* flesh, A breath that passes away and does not come again.

---

[46] 1 Peter 1:16
[47] Matthew 5:48

The Lord Sings Over You

Though God had every right to deal harshly with those who sinned, He extended mercy for generations as He pleaded with them to return to righteousness and guided them with warnings and promises. The Lord's goal was mercy. And why was He so merciful toward His people, who were caught up in iniquity? He remembered that they were only flesh. They were people struggling against human emotions, their passions, and the influences around them. They weren't divine, nor did they have a clear picture of the eternal values of life. They often went astray because the passions of their flesh lured them away from walking by faith.

You and I have the same problem. Though we have the internal guiding of the Holy Spirit, we battle our passions in the flesh, and at times these desires draw us away. When we know iniquity is in our lives and that we've violated the holiness of God, we want to run and hide. We see our guilt, and expect God to deal harshly. We struggle with the perceived anger of God, yet anger is not God's first choice. His first goal is to draw you back and cleanse you.

Don't mistake the mercy of God for apathy. God does indeed require holiness. God does indeed call us to leave behind the works of the flesh, and the passions that produce corruption in our lives. We know the Bible's warning / promise, "He that sows in the flesh will reap corruption, but he that sows in the Spirit will reap everlasting life.[48]"

I've heard the well-intentioned but misguided teaching that if grace is taught as it should be, it will sound like a license to sin. That is far from the truth. If grace is taught as it should be, it will show God's deliverance from sin. Rather than God punishing us when we fail, God reaches down and pulls us out of our sins. Here is the message of grace - **Psalm 40:2-3**

[2] He also brought me up out of a horrible pit, Out of the miry clay, And set my feet upon a rock, *And* established my steps.

[3] He has put a new song in my mouth -- Praise to our God; Many will see *it* and fear, And will trust in the LORD.

---

[48] Galatians 6:7-8

Grace pulls us out of the pit we have fallen into. It doesn't merely visit us in the pit and wink at our predicament. Sin is a pit. Yet I foolishly return to it again and again, each time thinking I can somehow walk on top of the mire. I ease back into sin and test the surface of the clay. It seems safe until I realize I can't step out. The more I struggle, the more I sink.

Have you ever stepped into miry mud or clay? I have. When I pulled my right foot out, the other was pushed deeper. I pulled the left foot out, and my right foot went deeper still. Each time one foot broke free, there was a moment of hope, but it faded when I realized that I continued to sink with each attempt toward freedom. Escape only came when someone outside of the clay pulled me out.

This is the trappings of the flesh. From a temporal perspective, we have the illusion that we can free ourselves, but with each step of progress, we continue downward into the mire.

Yet the Lord doesn't leave us to our fate. Once we look up and cry out for help, He rescues us and sets us upon the rock. That rock is Christ. While standing on the rock, we are safe. But the flesh continues to call, beckoning us with the promise of pleasure and the false assurance that we are stronger and won't sink on our next visit.

Even the godly suffer from this tendency to return to the mire. The Apostle Paul lamented over his tendency to do the things he knew he should not do, while neglecting what he knew he should do. He then warned that sin remains in our bodies of flesh and will war against our minds, seeking to draw us back into its captivity.[49] If the Apostle Paul struggled, it should not be a surprise when we find ourselves wrestling with the same things.

Like Israel in the Old Testament, God delivers us and gives us the word of instruction that could prevent us from repeating the same mistakes. Israel was delivered, and they promised to never stray again. Yet they did. They soon found themselves under bondage again, cried out for deliverance, and were rescued again. What the nation did so foolishly in the Old Testament, we do today

---

[49] Romans 7:23-24

in our own lives. But God is merciful and continues to deliver us when we repent. When we stray, God pulls at our heart, calling us to turn from our ways and back to Him. When we allow Him to lead us back, this is repentance.

Consider how God dealt with His people in the Old Testament. He called, wooed, and wrestled with His people. God's first option was not to punish, but to instruct. When they strayed, God sent His word to them with instructions to return. It was only after years of rejecting God's call to turn from sin that harsh action was taken. He reached down into the mire, but they slapped His hand away. When they refused to turn from sin, God allowed them to sink. But He did so with two promises. If you repent, I will rescue you, and I will not allow you to be utterly destroyed. So even when He allowed the consequences of sin to judge the people, He still made it clear that mercy was His greatest desire.

The same is true for you and I. God wants to take us out of the mire. Grace not only rescues us from the mire, but it teaches us how to live in a way that we can avoid the trap of sin. Spiritual maturity is when we cease from repeating the same pattern of behavior, stop sowing in our flesh, and begin investing our lives in righteousness so we can reach for the promises of God. Living is more than being delivered from the flesh. Just as there are consequences to living in the flesh, there are also great rewards in spiritual maturity.

There are those who look for a license to sin and turn faith into mere religion. Worldly religion seeks to appease our conscience while pursuing our own ways. True faith pursues what is eternal while learning how to leave behind what is worthless and temporary.

True faith separates us from the world (the process of living for the flesh) and sets us apart for God. In fact, that is what holiness means. To be holy means to be set apart. It is the believer setting themselves apart for God. Unholiness is to remove ourselves from God's will, the place where we belong, and to mix our lives back into the world.

Is Perfection Required?

If you ask people if God requires us to be perfect, most will say, "No." Nobody is perfect, right? You may have seen a bumper sticker on a car that says, "I'm not perfect, just forgiven."

What do you think? Must you be perfect to enter heaven? If you're like most people, you'll say, "No." But is that true? Consider these statements from the teaching of scripture:

You shall be perfect, just as your Father in heaven is perfect. Matthew 5:48

The purpose of roles in the church is to bring believers to become perfect and to measure up to the fullness of Christ. Ephesians 4:9-11

Paul said that he warns and teaches every person in wisdom that they may be presented perfect in Christ Jesus. Colossians 1:28

We labor that you may stand perfect and complete in all the will of God. Colossians 4:12

The spirits of just men are to be made perfect. Hebrews 12:23

According to Jesus, perfection is a requirement. According to the teachings of the Apostles afterward, the purpose of the scriptures and the doctrines we teach are to make the Christian perfect. Unless you are perfect, how can you stand before a perfect God? So the statement, nobody's perfect, is a recognition of the problem. We all recognize the impossibility of human perfection, yet perfection is still required.

I say all of this to point out the fact that you are unable to measure up to God's standard. It is impossible. Every effort you make is a work of the flesh. The reason? You are flesh. Jesus made the statement that on the Day of Judgment, many will come to him and show all their good works done in Jesus' name. They will have fed the poor, done wonders, and accomplished many of the things

Jesus instructed the church to do. Yet he declares to them, "Depart from me, you're a worker of lawlessness[50]."

How can a good deed done to the poor, or other good deeds be works of lawlessness? Jesus compares their good deeds to sin. Jesus isn't introducing a new concept. Even in the Old Testament, the prophets acknowledged that all our righteous acts are filthy in God's sight[51]. The reason? Jesus said it best. "It is the Spirit that gives life. The flesh profits nothing.[52]"

So what does all this have to do with yours and my struggle against sin? Simply put, you can't be perfect. Yet you must be perfect. In the flesh, your best isn't good enough. When you blow it and fail, you are no worse off than when you think you're earning favor with God.

Whether your work of the flesh leads to sin, or your work of the flesh is lawlessness masquerading as righteousness, you are still in need of divine intervention. And that is how you become perfect. Look at **Hebrews 10:12-14**

[12] But this Man, after He had offered one sacrifice for sins forever, sat down at the right hand of God,

[13] from that time waiting till His enemies are made His footstool.

[14] For by one offering He has perfected forever those who are being sanctified.

Verse fourteen describes your perfection. Because of Jesus' offering on your behalf, you are made perfect. If you are in the process of being sanctified, you are already perfected forever.

What does it mean to be sanctified? The biblical definition of sanctification is: to be separated from the profane, and to be cleansed, purified, and dedicated to God.

In other words, when someone surrenders to Christ, they are removed from the profane world that cannot please God, and are cleansed and made pure and perfect for the Kingdom of God. You

---

[50] Matthew 7:22-23

[51] Isaiah 64:6

[52] John 6:63

are still in the process of being sanctified. That is the process of spiritual maturity. But you are already declared as perfect because you are viewed through the works of Christ. Your works by human effort are sin, but the work of God in your heart and life is the righteousness of Christ.

When you sin, it is the work of the flesh. When you try to do good works by human effort, it is still the work of the flesh. The Lord's work in your life is to bring you into sanctification (or purity) so you can inherit the promises. Salvation and perfection is through Christ.

The promises are no different. We work the works of God by walking in faith. As Jesus stated, you must abide in Him as a branch connected to the vine. By yourself, you can do nothing, but if you abide in Him, you bear good fruit and accomplish the work of God[53]. It really is that simple.

A Father Delights in His Children

My hope is that this chapter changes your perspective on how God views you. Rather than viewing yourself as the object of God's scorn for your failures, think of yourself as a child of God. We've all heard of 'the fear of the Lord', but let's consider what that means.

The Bible says that the fear of the Lord is the beginning of wisdom[54], but we are also told that the fear of the Lord is our strong confidence, the fountain of life, and the pathway to true riches and honor. Our tendency is to think of the fear of the Lord as something to cower from. If not viewed correctly, people look at this term as something negative. That's why some water it down by saying the fear of the Lord means to show reverence to God. This completely obscures what the Bible is teaching, so let's take a moment to understand this principle.

The fear of the Lord is a good thing. The image God constantly paints in both the Old and New Testaments is that He is our father and loves us as a parent does his child. When explaining His care for

---

[53] John 15
[54] Proverbs 9:10

The Lord Sings Over You

Israel, God described the relationship as a father carrying his son to safety.[55]

I have children. When one is afraid, hurt, tired, or just wants to be picked up, I carry them. In my arms they feel safe, secure, and loved. At the same time, each one knows about the consequences of disobedience. When their behavior goes astray, I correct them with instruction. If it continues, I warn them. If they are determined to do what I know will harm them, I punish them to correct the behavior. The punishment is more profitable than the end result of rebellion; therefore it is a good thing.

My goal isn't to harm, but to correct. If words correct them, there are no further actions required. But if they insist on going their own way, I will prevent them. The consequences of punishment are much less harmful than the consequences of where their behavior will lead.

A child can't see the future. Their limited understanding and lack of life experience prevents them from seeing the harm of their direction. It's not possible to reason with a four year old, so I just tell them, "Here is the rule. Why? Because Daddy says so."

Even a teenager believes they know more than they do. Parents often fail to persuade by reasoning because we can see by experience the consequences they cannot see. Though a rebellious teen may be convinced there are no consequences, we have seen the end of their plan and understand the danger. The only thing they see is what they want, but not where that road leads.

When I correct my children, do I reject them? Hate them? Am I being mean? Of course not. It's an act of love. In fact, I love them enough to risk my own feelings to protect them. I accept their lashing out and mischaracterization of my intentions because I care more about protecting them from consequences than protecting my own reputation in their eyes.

Jesus made the statement, "If you being evil, know how to give good things to your children, how much more is this true for your Heavenly Father." By evil, Jesus is referring to what we've already discussed. We are flesh. We have a limited perspective and operate

---

[55] Deuteronomy 1:31

from a self-centered viewpoint. If I view discipline as an act of love and I am willing to protect my children at my own expense, how much more is this true about how God deals with me?

This was discussed earlier, but it bears mentioning again because it applies so well to this topic and our life of faith. The fear of the Lord is the beginning of wisdom because in the beginning, we are like children. Children obey because they are afraid of the consequences. Discipline corrects their behavior and the punishment is not worth the pleasure of disobedience.

Wisdom is making a decision to do what is right. In the beginning, a child does what is right because of the fear of consequences. But as a child matures into adulthood, they begin to understand what is right. As a young adult grows into responsibility, they recognize the value of doing what is right. A child does what is right because they don't want consequences, but the mature do what is right because it is good. Fear creates the beginning of wisdom, but mature wisdom does not require fear. In fact, righteousness becomes a joy.

The beginning of wisdom is where we consider the cost of bad choices before we make them, knowing we are accountable to the Lord for our actions. Mature wisdom is where we consider the value of what is right, knowing we'll stand before the Lord and see the treasure of His ways, and that His word is truly a fountain of life.

So we can see that even in correction, the Lord is delighting in our way. Chastisement is a delight to God. The delight is not in our discomfort, but in the maturity it brings. Chastening turns us away from the consequences and directs us toward the promises. That's why the Bible says that God corrects the children He loves and chastises those He delights in[56]. Also consider this passage from **Psalm 37:22-24**

[22] For *those* blessed by Him shall inherit the earth, But *those* cursed by Him shall be cut off.

[23] The steps of a *good* man are ordered by the LORD, And He delights in his way.

---

[56] Hebrews 12:5-11

The Lord Sings Over You

[24] Though he fall, he shall not be utterly cast down; For the LORD upholds *him with* His hand.

Keep verse 23 in the front of your mind at all times. Always remember that God delights in your way. Your journey through life is an exciting journey to the Lord, for it is His good pleasure to give you His Kingdom[57]. When you go astray, He pushes you back to the right path. When you're on the right path, God rejoices over you with delight. The Lord's goal is for you to inherit the promises that are found in His presence.

If you belong to Christ, everything in your life is focused on you glorifying God by reigning with Him and inheriting the promises. After all, the promises are given because God wants you to have His kingdom. Finally, look at **Zephaniah 3:17**

The LORD your God in your midst, The Mighty One, will save; He will rejoice over you with gladness, He will quiet *you* with His love, He will rejoice over you with singing."

What more can God do to express His love? Rather than viewing God as someone angry and waiting to lash out at your failures, picture him as a loving father, guiding you to maturity and fulfillment. Unlike flawed earthly fathers, our God has perfect motives and patiently leads without lashing out in anger. Keep in mind that it is the goodness of the Lord that leads you to repentance[58].

Repentance isn't groveling in failure. Repentance is a course correction. It's turning from our own way, and toward the way God is leading.

---

[57] Luke 12:32
[58] Romans 2:4

Let's get it right about Righteousness

This is a good time to talk about righteousness. People are often confused by terms like, imputed righteousness, infused righteousness, and other phrases that are meant to identify church beliefs, but often lead to confusion. A lot of this we have discussed in bits and pieces, but some things need to be clarified. Understanding righteousness does matter. How I view my ability to be righteous determines how I live out my faith.

Imputed righteousness

As we observed earlier, God used Abraham as the example of faith and how it affects our righteousness. By God's design, faith was revealed before the law. The reason is made clear throughout the New Testament. God showed how His righteousness is accredited to us before giving the law so that we could understand that righteousness is by faith and not by works. The Bible says that we were saved by grace through faith, and that it is not of ourselves.[59]

It is the work of God that reaches down and calls man out of sin, and places the righteousness of God within the hearts of those who believe. Righteousness is first accredited to us – or imputed. Then it is produced in our lives by the work of the Holy Spirit. It's important to understand these things because good doctrine is well balanced. To say we are credited with righteousness; therefore, we don't need to live rightly is a common but false belief. Yet because people only see certain passages without seeing the context, it's easy to draw incorrect assumptions.

It is also false to say that I must do something to become righteous. The Bible must be taken as a whole. Once I was asked who I believed, Paul who said faith is apart from works, or James who said faith is by works? In truth, both Paul and James provide the same teaching, but begin by addressing different audiences.

---

[59] Ephesians 2:18-19

Paul addresses those who seek justification by keeping the law. James begins by addressing an apathetic church who claimed to have faith but show no evidence. At the end of this discussion, we'll compare these to apostles and see that both are saying the same thing but addressing different problems.

The truth is that the Bible never makes us choose between contradicting teachings. Scripture is a complete revelation and is to be taken as a whole. The Bible tells us to be diligent to study so we can rightly divide the word of truth[60]. We rightly divide by taking a doctrine from the scriptures, examining it to understand how it applies to our life, and then examining each doctrine in light of the entire Bible.

It takes time and diligence to study the word. This is why God said he teaches us precept upon precept, line upon line, here a little, there a little[61]. Each time you study the word, you build upon what you've already learned. Incorrect assumptions are also corrected by the rest of scripture when we study. Just as the weakness of the law was man, the weakness of doctrine is also man. Once we add ideas to scripture based on personal opinions and assumptions, our doctrines begin to stray from truth. Yet the Bible corrects this when we diligently study. Consider **2 Timothy 3:16-17**

> [16] All Scripture *is* given by inspiration of God, and *is* profitable for doctrine, for reproof, for correction, for instruction in righteousness,
> [17] that the man of God may be complete, thoroughly equipped for every good work.

Notice one of the purposes of scripture. To correct. There's a saying that a little knowledge is a dangerous thing. This is also true when it comes to the Bible. New Christians bring a lifetime of assumptions to the word, but as someone studies faithfully, errors fall by the wayside as the scriptures correct our false beliefs. Most false teaching arises from people bringing in their personal beliefs

---

[60] 2Timothy 2:15
[61] Isaiah 28:9-10

and applying it to the Bible. Instead, we should be taking the Bible and applying it to our lives.

Misconceptions are found throughout Christendom, and you will find times when your own beliefs are corrected by scripture. Just because everyone around you believes something to be true doesn't make it true. God has provided a firm foundation in the word, and we should never reject scripture in order to hold to a pet belief.

Diligent study dismantles false beliefs. That's why we must study the whole word. We can't build a solid foundation with bits and pieces of the word.

This same issue comes into play when we discuss righteousness in the Christian's life. External beliefs coming in can muddy the waters, but the Bible clarifies itself. Let scripture be the interpreter of scripture.

Is righteousness an accounting term, or a legal declaration, or a practical way of living rightly? At times groups will claim one of these as the meaning of righteousness but miss the fullness of what the Bible teaches on this subject. It's all these things. Often people misunderstand because they are taught that the Bible says righteousness is only an accounting term – we are accounted as debt free, but then need to work to become personally righteous. Others say it's only a legal declaration, but not individual righteousness. We don't choose one or more. The Bible explains how all of these things apply to the Christian life.

Legal declaration

The Bible declares us legally just from our sins. This does not mean that the bible *only* declares us legally just. It is only one of the declarations of scripture referring to our righteousness, and it is the first step in our justification. Justification simply means, "The act of God declaring men to be free from guilt."

There is an interesting passage regarding this. Look at **Romans 3:25-28**

^{25} [Jesus,] whom God set forth *as* a propitiation by His blood, through faith, to demonstrate His righteousness, because in His forbearance God had passed over the sins that were previously committed,
^{26} to demonstrate at the present time His righteousness, that He might be just and the justifier of the one who has faith in Jesus.
^{27} Where *is* boasting then? It is excluded. By what law? Of works? No, but by the law of faith.
^{28} Therefore we conclude that a man is justified by faith apart from the deeds of the law.

Earlier we looked at sin as being an affront to the nature and character of God. To be right with God, we must be just. To be just is to conform to the requirements of the law so we are able to approach a holy God. But we are not just by nature, for human nature is corrupt. We were born with a bent toward sin. Some baulk at the idea that we are born with a sin nature, but as we have seen earlier, any parent knows children have a propensity to sin without seeing that behavior in others. It's part of the sinful nature we are born with. We use consequences to restrain behavior, but the heart is not changed. Though an acceptable standard of behavior is learned, the tendency to sin and act selfishly remains within each of us.

In the passage above, the Bible is addressing the problem of our guilt. God paid for our guilt with his own blood. The word *propitiation* simply means for one person to stand in the place of another. Once again, faith is the key to the whole process. By faith, we receive the gift of God. He becomes our righteousness, and took our guilt upon Himself.

Also note, God remained just. At no time is the law violated by grace. The legal requirements of the law remain in place regardless of God's expression of mercy. The wages of sin is death and the consequences for our sins are to bear the penalty of judgment. God will not violate the law. In society, when a judge is soft on sentencing a criminal, we are outraged. We consider it injustice to see a murderer or sex offender get a slap on the wrist. A soft judge is an affront to the law that was designed to protect citizens.

It's no different with God's law. The law demands judgment and we are guilty because we have broken the law. The Bible says that every sin will be judged by God – and indeed they have been – as explained in the passage above.

God remained just, while becoming our justifier. This is the sacrifice of Christ. He remained just by standing in judgment in our place, so that through His sacrifice, He became our justifier – or the one who declared us just before God. Jesus did this by becoming the one who was judged for our sins. We are declared just, but the penalty of sin was still satisfied – through Christ.

When God looks at you, He sees justice through Christ. It is a legal declaration. You are declared just, because the penalty has been paid through Christ. Legally you are free from the guilt of sin.

So is our imputed righteousness a legal declaration? Yes. But not *only* a legal declaration. We must first be declared not-guilty before we can become an heir. The promises of God are only to those who belong to Him. Consider **John 1:12-13**

> [12] But as many as received Him, to them He gave the right to become children of God, to those who believe in His name:
> [13] who were born, not of blood, nor of the will of the flesh, nor of the will of man, but of God.

Through Christ, we have the right to become the children of God. The guilty have no rights. A convicted felon is led away in handcuffs and no longer has the normal rights to citizenship. The same is true with becoming a citizen of heaven. We have no right to become a child of God, citizen of heaven, or joint heir with Christ, until we are declared just. To be just we must be perfect under the law. Our imputed righteousness is a declaration of justice. The penalty was paid through Christ and He was declared guilty for our sins so that we could be declared just before God.

Accounting of righteousness

Jesus made a declaration on the cross moments before his death. He cried, "It is finished." The words he actually declared were in Greek. The word was 'tetelestia'. Tetelestia is a Greek word used in accounting. When someone paid their debt, this word was written on the records. It literally means, "Paid in Full". Jesus was accounted as the debtor so that we could be credited with his righteousness. Look now at **2 Corinthians 5:21**

> For He made Him who knew no sin *to be* sin for us, that we might become the righteousness of God in Him.

In Christ, we become the righteousness of God. It is not our righteousness. It is God's righteousness credited to our lives. The Apostle Paul addressed this in his own life. He was a Pharisee. Not all Pharisees were evil. Some truly tried to keep the law in sincerity and by faith. Nicodemus is a good example. He's stood up for Jesus when the other Pharisees were trying to find a way to arrest Him[62] and he came to Jesus to understand the scriptures[63].

Like all other religious people, the Pharisees were only condemned when they chose to seek self-justification. They tended to rely on their own works to become righteous. The Apostle Paul was such a man until God intervened to show him mercy. Once he saw the truth of Christ, he abandoned his old ways and made the following statement, "I count all things as garbage that I may gain Christ and be found in Him. Not having my own righteousness...but that which is from God by faith.[64]"

Here is a man who lived to fulfill the law by his own efforts, now saying we cannot be righteous by our own works. In fact, Isaiah 64:6 tells us that all of our righteousness is filthy rags in God's sight. Like Paul, everything we do for God is garbage. It's worthless and worthy of nothing but the trash heap.

It sounds harsh and often offends people, but any student of the Bible knows that God will offend those who look anywhere but

---

[62] John 7:51
[63] John 3:1
[64] Philippians 3:8-9

to Him. Anytime someone looks to their own efforts as a method to increase their own righteousness will only produce worthless works. As Jesus said, "The flesh profits you nothing," and "unless you abide in me, you can do nothing." Righteousness is found in Christ, and unless your righteousness is the righteousness of God, it is worthless.

Righteousness is credited – or imputed to us. Let's go back to the example of Abraham again. Look at **Romans 4:20-25**

> [20] He did not waver at the promise of God through unbelief, but was strengthened in faith, giving glory to God,
>
> [21] and being fully convinced that what He had promised He was also able to perform.
>
> [22] And therefore "it was accounted to him for righteousness."
>
> [23] Now it was not written for his sake alone that it was imputed to him,
>
> [24] but also for us. It shall be imputed to us who believe in Him who raised up Jesus our Lord from the dead,
>
> [25] who was delivered up because of our offenses, and was raised because of our justification.

It can't be denied that the Bible teaches that our righteousness is imputed – or accredited to us. And this is done without any works on our part. Faith is not an act of work. Faith is given to us by God. The Bible says that the Lord has measured each person a portion of faith[65]. Then we are told that God reveals Himself to us by faith. Then we receive Christ by faith. From beginning to end it is the work of God. The only time man is involved is when he resists God and tries to justify himself by his own methods. Methods which God rejects.

According to the scriptures we've examined so far, God declares us righteous legally, and He credits (imputes) His righteousness to us. Now let us look at practical righteousness and how it affects our lives. To understand this, we should look at the

---

[65] Romans 12:3

Let's get it right about Righteousness

two approaches to this subject given by the Apostles Paul and James.

Practical righteousness

Righteousness is not only being counted as right before God, but also doing what is right as God commanded. The Bible says that the one who knows to do good and does not do it, to that person it is a sin[66]. It isn't possible to live a righteous life while refusing to live out the Christian life. So is it our actions that make us Christians? Or is it our actions that reveal the new life God has placed within us?

This is the conflict being addressed by both Paul and James. The Apostle Paul wrote the books of Romans and Ephesians, along with approximately two-thirds of the New Testament. The book of James is the only letter we have that James wrote to the church. Let's look at a few passages that are often misunderstood as a contradiction.

Since we are digging into the writings of two apostles, we'll use a few more scriptures in this section, but don't let this overwhelm you. We'll start in Romans 4, but let me first mention what Paul is discussing prior to the beginning of this chapter. He begins in chapter two with a discussion about circumcision and how it pointed to the covenant of Christ. After a detailed explanation in chapter three, he makes the statement, "Therefore we conclude that a man is justified by faith apart from the deeds of the law."

To understand what Paul is addressing, take a little time to read Acts 15. As the gospel spread, many gentiles (or non-Jews) came to faith. Jewish Christians still believed the law was applicable in order to be in God's covenant. They were raised in that mindset and had a hard time grasping that the Old Covenant was replaced by the New Covenant. In the past, gentiles had to convert to Judaism and be circumcised in order to enter God's covenant.

These well-meaning, but badly misinformed Jews were going into churches and telling the gentiles that they couldn't be saved unless they were circumcised according to the Law of Moses. Paul

---

[66] James 4:17

addressed this heavily in the book of Galatians when he said, "You who attempt to be justified by the law have fallen from grace and are estranged from Christ." In this passage, Paul is specifically addressing gentile Christians who were being circumcised thinking they were meriting God's favor.

In other words, to attempt to justify oneself by something they do by human effort is a denial of the faith. In this case it was circumcision, but it could be anything we think we are doing to earn God's favor. So as we examine the passage in question, keep this in mind. Paul is addressing this specific issue. He is not saying Christians will not have works. In fact, he says the opposite throughout his letters to the churches. He is addressing the belief that works justify us, rather than trusting in the work of Christ – who is our only justification. Now look at **Romans 4:2-10**

> [2] For if Abraham was justified by works, he has *something* to boast about, but not before God.
>
> [3] For what does the Scripture say? "Abraham believed God, and it was accounted to him for righteousness."
>
> [4] Now to him who works, the wages are not counted as grace but as debt.
>
> [5] But to him who does not work but believes on Him who justifies the ungodly, his faith is accounted for righteousness,
>
> ...
>
> [9] *Does* this blessedness then *come* upon the circumcised *only*, or upon the uncircumcised also? For we say that faith was accounted to Abraham for righteousness.
>
> [10] How then was it accounted? While he was circumcised, or uncircumcised? Not while circumcised, but while uncircumcised.

Abraham was credited with righteousness before entering the covenant of the Old Testament through circumcision. Therefore, Paul is pointing out that the law introduced through the covenant was not the source of Abraham's righteousness. God was the source of Abraham's righteousness, and it was given without any effort on man's part. It was merely believing God – by faith. Circumcision came as God introduced the covenant and Abraham obeyed – another act of faith. But he was already just and righteous before doing any works, religious practices, or obeying the law.

The verses I skipped speak about God not imputing sin, but forgiving us and giving grace. If you look at this passage in the context of Paul's entire thought, it's clear that the issue is the false belief that our justification is obtained, in whole or in part, by human effort rather than by faith in Christ's completed work on our behalf. God, in His foreknowledge, revealed justification by faith to Abraham before commanding him to be circumcised.

Let me summarize again for clarification. Circumcision, which we discussed earlier, was the sign of the seal of the covenant. However, it was *not* what made Abraham righteous. Abraham was declared righteous and justified when he believed God. When it came to entering God's covenant, the circumcision was man's submission to God. The act of circumcision didn't make Abraham right with God. Abraham was *first* accredited with God's righteousness, and then he entered the covenant.

This is the same truth taught in the New Testament. We are first declared legally just because our debt of sin was paid, then we are made righteous by being given the righteousness of God, and then we are called to act according to that righteousness by good works. It is God's faith, God's righteousness, and the works that God prepared before we were even born. Then we are called to walk in God's good works. This is explained in **Ephesians 2:8-10**

8 For by grace you have been saved through faith, and that not of yourselves; *it is* the gift of God,

9 not of works, lest anyone should boast.

10 For we are His workmanship, created in Christ Jesus *for good works*, which God prepared beforehand that we should walk in them. (Emphasis added)

Notice again that grace comes first. We are made right through God's mercy by faith, and there is nothing we have done to make ourselves righteous in any way. Why? Because as we saw earlier – no flesh can glory in God's presence. The same is taught here when Paul says, "Lest anyone should boast."

Where is our justification? By works? No. Just as Abraham was justified prior to being circumcised or doing any action, we are saved and declared right by God and welcomed into His Kingdom prior to any acts on our part. God opens our eyes through faith, and we either believe and accept His grace, or we reject it. Sometimes that rejection is man declaring that he can't believe God's grace is sufficient, and he attempts to use his own efforts in place of Christ's completed work. True faith is believing on Christ for our justification and righteousness; however, it doesn't end there.

We are God's workmanship. He created us in Christ by the miracle of His own power. Did God save us so we could live in apathy? No. He created our new nature for good works. Works that God prepared beforehand that we should walk in them. In other words, God created us, redeemed us, made us into a new eternal creation, prepared the way for us to do good works, and He now calls us to walk where He has prepared the way.

We'll examine works in more detail later, but for now, take note of the fact that Paul is teaching that we are created for good works, and we are called to walk in obedience. Now let's look at how James addresses the same issue. Look at **James 2:14-26.** It's a long passage, but full of good instruction.

[14] What *does it* profit, my brethren, if someone says he has faith but does not have works? Can faith save him?

[15] If a brother or sister is naked and destitute of daily food,

[16] and one of you says to them, "Depart in peace, be warmed and filled," but you do not give them the things which are needed for the body, what *does it* profit?

[17] Thus also faith by itself, if it does not have works, is dead.

[18] But someone will say, "You have faith, and I have works." Show me your faith without your works, and I will show you my faith by my works.

[19] **You believe** that there is one God. You do well. **Even the demons believe** -- and tremble!

[20] But do you want to know, O foolish man, that faith

without works is dead?
²¹ Was not Abraham our father justified by works when he offered Isaac his son on the altar?
²² Do you see that faith was working together with his works, and by works faith was made perfect?
²³ And the Scripture was fulfilled which says, "Abraham believed God, and it was accounted to him for righteousness." And he was called the friend of God.
²⁴ You see then that a man is justified by works, and not by faith only. (Emphasis Added)

Is James in disagreement with Paul? He is not. It can appear that way if you only look at a few isolated verses, but if you look at both Paul's writing and what James wrote here in context, you will see that they are in full agreement.

What is James addressing? He's confronting those who are apathetic to the needs of others within the church. These people who claim to be children of God are walking past those in need within the church, and doing nothing to help them. Believers are passing by and casting a few meaningless words toward those in need. While they have extra food and clothing, they hoard what they have and say, "Be warm and full." An empty blessing. They have the blessing God provided in their possession. They care more about their closet than the needs of people in their very circle of fellowship.

James then goes on to make a few comparisons. With empty words, these people claim to believe God, but the evidence of their life is contradictory. To drive home this truth, James points to demons. You say you believe? Big deal. Demons believe and tremble, but what profit is it? Even a demon can believe in God, so us claiming to believe in Him means nothing. James calls this type of faith dead.

Consider the weight of the words of James. The Bible calls the works of the flesh dead. Everything about our life before Christ was called dead. We were dead. Our spirit was dead. Our faith was dead.

It was dead because it was rooted in the flesh that is cursed by sin and destined for the wages of that sin – death.

Life does not come until the Spirit breathes life into our dead soul. This is why the Bible says things like, you have been made alive in Christ, you were buried in the likeness of Christ's death, and then raised in newness of life. Or we are like a grain of wheat. It must fall into the ground and die before it can have life. When we die to our body encased in lifeless sin, God raises us by faith and makes us alive, together with Him.

Human faith is dead. Mustering up faith by your own efforts is dead. People who sit in the church and say, "I believe the Bible," but never surrender to its life-changing message are dead. Consider the words of **Hebrews 4:2**

> For indeed the gospel was preached to us as well as to them; but the word which they heard did not profit them, not being mixed with faith in those who heard *it.*

These people heard the word, but did not benefit from it because it was not received by faith. They died in their sins. In this passage, Israel is the group of people who heard the word. They had a pretense of belief, but when God put them to the test, they refused to obey. Their faith was dead and they all died while wandering in the wilderness.

In the same way, James is drawing a contrast between dead faith and true faith. Dead faith is human beliefs, but living faith is God-breathed. It's alive because it was given to us by the Spirit. Human beliefs cannot save, but true faith calls us to obey God and surrender our lives to His will. We believe His promises, so we don't feel the need to cling to our possessions, ambitions, or anything else that prevents us from obeying.

James is confronting those in the church who claim to be Christians, but show no more works than the enemies of God. That's the evidence against someone's claim to faith. After showing a stark example of worthless faith, James moves on to the example of Abraham's life to show how true faith stands out differently. **Dead** faith is demonic and apathetic. True faith stirs the love God has poured out in our hearts and calls us to action.

Abraham truly believed, and what happened? He was willing to do whatever God asked of him – even to the point of offering Isaac, his only son, upon an altar. In hindsight, we know what God was doing, but Abraham did not.

It's interesting that James chose the same examples Paul used. Most likely, James is addressing a church that has done as we see in our churches today. They are picking and choosing only the scriptures that don't interfere with their lives. Therefore, James is taking the instruction Paul gave them, and is expounding it more clearly. He is being blunt and brutally honest so those who misapply the scriptures can't miss his point.

Let's look closer at the illustration James used. It's likely he's referring to what Paul taught in Romans. It could have been any church Paul started or taught in. Human nature exists within the church and attempts to turn the word into a selfish gospel.

When using the illustration of Abraham and Isaac, Paul explained that Abraham believed God, who was able to give life to the dead[67]. This is important, for it gives an insight into Abraham's view of God. By promise, God declared, "In Isaac will your name be called.[68]"

Isaac was the life through whom the promise would be carried for generations to come. After telling Abraham that the promise was in Isaac, God then called Abraham to sacrifice his son on the altar. Without wavering, the Bible said Abraham rose early in the morning and set out to find the mountain where God had directed him. Though it was not known at the time, that mountain would be named Golgotha and would be the place where Jesus was crucified. Again we see the Old Testament foretelling God's plan through Christ.

---

[67] Romans 4:17
[68] Genesis 21:12

Abraham journeyed three days until he found the mountain, and then said to the men who came with him, "You stay here. The lad and I will go and worship, and we will come again.[69]"

That's an interesting statement. This tells us that Abraham had two possibilities in mind. One, God would have to raise Isaac from the dead. Two, God would have to provide a substitutionary sacrifice. Until God stopped Abraham's hand as he plunged the knife, he did not know which it would be. But God stopped him and declared that Abraham had proven his faith and not withheld the son whom he loved from the Lord. Abraham saw a ram caught in a thicket, and that became the sacrifice in Isaac's place.

It wasn't Abraham's son that would die for sins. Jesus, the Lamb of God, was foreshadowed in the sacrifice of the ram in Isaac's place. The true sacrifice was to come in Jesus Christ. The thicket became a crown of thorns and He ascended that same hill and God did not withhold from us the Son He loved. But Jesus became the redemption that pardoned Abraham and all those who are called God's children.

This is the example James is pointing to. Abraham proved his faith by not withholding what he loved. In fact, he was willingly giving back to God the very blessing and promise God had given him. He believed God enough to give back as God required. Yet within the church, James saw those who claimed to be people of faith, but wouldn't even give a spare coat to someone in need. This was not the life-changing faith of Abraham.

So we don't miss the point James is about to make, he says, "Some will say they have faith... Show me your faith without your works and I will show you my faith by my works." From this statement he goes on to explain the difference between true faith and dead faith. Dead faith is empty words without evidence of works. True faith produces good works. This is so because it's the work of God in our heart that calls us into the work God has prepared beforehand – that for which we were created in Christ Jesus to do.

69

Also keep in mind that there are no good works outside of what God produces. Remember those who presented their deeds to Jesus and He declared, "You are a worker of lawlessness"? There are good deeds done through human effort, and there are good works done through God's plan and foreknowledge. We are saved for good works. Those who shun God's path of obedience have no right to claim to be followers of Christ. Nor do those who try to create their own righteousness by good works and human effort.

Works will be examined more clearly when we discuss it in two chapters. For now, let's look at works as the evidence of faith. James is not saying we earn salvation through good works. He is saying if we have true faith (for we are saved by grace through faith), it will produce good works. When I am obedient to God, I know I'm justified for my works prove that my faith is true.

Jesus also testified to this when He said, "By their fruit you shall know them." Love is of God and is the fruit of the Spirit. If the fruit of the Spirit is absent, the Spirit is also absent.

This teaching by James is not for you and I to judge the fruit of others. It is for you and I to judge ourselves. As Paul said, "Examine yourselves to see if you are in the faith." I don't know what God has called someone to do, and if they are serving God as they ought, I may never know. According to the Bible, those who broadcast their good works have their reward – the praise of others. But those who serve in secret God promises to reward openly.

Unless God calls you to serve in an area where you are in the public eye, few people will know your service to God. And you can't know what someone else is doing or is called to do. A mother nurturing her children and teaching them how to love God is making disciples. Who will know other than her and those in the same home? So, the purpose of this passage is not for us to look around and see who is of faith, but to look inward.

These things are given so you and I can examine our lives and see if our faith is genuine. If we have been taught incorrectly, this gives us instruction. It may be that we never understood our calling and now realize we've fallen into apathy. James' words become a call to action. Even true faith can be obscured by getting caught up in the selfish cares of the world. This is why the Bible reproves and corrects, while giving instruction and doctrine[70].

Both Paul and James are teaching the same thing. While Paul is battling a false faith masquerading as good works, James is battling a false faith masquerading as apathy and easy believe-ism.

Infused or Integrated Righteousness

I saved this topic for last because it's something that needs to be addressed after understanding how the Bible defines righteousness. Before we can look at what righteousness is not, we must first understand what it is. I'm sure this has different connotations to different people, so I'll define it based on my own experiences. Infused righteousness is the idea that mankind becomes good and can produce good by human effort. The idea is that God saves us, and then we must do righteous acts and produce good works to continue toward complete justification. It is the belief that we partner with Christ to produce righteousness.

Infused righteousness is the belief that God infuses our bodies with righteousness and we continue to become better by good works. The Bible has much to say on this topic. We've already seen that Paul stated, "Not having my own righteousness, but that which is in Christ." He also makes an interesting statement in **Romans 7:18**

For I know that in me (that is, in my flesh) nothing good dwells; for to will is present with me, but *how* to perform what is good I do not find.

The truth is that God is the source of righteousness. Man cannot produce righteousness. He takes what is given, and lives according to God's own goodness. Even Jesus refuted this idea. Remember when we looked at the rich young ruler? When he looked at Jesus from a human perspective and called Him good, Jesus rebuked him saying, "Why do you call Me good? There is one good and that is God." But later when Jesus was pointing to His

---

[70] 2 Timothy 3:16-17

Let's get it right about Righteousness

divinity and calling for people to follow Him, He declared, "I am the good shepherd."

In the first instance, the focus was on human goodness, but the second is focused on Jesus' divinity. The flesh profits nothing. The Spirit gives life and peace. Each time someone looks toward the flesh, the Bible rebukes them. But when the Spirit is the focus, it is called truth. Righteousness isn't what we do, but rather when we yield ourselves so God's goodness reigns without hindrance.

We are never called to make our bodies good. Nor does the Bible ever call our bodies good. Nor does the Bible remotely imply that righteousness is infused into us. Paul lamented the sin that dwelled in his members – the flesh of his body. Then he cried, "Who will deliver me from this body of death?" Finally, he gives the answer in **Romans 7:25**

I thank God -- through Jesus Christ our Lord! So then, with the mind I myself serve the law of God, but with the flesh the law of sin.

In a later chapter, we'll discuss what it means to walk in the Spirit, but in this situation, Paul indicates our minds are the battle ground for resisting the flesh and serving God. The flesh always serves sin. The mind, if in Christ and in the Spirit, serve the law of God. Serving God is always through abiding in Christ so that we can walk in the path of good works God has predestined for us to walk in[71]. It's not your works or your righteousness. Everything in scripture focuses on God's works created for you, God's righteousness placed within you by the Spirit inside you, and your need to die to your own works and live by walking in faith.

Each time we see our bodies mentioned in scripture, it is in reference to bringing it under subjection. "Do not yield your body as an instrument of sin, but yield to God." "I discipline my body and bring it under subjection." "I am crucified with Christ." This theme continues throughout the New Testament. Though our inner man has been redeemed and made alive in Christ, sin remains in our physical bodies until the time of adoption. Look at **Romans 8:23**

---

[71] Ephesians 2:10

Not only *that,* but we also who have the firstfruits of the Spirit, even we ourselves groan within ourselves, eagerly waiting for the adoption, the redemption of our body.

Our bodies will one day be redeemed, but for now, we wrestle against the flesh so it doesn't recapture our mind and bring us back into captivity to sin[72]. There is nothing to infuse. We receive the Holy Spirit, and He is our righteousness. The Spirit convicts us of sin, righteousness, and judgment[73]. The world is convicted, but so are we. If the Spirit is in us, we are convicted of sin, we are instructed in righteousness, and we are shown good judgment – the ability to see right from wrong according to scripture.

According to the Bible, God has already given us all things pertaining to life and godliness through His divine Spirit[74]. Our role is to bring the flesh under subjection so the things of the Spirit can reign unhindered in our lives.

When we look at the Bible's teaching on righteousness, we can see that true faith first declares us just, then credits us with God's righteousness, and finally calls us to righteous works. We do not choose only one, nor do we neglect any part of righteousness. All are in agreement and necessary for our walk of faith.

As we shall see in the chapter on works, once we are yielded to God's will, good works are the natural result. Walking in the will of God is a partnership of faith, righteousness, and good works.

---

[72] Romans 7:23
[73] John 16:8
[74] 2 Peter 1:3

Let's get it right about Righteousness

Simply Loved

Before we look at works, it's important to understand the love of God toward us. It's vital to understand that works do not create God's love and gaining favor is not the purpose of our works. What makes God love me? Nearly every person has asked this question. Most people go through life hoping they are doing enough to merit God's approval. Even those who know that God's grace is unmerited may still struggle with living like it in their everyday life. This knowledge needs to make the six-inch journey from the head to the heart.

When people fail, they feel they have disappointed God. In their weakness, they either do something they know is wrong, or don't do something they know they should. The next thought is the perceived angry stare of God.

When Adam and Eve sinned, what did they do? What did God do? Did God say, "You blew it," and then turn His back on them? No. Did God hide from Adam and Eve? No.

Adam and Eve hid from God. They fell short of God's glory intended for them when they bought into the false promise that if they rebelled, their actions would make them like God, to know good and evil. When they committed themselves to pursue the lie, their eyes were indeed opened. And what was the first thing they saw? When they knew good and evil, they saw their own nakedness and shame. Shame drove them away from God. After the fall, Adam and Eve recognized their own inability to measure up to God's perfect character, and they no longer felt welcomed in God's presence.

This is what happens in our lives when we recognize our inability to measure up to the standard of God's character. Just as with Adam and Eve, God pursues us as we attempt to hide from Him. And His goal is not to punish, but to cover our sin and restore fellowship with us.

Anyone who attempts to merit God's favor by perfect living and perfect works has missed the point of the Father-child relationship. I love my kids. Even when they fail me, I still love them.

When they rebel, I have to deal with their behavior, but I still love them the same. There is a strain on our relationship if they are misbehaving. When this happens, it isn't love that is lost, but the fellowship.

We falsely measure love and God's favor based on our immediate circumstances. If I feel pain, God must not love me. If I sin, God must not love me.

Peace, comfort, prosperity, and happiness are not the evidences that God loves me. The evidence God loves me is the cross. I need no more proof than this – a holy God cared enough for me to step into the world as a humble man, fulfilled the requirements of the law, and then bore the penalty of the consequences of sin on my behalf.

People try to come up with illustrations to explain God's love, but they all fall short. For example, there is a story about a drawbridge keeper who took his son to work. His son wandered out on the bridge and a ship came by. As the father was raising the drawbridge, he saw his son had wandered onto the bridge and then had to make a decision. If he kept raising the bridge, his child would be killed, but the people saved. If he rescued his son, the ship would hit the bridge and the passengers would die. To save many passengers, he sacrificed his son.

There are many variations and for some people, it conjures up emotions of sacrifice. But the story is fundamentally flawed. First, God wasn't caught by surprise. Nor was the son an unexpected victim. Nor do people pass by in safety, saved from a death they knew nothing of. According to scripture, God chose us through Christ before the foundation of the world.[75] Jesus said He willingly laid down His life and it was for this purpose that He came into the world.[76]

There is no adequate illustration to explain the love expressed through the cross. Indeed, we need no illustration. The cross is the picture of God's love. And once we pass through the cross, we've passed from the existence of death in the flesh to the new life in the

---

[75] Ephesians 1:4
[76] John 18:37

Spirit. As John 1:12 puts it, through Christ we have the right to become children of God. Someone who has been born into God's kingdom by the Spirit is a child of God. Sons and daughters don't have to merit their relationship with their parents. The closeness of that relationship is affected by our maturity, but the love God expresses toward us is not.

Consider this passage from **John 15:14-15**

[14] "You are My friends if you do whatever I command you.

[15] "No longer do I call you servants, for a servant does not know what his master is doing; but I have called you friends, for all things that I heard from My Father I have made known to you.

This is not a new concept, though it was not well understood until after Jesus revealed the Father. Jesus made the statement, "If you have seen Me, you have seen the Father."

Most people look at our heavenly Father as a stern disciplinarian that only shows up when He is taking something away, scolding us, or punishing our shortcomings.

Others look at God as though He is a chummy buddy. You see t-shirts with phrases like, Jesus is my BFF. How can our relationship with the Father be like a friendship, yet without demeaning God to the level of a pal who has no more influence on our lives than a friendship among peers?

Friendship with God isn't complicated, but can be understood. The Bible says that Moses spoke to God face to face as a man speaks to his friend.[77] Yet the relationship God had with Moses wasn't always this way. Moses began in fear, but as he walked with God, the relationship grew into friendship. And that friendship didn't exempt Moses from obedience and even rebuke. God still held Moses accountable when he disobeyed.

To better understand how God can be the authority over us and yet a friend, let's look at the human relationship God compares His relationship to. Fathers. This comparison would apply to both our parents.

---

[77] Exodus 33:11

A child begins life immature and incapable of making wise choices. Infants need constant care and nurturing. As children grow into the next stage of life, they look at the attention they've received and begin to expect everything to be a self-centered experience. Children are a joy to parents when they are responsive, but when they pursue the things they cannot do or have, conflict arises. Love isn't dissolved, but the relationship can be strained.

The back and forth relationship continues through adolescence. But something wonderful happens when kids reach maturity. The parent becomes a friend. As children begin to adopt values and responsibilities, the requirements of parenthood eases, and the two become much closer.

This is why Jesus said, "You are my friends if you do what I've commanded." When a Christian matures and begins to adopt responsibility and then values what is good, the closeness of our relationship with God blossoms into a close friendship. The friendship does not nullify the commands, but rather causes us to appreciate the commandments of God. We appreciate the word because we see value. Our temporal self-centered perspective shifts with the understanding of the eternal perspective.

When I live as though eternity doesn't matter, I am not valuing what God values. The Lord then has to focus on correcting behavior. Eternity does indeed matter. God's goal is to guide each person's life into maturity so the kingdom can be in our grasp. Our Heavenly Father / child of God relationship is either focused on walking the path of this life together in fellowship, or getting us off the destructive road of the flesh and onto the eternal path of the Spirit.

Some children mature earlier than others, and some never mature at all. An immature adult who continues to make foolish choices still grieves his or her parents. But that doesn't mean they are no longer family.

Let me use a story to illustrate this. A foolish son approached his wealthy father. He didn't love the relationship. He only valued what his father possessed. To his father's grief, he said, "I don't want to wait until you die. Give me my portion of the inheritance so I can leave and make my own way."

The family business was looked upon as a hindrance to his life's ambition, and he was sure he understood the world and knew better than his father. The man tried to give good advice, but the son was stubborn and unwavering. Though the father knew the consequences of the choice, he gave in, sold enough of his business to divide the inheritance to his son, and let him set out on his own.

It was difficult watching the young man walk away. It was hard to tell which hurt worse, the fact that he knew his son was heading for disaster, or the fact that his son didn't return his love. The young lad didn't even recognize how everything in his father's life was born out of love for his children. He could only see correction, having to do things he didn't want to do, and being oppressed by what he thought were meaningless rules.

The father could have used the inheritance as a tool to keep his son under control, but a forced relationship wasn't what he wanted.

For years the boy lived like a king. He had many friends and spent his money living it up. One day he went for more money and found the coffers empty. The parties ended and he began struggling to get by. The friends he had spent his money with turned their backs on him and left to find other sources of amusement.

Things grew worse. The area fell under a drought. A year rolled by and the drought became a famine. Farmers had no crops, so he couldn't find work in the area. In his desperation, he took the worse job imaginable. He took a job feeding pigs and hogs. The young man was a Jew, and the Jews could have no dealings with unclean animals such as swine. But what choice did he have? There were no other jobs to take.

Food became scarce and one day as he was feeding the pigs, the hunger pangs got the best of him. The rations he could buy with his meager earnings wasn't even enough to feed him. He scooped out a handful of the slop and ate the food intended for the pigs.

When his belly was full, the realization of his situation hit him hard. The paid servants of his father's house had enough food to spare, but he was living among the pigs and eating what was not fit for human consumption. Suddenly he came to his senses. He would be better off sacrificing his pride and returning home. He would apologize for the cruel words he said to his father, and express how he was not worthy to even be called a son. If his father would just give him a job as a servant, he would be better off than in this place.

The old man peeked down the long and dusty road leading up to his vineyard. As he worked and checked on the other workers, he often passed by this road. Each time he would look to see if by some chance his son would come home. Sometimes he would stop and watch the road for hours, wondering about the fate of his son. After making his rounds, he wandered to the road again and stopped to watch.

This day he saw something different. Off in the distance a figure walked toward the family home. He thought the walk looked familiar and he strained to see. The emaciated man hung his head down as he walked, but there was no mistaking the stride. It was his son!

The old man cast off all dignity, and sprinted down the road toward the lad. At some point, the boy heard footsteps and stopped. He dropped to his knees and called out to the father, who was still running down the road. "I'm not worthy to be called your son," he cried out. Before he could finish his prepared speech, his father reached him and fell on his neck with joyful tears.

For a long time he ignored the foul odor of his son, but when the two arose from the ground, the father called for the servants to bring clean clothes and a ring for his finger – the ring given only to those called family.

I'm sure you recognize the story. It's often called the prodigal son. It's the story Jesus used to illustrate God's love toward us. The truth is that to some degree, it is every son and every daughter. It is a picture of God's perfect love toward us, and it's one of the richest illustrations in the Bible.

What did the son do to become worthy of the Father's love? Some would say repent, but that misses a significant part of the story. Each day the father watched for his son's return. The love was already there. The young man was loved, even while he was filthy, rebellious, and living among the swine. He couldn't experience that love until he repented, but the father loved him even while he was in rebellion.

After returning, the older brother showed just as much resistance as the younger one had previously done. Though he didn't rebel and demand his father's money, he did miss out on experiencing the fellowship of love. When he heard the music and celebration, he was angry. He refused to come in to be part of the fellowship, and the father had to come out seeking him. "Look at what I have done for you," he said to his father. He looked at his labors and compared himself to his brother. He thought his brother was unworthy to have such favor with his father. He was right in that regard. Both sons were unworthy, both sons were loved, and the father pursued both of them with the offer of fellowship. The Father's love was never based on worthiness.

Whether we run from God and miss the joy of the relationship, or we work ourselves to exhaustion, we have the exact same need. To the people around us, a laboring Christian may appear spiritual. But in reality, both the wanderer and the legalist have the same need. The symptoms may be different, but both have the same problem. Both also have the same solution.

What kept the prodigal son from enjoying fellowship with the father? He followed his own ways. He suffered the consequences of his actions and he squandered his inheritance, but he was still a son. All he needed was to receive the father's love that had been there all the time.

What kept the legalistic brother from experiencing fellowship at the end of the story? He looked to himself, his labors, his lack of failure, and his superiority. Rather than meriting love, these became a barrier to love. All he needed was to accept the fathers love and join the fellowship.

Just like in the parable of the prodigal, our church culture has the same problem. It's easy for the one who is at their wits end to realize their need, but it's hard for those who feel they have merited something to recognize their own need. This is why Jesus told the spiritual leaders of his day, "The prostitutes and sinners will enter the kingdom of God before you."[78]

Like the son who thought he stood on obedience, the spiritual leaders Jesus addressed were standing outside the fellowship and scorning the sinners – those who had done what they would never do. They then scorned Jesus for treating them like family. "Why does he eat and drink with sinners?" they complained. In their eyes, the lowlifes weren't worthy of fellowship, so they excluded themselves from Jesus' company.

The good news is that whether we have stayed in the congregation of the behaving, or have wandered far away from God, His love remains true. Our heavenly Father wants you to experience true fellowship with Him.

Think about an earthly king or dignitary. When the President arrives, people are intimidated. When I was in the military, we had high ranking generals visit from time to time. Everyone panicked when the general came to town.

One time a general visited our base and walked around to see the soldiers in daily life. He walked up to a soldier washing mud off his boots with a hose. "How are you doing, soldier?" he said.

The soldier casually said, "Fine," but then he looked up and saw the stars on the officer's collar. He snapped to attention, still holding the hose in his left hand while saluting with his right. Water poured out of the hose, and doused the general.

He looked down at the stream of water hitting his leg and calmly said, "You can drop your salute. And that hose, please."

It was good for a laugh, but illustrates how intimidating authority can be. When a high ranking officer walks through, many people act as though they are afraid of the person, but what do you think his children do when he walks in the door? Unless he's a cruel man, his kids aren't intimidated. To them, he's just daddy. The same is true for every king, emperor, and world leader in history. Those under his authority may live in fear, but most likely his children run to him and climb into his lap.

---

[78] Matthew 21:31

This is the picture we should have of God. He is God, ruler of heaven and earth, and one day every knee will bow, and every tongue confess that He is Lord. But to us who already know Him as Lord, He is also our friend and father, and we His children.

Though we stray, we are not disowned or cast down. When we're entangled in our failures, He picks us up and restores us to the fellowship. Like a loving father, God corrects us to protect us from eternal consequences, but He also never ceases to love us as His children. And as we mature into obedience, we are no longer limited to looking to Him as a toddler does. We learn to be responsible and live in the promise, "You are my friends if you keep my commandments."

Obedience is not to gain favor. Obedience is not to make God love us more. Obedience is the result of us loving God who first loved us. Obeying out of fear misses the whole point. And it misses the mark. When someone loves another, they want to do the things that please the other. Love isn't trying to merit someone's approval. I love my kids; therefore, I do things to please my kids. I do it for no other motivation than as an expression of affection and to see them enjoying life.

How my children respond does not change my love for them, but it does affect the closeness of our relationship. A child who reaches out to her father will have a closer relationship than the child that rebels or simply stands aloof. It's not the love that is different; it's how a child responds that makes them closer or more distant. In the same way, how the Christian responds to God and His word affects how close their relationship with God will be.

This is not an abusive relationship we have with God. An abused spouse may do something that pleases her husband, but it's out of fear, not love. When two people love each other, they give to each other. The gift isn't payment, nor does it require payment. A gift ceases to be a gift when payment is expected.

If you serve God out of an obligation or because you think God will owe you a return favor, it isn't love. God first loved you and expressed that love through the cross. Because He first loved us, when we recognize that love, we express our love to Him by the things we do and the way we act.

People who repent because they are afraid of hell have missed the whole point. In fact, that is human repentance. It becomes mankind trying to rescue himself by changing his own mind. True repentance is responding to God's call as He draws us to Himself. It's a call to fellowship, not to flee hell. God so loved you that He gave of Himself through the Son to reconcile you to the fellowship He created you to live in. If you so love God, you'll give your life to Him as an expression of love. Then you have both sides giving to each other, and true fellowship begins.

God first loved you, so the only thing preventing the fellowship of love is your willingness to receive that love and to abide in love by given back with a life obedient to His commands which flow from His nature.

Works to Walk In

Good works are an integral part of the Christian's life, but we must approach works with the right heart. Overcoming laziness isn't the only problem when it comes to works. We must also guard against wrong attitudes, over extending ourselves, and turning works into idolatry. Yes, works become idolatry if we are trusting in good works as a means to reach God. Works are not what makes us right with God, but they are the outflow of walking with God.

We'll dig into the Bible's explanation of works in a moment, but I'll first start with a true story about burn out to illustrate the danger of working outside of God's design for you.

Burn out

Burn out is the result of missing God's call and overloading ourselves with human effort. For an example, consider this true story. Many years ago a pastor friend of mine came to my house to visit. Let's just call him Pete. When I answered the door, I could tell something was heavy on Pete's mind. We engaged in the typical small talk for a few minutes before we got to the real reason for his visit.

After explaining the stress of being overloaded with responsibilities, Pete said, "I just don't know what to do. I'm so stressed out and burned out, I don't know how to handle it all." He went on to explain the dozens of tasks he had taken on at church. It was a small church going through some growing pains. Like many small churches, it is difficult to fill the labor needs of the programs. Wanting the church to thrive, he took on each need as it arose, and people became very dependent upon him. Pete was trying to make the church succeed through his own efforts.

Once he finished expressing his current dilemma, I said, "Think about your gifts. If you could narrow your calling down to a few words, what do you believe you've been gifted by God to do?"

Without hesitation he said, "I know I've been called to be a discipler and an encourager."

"Perfect! Now let's look at the duties in the church you have taken on. With each task I want you to ask yourself two questions. Is this something that fulfills my calling? If the answer is 'no', then ask, Is this something that hinders my calling? Anything that doesn't pass the test on both of those questions should be dropped from your life."

As we went down the long list of duties, it became clear that nearly every task failed the test. He was like a juggler trying to keep two dozen balls in the air. He was so busy keeping the things going God had not called him to do that he didn't have the time or energy to do what God had called him to do.

I said he should drop all these jobs and let others bear their share. After all, God appoints each person in the church to do a specific work that they have been gifted and called to do. My advice was hard for him to accept because it was difficult to get enough workers to fill all the needs he saw. Pete even protested by saying, "If I drop this duty, what if no one comes behind me and picks it up?"

"Then it isn't important enough to the church to keep it going," I said. "A small congregation can't do everything. Determine what is the most important, call others to step up, and let everything else go until God raises up those who are gifted to do it."

It's hard to discern where to draw the line. I love being active in ministry, but I learned long ago to say 'no' when I'm being asked to overextend myself. When I'm doing what God has equipped me for and called me to do, I am energized. When I take on the things God hasn't called me to do, it becomes a burden. Sometimes people get upset, but I just explain that I can't put another iron in the fire until I take one out. And I can't remove the things I know I am called to do.

A well-meaning Christian once told me, "Where ever you see a need, you have a call of God."

Sounds good, but this simply isn't true. I see thousands of needs all around me, but I can only meet the ones the Lord has called me to do. It may be a call of God for someone, but every need isn't a call of God to every Christian. The truth is, if you try to do

134

everything, you accomplish nothing. Narrow your focus to what God has equipped you to do, and do not allow your life to be crowded and distracted from that mission.

Burn out in the church is when Christians allow themselves to be overwhelmed by the things God has not brought into their life. We aren't called to 'get busy for God'. We are called to labor as the Lord has called us. There is a difference.

So how do we know which things are God's call, and which things are not? It's a trick question for identifying our works isn't the first step in discerning God's will. The starting point of finding God's will is not deciding which duties to take on. It begins with seeking the Lord and equipping ourselves spiritually. As we learn to walk with God, we will also discover the good works He is leading us to walk in. Seeking for works before establishing our hearts in righteousness only leads to confusion, frustration, and meaningless works.

Having said these things, let's begin looking at how we approach works.

Attitude is Everything

You've probably seen the person who works hard, but complains constantly about their tasks. When asked to take on responsibilities, they will do it, but then vent their displeasure the whole time they are working. Consider **Philippians 2:12-16**

[12] Therefore, my beloved, as you have always obeyed, not as in my presence only, but now much more in my absence, work out your own salvation with fear and trembling;

[13] for it is God who works in you both to will and to do for *His* good pleasure.

[14] Do all things without complaining and disputing,

[15] that you may become blameless and harmless, children of God without fault in the midst of a crooked and perverse generation, among whom you shine as lights in the world,

[16] holding fast the word of life, so that I may rejoice in the day of Christ that I have not run in vain or labored in vain.

There is much to glean from this wonderful passage. The first thing to note is the phrase, "Work out your own salvation with fear and trembling."

This passage is *not* saying to work *for* salvation. It's to work *out* the salvation we have already been given. This is self-evident seeing that just after this we are told that we are children of God, and He is working in us to do His will. A child of God is already in Christ. God within us is evidence that we already belong to Him. The Bible says that the Christian is the temple of God and that the Spirit of Christ is within us[79], and the God has sent His Spirit into our hearts to call out to Him as our Father.[80] Therefore, we are already possessors of salvation before this command applies to our lives.

We are called to work out (or labor) with fear and trembling. This relates to our earlier discussion on the fear of the Lord. The fear is knowing we will give an account for everything we've done in our body after God redeemed us.

The Bible says we will all stand before the judgment seat of Christ and give an account[81]. The unredeemed will stand before a different throne to be judged for sin[82], but we will be judged according to our deeds. Our judgment will not only be for what was done in the body (See 2 Corinthians 5:10), but our works will also be judged for eternal merit. Look at **1 Corinthians 3:11-15**

> [11] For no other foundation can anyone lay than that which is laid, which is Jesus Christ.
>
> [12] Now if anyone builds on this foundation *with* gold, silver, precious stones, wood, hay, straw,
>
> [13] each one's work will become clear; for the Day will declare it, because it will be revealed by fire; and the fire will test each one's work, of what sort it is.
>
> [14] If anyone's work which he has built on *it* endures, he will receive a reward.

---

[79] 1 Corinthians 3:16
[80] Galatians 4:6
[81] Romans 4:10 and 2 Corinthians 5:10
[82] Revelation 20:11-15

Works to Walk In

15 If anyone's work is burned, he will suffer loss; but he himself will be saved, yet so as through fire.

Don't miss this important point – some of our good works will not survive the test of God's fire. These are the things we have done outside of God's will, or the things we have done with bitter attitudes. Human efforts will be burned up. God's work laid for us to walk in will not. One thing this passage makes clear is that the foundation of our life must first be laid in Christ before works can even be considered for merit. All good works must first be built upon a life of faith. Salvation is already given. We begin walking in fellowship with God, and only then can we have good works.

Not every good deed will be rewarded. Wrong motives, bad attitudes, works by human effort, things done for the praise of men, these will all be counted as the wood and hay. Any work not produced by God working through us is not counted as precious. We still are bought with a price, so works are necessary – even in the life of someone with a bad attitude. We'll see the scriptures teaching on this shortly. But first we must realize that crowding our lives with busyness in the church is not rewarded.

Consider the reality of this truth. Think back to Pete. God called him to disciple (teach others how to mature in Christ) and to be an encourager in the church. Those are precious stones, gold, and silver. What God produces will always have eternal significance. However, the tasks that crowded his life appear good to those who don't know Pete's calling, but to God they are nothing but wood, hay, and stubble.

Pete labored and labored hard. He was busy for God and working in the church. But because these busy things prevented Pete from fulfilling God's will, they will be counted as worthless labor. Working hard may appear noble, but consider that Pete was doing many things God had not called him to do, but was not able to do the two things God had called him to do. Doing things that were contrary to God's will crowded his life and prevented him from doing God's will. We aren't measured on how much we work, but how we walk in the works God prepared beforehand for us to walk in.

The same is true for those who grumble through their work, complaining about what God is making them do. Or complaining about how things aren't going their way. Sometimes people complain because they aren't getting the recognition from others they feel they deserve. Maybe they are complaining about what they missed out on because they were having to do something that required time and commitment. The Apostle Paul referred to this when he said, "If I do this willingly, I have a reward, but if against my will, I am still obligated by the gospel.[83]"

Your redemption was a labor of love from Christ. Let your service be a labor of love toward Christ.

Merit / idolatry

For many, the next sentence will seem like an odd statement, but we'll see how this truth draws from scripture. Working for God's approval is a form of idolatry. This is true for those who think they can earn salvation, but it's also true when we think we must do something to please God after our redemption.

Think about the purpose of idolatry. Someone makes a sacrifice before an idol to appease the gods or a god. They are taking their works, and presenting it as an offering. The hope is that either the god or gods won't be angry, or that they will be pleased enough to offer a blessing to the worshipper.

This problem goes all the way back to Cain and Able. Able's offering to God was accepted, but Cain's was not. Anger boiled in Cain's heart and he murdered his brother. The Bible says that Cain killed his brother because his own works were evil and his brothers were good[84].

Both men offered what they believed to be good, so why was Cain's offering rejected as evil?

---

[83] 1 Corinthians 9:17
[84] 1 John 3:12

One brother was a master gardener, and the other tended to the flock. The gardener, Cain, sweated over his work as he planted, tilled the soil, nurtured the plants, and produced the fruit of his labors. He then took the best he could produce and brought them to God as an offering. He must have been proud when he laid before God his best fruit and vegetables, because they were fit for a king. Disappointment hammered at Cain's ego when God refused to accept his hard work and the best he had to offer.

Able, on the other hand, didn't sweat over the soil. He simply guarded the flock from wild beasts, and led them to good pasture. When it comes to raising cattle, you aren't producing the livestock, you are keeping anything from interfering with their growth. In the Old Testament, God often used livestock as a blessing to His people. He would increase their flocks, and bless them with health and abundance. And then God called for the best of the flock to be taken and sacrificed as an atonement. As we've already seen, this was a foreshadowing of Christ.

Able obeyed God's mandate to offer the best God had given him and give it back to God. Able's work wasn't to make cows, but to protect what God had given him and allow it to be blessed without interference. God gave Able in abundance, and then called Able to give back to God what God had produced and given.

Cain disobeyed the mandate to offer a proper sacrifice. Instead, he looked to himself as the source of the offering. He worked hard, gave his best effort, utilized all his skills, and then gave God the works of his hands. He discovered that man, at his best, cannot measure up to God's requirement. Able submitted to God and trusted in God's goodness as an acceptable sacrifice, but Cain decided to offer something he thought was better. Which turned out not to be better in God's sight. As we have already seen, It's just as the Bible says in **Romans 4:4-5**

⁴ Now to him who works, the wages are not counted as grace but as debt.

⁵ But to him who does not work but believes on Him who justifies the ungodly, his faith is accounted for righteousness,

We've already viewed this passage, but because it is a key to understanding the Christian's works, it's important to keep this principle in sight. What made Able's works righteous? The grace of God. He believed God and didn't take upon himself the work of meriting favor with God. His offering was an act of faith – believing God and giving an offering that acknowledged God as the provider.

What made Cain's works evil? It's the same as we are taught in the New Testament. The one who works doesn't earn grace. He only counts his labors toward his debt. A debt that cannot be paid by man. According to scripture, our work is counted as debt, not merit. Able believed God and was declared righteous. Abraham believed God and was accounted as righteous. Neither labored for acceptance, but rather acted in obedience while depending upon God for grace. Grace simply means, unmerited favor.

In the same way, if we are depending on our deeds or works in order to please God, we have stepped outside of faith and have made the labor of our hands the source of righteousness instead of God. That's why it's idolatry. Our works become the source of goodness rather than God being the source of goodness. Or you can substitute goodness for righteousness. The same principle applies. This is the trap the Galatian church fell into. Look at **Galatians 5:4-5**

> [4] You have become estranged from Christ, you who *attempt to* be justified by law; you have fallen from grace.
> [5] For we through the Spirit eagerly wait for the hope of righteousness by faith.

In their situation, the men of the church attempted to become righteous by keeping the Old Covenant law of circumcision. In Cain's situation, he looked to his skills and hard work to earn God's favor. In the church, people think they can earn righteousness by tithes, church programs, saying certain prayers, or various other practices. Those who look to their efforts to obtain righteousness have fallen from grace. Grace is given to us by faith – believing God. We wait eagerly for the hope of righteousness that will one day be fulfilled in us. And we do this through the Spirit – abiding in Christ and walking in obedience.

Is tithing, reading the Bible, working in ministry and all the other things we do as Christians a waste of our efforts? No, but it is *not* what makes us righteous. Our righteousness is found by faith in Christ. As we saw earlier, faith is active and calls us to obedience. Human belief can be passive, but true faith always shows the fruit of obedience to God.

The point is that you and I are not working to become righteous. We are taking what God has created and given to us, and fulfilling His will through obedience. We are righteous in Christ; therefore, we walk in righteousness in the Spirit. That walk of faith is paved with good works – but works are not what we worship, nor is it what we place our trust in. We trust in Christ alone.

Sometimes it can seem like a fine line, but it really boils down to having the right heart. Having a heart that is dependent upon the flesh and the efforts of the work of our own hands is to trust in something other than God, which is a form of idolatry. The Bible says, "Whatever is not of faith is sin."[85] Faith comes first. So even works are accounted as sin if they are not born out of faith in Christ. God deals us the measure of faith, and everything of God comes through faith.

Works do not produce faith, but faith does produce works. The difference is God working in you to do His good will, or you working without God in an attempt to merit (or earn) His favor. One is as the offering of Cain, and the other as the offering of Able.

Works are prepared by God beforehand

Now that we've looked at the importance of giving back to God what God has given, let's also look at laboring in what God is doing. Whether we are looking at the concept of laboring or sacrificing, the principle is the same. It begins with God and ends with Him. Just as Jesus is the author and finisher of our faith[86], the

---

[85] Romans 14:23
[86] Hebrews 12:2

Lord is also the author and producer of our works. Let's look at a few key passages. Begin by looking at a passage we saw earlier: **Ephesians 2:8-10**

[8] For by grace you have been saved through faith, and that not of yourselves; *it is* the gift of God,

[9] not of works, lest anyone should boast.

[10] For we are His workmanship, created in Christ Jesus for good works, which God prepared beforehand that we should walk in them.

Much is revealed in verse ten. I often hear people quoting verses eight and nine, but we can't neglect what comes after. The Bible does not teach that man is exempt from work. It teaches the proper role of works. Works can't save. Works can't merit God's favor. Works have no role in producing faith or righteousness. However, neglecting God's path of good works is rebellion against His calling. True faith and righteousness will produce good works. Anything short of that is man's resistance to God's will.

There are works, and there are good works. Religion is filled with works, but only God can produce good works. We call man-made works good based on the human perspective, but true good comes from God. Just as Jesus said no one can be called good except God, no work can be truly good except that which is from God.

When you come to faith, it is God's work. God not only saves, but He produces a new life, gives us a new nature, and then we show the evidence that we are His workmanship by our actions. You are a new creation, created for good works.

You can see that rather than works producing faith or righteousness, the opposite is true. We become God's workmanship to produce good works. Faith produces works, not the other way around.

Take note of a very important principle in verse ten above. I've reiterated this several times, but it's an important principle that we cannot overlook. God prepared the works you are called to do beforehand, and you are called to walk in God's prepared work. This is important for a lot of reasons.

First, it is not what you are doing for God. It is what God is doing and He is calling you to join in His labor. The path is already laid out. Your role is to just walk in God's works and do as He opens the door and provides opportunity.

Also notice where the dependence lies. God is not depending on you. You are depending upon Him. Not only that, but it takes the pressure off you and gives you rest from your own labors. You will succeed when you are walking in His works. The way has already been made. You have already been equipped.

When Jesus was mentoring the disciples, He sent seventy out to labor. He paired them up and sent them to the fields of ministry that were already prepared for their arrival. Jesus even said, "I send you out to reap where you have not sown. Others have labored and you are entering into their labor." This is the call to works. The way has already been made and you are just being called to labor where the Lord is sending you.

Consider how Jesus prepared the disciples for work. He taught seventy disciples, sent them out to work, and then taught them again as He prepared them for other work. They returned rejoicing in success. You also are called to become a disciple of the word, then go out to labor where God calls, and then continue in the word. We cannot expect God to reveal His work to us if we are neglecting His word. Yet when we are faithful, we'll see God move in amazing ways, so that we too return while rejoicing in the fruit of our labors.

This doesn't mean success is always easy or that our efforts are pain free. Let me give you another example from Jesus and His disciples.

After seeing an amazing miracle of Jesus feeding five-thousand men with a few loaves, the disciples were put to the test. Jesus ended the day by telling His disciples to get in a boat and row to the other side of a large lake. He said he would meet them later. Jesus then went up to the mountain to pray.

The Bible says a great wind storm arose and blew against the boat. The natural response for most fishermen would have been to allow the wind to drive them back to shore, and wait out the storm.

It was a test of obedience. The disciples rowed against the wind for over nine hours. All the time, Jesus watched from the mountain[87].

These men had to be exhausted and discouraged. They had worked as hard as they could, but made little progress. In fact, they probably were losing ground. Yet they remained faithful to the instruction they were given, "Go, and I will meet you."

Nine hours into the storm, Jesus came down from the mountain, walked out on the sea, and got into the boat. He calmed the storm and Jesus took them to the other side.[88] Their labors did not produce success. The work showed faithfulness and obedience. In God's timing He produced success and completed the work.

That is works at its core. We may find ourselves laboring against all odds, but if we know we've been called to a mission, we'll remain faithful. Hardship separates the called from the seeker. I can always tell who is truly called and who is emotionally driven or seeking some type of fulfillment. When ministry becomes work and success is scarce, only the called persevere.

The one seeking fulfillment will stay as long as they feel encouraged. But those who look to Jesus, the author and finisher of our faith, will not be discouraged when times get hard. When we know God is accomplishing His will, we take heart and stay the course. Earlier we looked at **Hebrews 4:2**, but now let's read it again and bring in the works of verse 3:

> [2] For indeed the gospel was preached to us as well as to them; but the word which they heard did not profit them, not being mixed with faith in those who heard *it.*
>
> [3] For we who have believed do enter that rest, as He has said: "So I swore in My wrath, 'They shall not enter My rest,' " although the works were finished from the foundation of the world.

This passage is drawing the contrast between the Children of Israel, who rebelled against God, and the Church in the New Testament. The ability to succeed in fulfilling God's call was available

---

[87] Mark 6:48

[88] John 6:21

to them as well as to us, but they didn't receive the word by faith. The question to the church is, "Will we receive it by faith?"

Verse three tells us that they failed to finish the work and enter God's rest – even though the works were finished from the foundation of the world. In other words, God established the work and made the way of success in His purpose and plan before even creating the world. The way has been made, but they didn't find it because they couldn't trust the Lord. Their calling was to go where God was leading and walk in the works God had already established.

The scriptures teach that Jesus is our rest. We enter God's rest by ceasing from our own labors, and trusting in the completed work of Christ.

God's work will be accomplished. It isn't dependent on you. The work has already been finished, but you and I have the privilege to walk in those works, which God prepared beforehand. We benefit from believing God and walking in His works. We are rewarded for faithfulness, not success. Success belongs to God, but faithfulness and obedience belongs to you and I. Look also at **Romans 8:29-31**

> [29] For whom He foreknew, He also predestined *to be* conformed to the image of His Son, that He might be the firstborn among many brethren.
> [30] Moreover whom He predestined, these He also called; whom He called, these He also justified; and whom He justified, these He also glorified.
> [31] What then shall we say to these things? If God *is* for us, who *can be* against us?

When the topic of predestination comes up, people often get negative images and ideas. I meet people who say, "I don't believe in predestination." Perhaps a better way of putting it would be, "I don't believe in a man-centered view of predestination." If we don't believe in predestination – God's foreordained plan, then we have to reject the scriptures. Predestination is not a negative thing and it doesn't turn us into robots. It's the pathway God has made beforehand so you can see good works fulfilled in your life.

Predestination shows the amazing foreknowledge of God, and the truth of His power to accomplish His will.

In the passage above, we see that God's foreknowledge and plan is the hope we have of accomplishing our own calling. It is our confidence. If God is for us, who can be against us? What can be against us? If I'm faithful and obedient, I will fulfill my calling and enter the promise of Christ. I will become a joint heir with Christ. How can that be looked upon as something to shun?

Knowing that I've been predestined to conform to Jesus' likeness gives me the confidence that the path to spiritual maturity is laid before me. All I have to do is walk where God leads and obey in faith. The same is true for you. Everything we need to become what God wants us to be is open and available for any who obey.

The same is true for works and ministry. Nothing on earth can prevent me from accomplishing all that God has called me to do. Like the disciples rowing against the wind, I may struggle, but I struggle with hope and confidence. God's work will be accomplished. If God is for me, who can be against me? I only must wait on the Lord to enter my works to do His will.

To be predestined does not eliminate our call of obedience. It's our confidence that when we obey, God has built His plan into our path so we can't miss out on any good thing. Disobedience is to follow our own path that leads nowhere, but obedience places us on God's foreordained path that leads to every promise.

Even when our works look like a failure, God is able to transform this into a fruitful accomplishment. Let me give you a real world example from the life of Jim Elliot.

Jim Elliot was called to the mission field. God laid Ecuador's Waodani Indians on his heart. From 1945 to 1956 he studied and prepared for the mission field. After more than a decade of working toward the goal of reaching this remote group of people, he made initial contact and was encouraged by their friendly manner. His mission team loaded up a boat and launched out to begin his mission work.

Ten warriors waited for the boat and ambushed the mission team. Jim and his four companions were killed before they could say a word about the gospel.

When I first heard this story, I couldn't imagine how God could allow such a tragedy. That is until I heard the rest of the story. His wife and fellow missionaries showed what true faith is. Instead of wanting revenge, or running away in defeat, they came up with a plan to finish the work. Though they grieved their loss, the mission team returned to the Waodani people and used Jim's death as an example between how the world reacts and how the Christian reacts. They stunned the warriors and villagers by expressing forgiveness and the love of Christ.

In the end, the village received the gospel, and the man who drove the spear into the heart of Jim Elliot heard the call of God and became a pastor. This man reached more people in Ecuador than the mission team could have done by their own plans.

Because Elizabeth Elliot and the rest of the mission team remained faithful, they saw God turn a tragedy into an amazing work. The Bible speaks of those who are killed for the name of Christ and says that even though they have passed from the earth, their works follow them.[89] Though Jim Elliot never saw results from his calling, the works follow him into heaven and he'll reap the fruit of his faithful labors.

This may be a hard example, but it shows that our labors are never in vain as long as we are walking in the call of God. What looks like defeat is God's tool for victory, and what looks like an impenetrable wall is an open door. Consider Jesus' words to the faithful few in the church of Philadelphia from **Revelation 3:8**

> I know your works. See, I have set before you an open door, and no one can shut it; for you have a little strength, have kept My word, and have not denied My name.

When God opens the door, no one can shut it. The opposite is also true. Unless God opens the door, we are battering fruitlessly

---

[89] Revelation 14:13

against a wall if we try to open what God has shut. The open door is to those who keep His word and hold true to His name.

Though we may not be called to lose our lives, we do know that no barrier can stand. There will be barriers, walls, and challenges. They are beyond our strength, but nothing can stand against the will of God. As Jesus said, "The gates of hell will not prevail" against you. A gate is a defensive barrier. It is the closed door that protects a city from invasion. Yet God has the power to open anything He chooses.

We too will see this if we keep His word and honor His name. God has already made the way. He now calls for those who are faithful to walk in it.

The Reward of Our Labors

God desires to bless each person with rewards, but you are not rewarded for the amount of work you accomplish. Yes, I know. This is counter intuitive. The mindset of most people is drawn from our culture. But God isn't concerned with how busy you are, but how faithful you are. We are about to look at scriptures that will blow most Christian's ideas of works and rewards out of the water. In fact, let's begin with the words of Jesus. I'm sure that when He instructed His disciples on works, they were caught by surprise. Jesus had a way of pulling the rug out from under people's misconceptions. Look at **Luke 17:7-10**

[7] "And which of you, having a servant plowing or tending sheep, will say to him when he has come in from the field, 'Come at once and sit down to eat'?

[8] "But will he not rather say to him, 'Prepare something for my supper, and gird yourself and serve me till I have eaten and drunk, and afterward you will eat and drink'?

[9] "Does he thank that servant because he did the things that were commanded him? I think not.

[10] "So likewise you, when you have done all those things which you are commanded, say, 'We are unprofitable servants. We have done what was our duty to do.' "

This is another one of those hard sayings Jesus often dropped into His teachings. One thing is certain, He wasn't worried about how many people followed. Jesus' concern was that people followed Him for the right reason, and that they understood the truth of what it meant to be a disciple. Consider this passage found in **Mark 8:34**

> When He had called the people to *Himself,* with His disciples also, He said to them, "Whoever desires to come after Me, let him deny himself, and take up his cross, and follow Me.

This is a message few preachers will proclaim from the pulpit today. To do so would send away the masses, for the only people who would stay are those truly interested in being a disciple. When crowds gathered, Jesus often taught hard sayings and on one occasion, most of His disciples turned their backs and left Him.[90] Even those who stayed acknowledged His teaching was hard, but they also recognized His way was the only thing of eternal significance[91].

Why would anyone want to choose a lifestyle that requires we deny ourselves and take up a cross? Why would anyone want a faith that says we must lose our life? The answer is in the next verse. **Mark 8:35**

> For whoever desires to save his life will lose it, but whoever loses his life for My sake and the gospel's will save it.

Jesus is asking His disciples to believe this one basic truth. This life is valueless unless it is lived in light of the life to come. The world is passing away, along with all the pleasures and investments made in it. We are being asked to give up the things we're destined to lose in order to gain the things that are eternal. And the Bible says not to look at the things that can be seen, for they are only temporary. The things that can't be seen with physical eyes are eternal. [92]

---

[90] John 6:66
[91] John 6:60-68
[92] 2 Corinthians 4:18

Only those who believe the word can do this. If I don't believe in what I can't see, I will not be willing to give up what I can see. God reveals the eternal to us through His word. Only those who believe the word can let go of their own life and take hold of the life God is offering – one that will not pass away.

Why would I want to take up a cross when the world says, "Go for the gusto?" This is why the way of the cross is foolishness to the world. Until someone sees through eyes of faith, the true Christian life doesn't make sense. The true Christian life isn't gathering treasures on earth, but inheriting the promise of heaven.

Many will say that God wants to bless us here and now. In some cases, yes. But that is never the focus of the Christian life. In fact, Jesus warned that we should not lay up for ourselves treasures on earth[93]. The Bible also warns that when wealth becomes our focus, we stray from the faith and it creates many sorrows[94].

Some claim that Jesus was rich and wants us to be rich. However, that is far from the case. According to scripture, Jesus was dependent on others to provide for His physical needs.[95] Also consider the humble examples Jesus gave. He was born in a borrowed manger[96]. When taxes were due, Jesus sent Peter to catch a fish that would have a gold coin. So He paid taxes with borrowed money.[97] His first miracle was to turn water into wine with borrowed jugs[98]. Twice Jesus fed the multitudes with borrowed fish and bread[99]. During His triumphant entry when He proclaimed Himself as the King riding on the donkey, it was with a borrowed colt[100]. For the last supper, Jesus sent the disciples to borrow a

---

[93] Matthew 6:19-20
[94] 1 Timothy 6:10
[95] Luke 8:3
[96] Luke 2:7
[97] Matthew 17:27
[98] John 2:6
[99] Mark 6:38 and Mark 8:8
[100] Matthew 21:1-5

Works to Walk In

guest room[101]. When He was crucified, Jesus was put into the borrowed tomb of a rich man[102].

Where is the wealth? True riches are not material possessions. Jesus said that how we treat money and wealth is a test. If we fail to be faithful in unrighteous wealth (money), who will commit to us the true riches (our eternal inheritance)?[103]

Once we have an eternal perspective, we'll also have the proper view of money and the things of the world. If physical possessions become a priority in our lives, we lose perspective and begin pursuing the wrong things.

Money and wealth is not the reward of God. God does indeed bless as He sees fit, but not everyone will be given excessive material wealth. If materialism is the reward, we'd be short changed when our time on earth is done. Keep a balanced perspective. Our life shouldn't be centered upon living to make money or gather possessions.

We need to provide for our families, and the Bible encourages work. The Bible calls the man who refused to work to meet his family's needs a person who has denied the faith, and worse than an unbeliever[104]. Making money is not condemned, but investing your life to obtain wealth is condemned.

Why we are rewarded

Now that we've looked at the importance of serving Christ and not money, let's look at why God rewards us. Jesus made it clear that our efforts are expected and not praiseworthy. When it came to following Him, Jesus instructed the disciples to consider the cost. The Christian walk isn't easy. Many struggle with the cost of discipleship, but the eternal inheritance will more than make up what we've lost. The Apostle Paul put it this way, "The sufferings of

---

[101] Mark 14:12-15
[102] Matthew 27:58-60 and Isaiah 53:9
[103] Luke 16:11
[104] 1 Timothy 5:8

this present time are not worthy to be compared with the glory that shall be revealed in us."

But how do we obtain that promise seeing Jesus said we should not think we deserve a reward for doing our duty?

We are bought with a price, and when we accept the new life God has given, we should also have considered the cost of what we are losing. We lay down the things we once valued so we can reach for the things that are of true value. But how do we reach for it?

Let's revisit a passage we briefly alluded to earlier, **1 Corinthians 9:16-17**

> [16] For if I preach the gospel, I have nothing to boast of, for necessity is laid upon me; yes, woe is me if I do not preach the gospel!
>
> [17] For if I do this willingly, I have a reward; but if against my will, I have been entrusted with a stewardship.

Consider what is being said here. First, Paul was called to preach the gospel. Though we are not all called to preach, we are all called to the work God has prepared for us. Necessity is laid upon us to fulfill the will of God and each of us will be held accountable for what we've done. However, the reward is not in doing the work, but our heart of faith and obedience. If I serve God willingly, I have a reward. But if against my will, I am still required to do what I have been entrusted to do. It's the cost of discipleship.

The reward is in a heart of faith, obedience, and a willingness to serve God. I have been redeemed. Jesus suffered on my behalf. He endured the cross while despising the shame He had to endure, but He persevered for the joy set before Him. That joy was in knowing that my life would be spared and reconciled to Him. Seeing how He endured being beaten until he was almost unrecognizable, and then nailed to a cross, is it too much for me to take the new life I've been given and honor God by doing His will? Also consider this wonderful passage in **Hebrews 11:6**

> But without faith *it is* impossible to please *Him,* for he who comes to God must believe that He is, and *that* He is a rewarder of those who diligently seek Him.

I believe, therefore I seek. Just as God told Abraham, "I am your exceedingly great reward," I cling to that same word. When I know Him, I find true riches and the treasure of heaven. Knowing God is what life is all about. It shapes me into something of value while revealing to me how much God values me – and values you.

God is your reward. Those who want things will never be satisfied, but once someone is satisfied in the Lord, the desire of their hearts is established in the right things with Christ being at the center of it all.

God wants you, not what you can give Him. In the same way, if we are only concerned about what God has in His hand, we miss the true treasure of fellowship with Him. God indeed rewards us and the Bible is filled with the promises of inheriting the kingdom. However, none of that has value outside of fellowship with Him.

When my kids were very young, their grandparents gave many gifts. It bothered me, but I put a stop to the gifts when my children's first words were, "What did you bring me?" No hello. No hugs. They weren't excited about seeing their grandparents as much as they were excited about getting something new. When the item wasn't something they valued, the visit was a disappointment.

Now they enjoy the fellowship with their grandparents. Presents arrive on occasions, but it is an added bonus and not the meaning behind the relationship. When they focused too much on materialism, they missed the value of knowing their grandparents and treasuring the time they spent together. Now they aren't dependent upon a gift in order to enjoy the time together.

Love God, not just what you can get from Him. The relationship is the treasure. All else is extra blessings to enjoy, but not the meaning behind the Christian life. God wants to bless and reward us. Jesus said that God delights in giving us the kingdom. But that kingdom is not the best part of heaven. Fellowship with God is the focus and our exceedingly great reward.

God has given salvation to you as a gift purchased with His own blood. Let your life and ministry be a gift to go with a heart of gratitude. True love is when two people give to each other. A husband that demands a wife to meet his expectation doesn't find love. A wife that requires her husband to meet her needs and expectations doesn't find love. That is two people taking from each other. But when a husband gives of himself to his wife as a gift, and a wife gives herself to her husband as a gift, true love blossoms. Demanding love doesn't produce love.

The Bible uses marriage as an illustration for Christ's love for the church. He gave Himself for her, so His love has been revealed. Now the members of the church, which includes you and I, should give themselves to God as a gift of love. Then the relationship is complete. A completed relationship is the best reward we can discover.

There is so much in the Bible on how to do good works that it can't fit into a single chapter. Take some time to search the New Testament for works and discover how you can express your faith and love through action. Never lose sight of works being a gift of yourself and not a merit system. Once you understand how works is an expression of love, you'll maintain a healthy perspective.

Simple and Accurate Bible Interpretations

It has been said that the Bible can be interpreted many ways by many people. The world is filled with cults, pseudo Christian groups, and various organizations. Each claims to have the truth and many claim to have discovered hidden truths that give them the inside angle on spiritual enlightenment.

How do we know who is right and who is wrong? Can we know with certainty? Yes, you can know the truth. Most have heard, the truth shall make you free, but that begins with how to know the truth. Look at this passage in **John 8:31-32**

> [31] Then Jesus said to those Jews who believed Him, "If you abide in My word, you are My disciples indeed.
> [32] "And you shall know the truth, and the truth shall make you free."

If you abide in the word – learning and obeying the word – you'll be a disciple indeed. And then you have the promise that you shall know the truth. You *shall* know the truth. That promise is to those who abide in the word. A disciple indeed will discover how to accurately interpret and how to avoid misconceptions and recognize deceptions from misapplied scripture.

Avoiding Deception

How do we know who holds the truth since every group makes this claim? Let's begin by looking at the words of **1 John 4:1**

> Beloved, do not believe every spirit, but test the spirits, whether they are of God; because many false prophets have gone out into the world.

Jesus made the comment, "I have not come in my own name and you did not receive Me, but if one comes in his own name, you will receive him.[105]"

This is a strong clue for us to know who to be on guard against. Any who present themselves as the source of knowledge or claim to hold a secret for knowing God or finding enlightenment, that's a banner revealing their true motives.

A true teacher from God will point to Christ, and seek to grow you into spiritual maturity. Those who make followers dependent upon themselves as the teacher have strayed from God's plan. Teachers who point to themselves are not of God. Even if they perform miracles, this is not the evidence they are of God. Consider the words of Jesus in **Matthew 24:24-25**

> [24] "For false christs and false prophets will rise and show great signs and wonders to deceive, if possible, even the elect.
>
> [25] "See, I have told you beforehand.

During the world's greatest time of trial, miracles and signs will be performed by demonic forces (See Revelation 16:13-14). The signs are intended to cause those who are not faithful to the word to become followers of miracle workers or the religion they represent. But notice what Jesus said, "To deceive, if possible, even the elect." It's something God allows in order to separate the faithful from those who are not truly disciples.

The elect are those who are grounded in truth. They are children of God, born of the Spirit, and grounded in the word. Even they will find the deception to be persuasive, yet they will not be deceived. Why? Because once they see the teacher leading them away from the truth, they will reject the teacher and his or her miracles, and cling to the truth of God.

The Bible informs us that the spirit of the prophets are subject to the prophets[106]. In other words, what is being revealed in the name of God is to be tested by what has already been revealed by God. It was Jesus who said, "Heaven and earth shall pass away, but my word will never pass away."

When someone claims God is doing a new thing that contradicts what God has already said, either the prophet is telling

---

[106] 1 Corinthians 14:32

the truth and God's word is false, or God's word is true and the prophet is false. We have to decide which we believe. Sadly, many choose the false prophet and his show of lying wonders, and then cast the word of God behind them. But the elect will hold to the word.

Let me give an example. Several years back a friend invited me to a revival service led by a man who claimed to have a special anointing from God. I declined at first, but he insisted that I would not be disappointed and said I had to see the miracles this man performed. Upon much insistence, I went.

For several weeks prior, my friend had been requesting prayer for a brain aneurism discovered in a checkup. He asked everyone he knew to pray for him. On the first night I attended, the healing preacher started getting words from God. Naturally, I was skeptical, but when my friend was called by name, I was caught off guard. The preacher identified his ailment accurately and then performed a healing – or so he claimed.

As the service went on, people were called by name and diseases were identified. Before our very eyes shorten legs were lengthened. It was a well-crafted show. It was so well performed that I began to question my own skepticism. I went back several nights and was impressed with this man's abilities. Even his teaching seemed biblical.

In a moment, everything changed.

The healer preached a very unbiblical sermon. He directly contradicted the scriptures and claimed his word was directly from God. The man had spent several days gaining trust and then used that trust to propagate a different gospel. The Apostle Paul warned a church that he founded, "Even if we or an angel from heaven come to you and present another gospel, which you have not received, let him be accursed."

Think for a moment about the impact of that statement. [107] The apostle who wrote two-thirds of the New Testament is telling the church that if he loses his mind, comes back, and teaches a

---

[107] Galatians 1:8-9

contradictory message, don't believe him. Instead, count him as accursed by God.

We must take this very seriously. Jesus said that it is the word we have received that will judge us on the last day[108]. Since our lives will be evaluated against the scriptures, it stands to reason that we should look to the scriptures as our standard today.

After this man contradicted the Bible, I began to look closely at his miracles. I made startling discoveries. First, I noticed he used sleight of hand to distract the audience. When he said, "Look over here," I began to be suspicious. When someone came up, he would sometimes lead them to the opposite end of the front of the church. He would then say, "Everyone face this man and stretch out your hands toward him." It was a clever diversion. I started looking in the opposite direction. I saw his assistants pointing to people and giving hand signals. Sure enough, in a few minutes he would call that person by name and identify their illness.

The whole revival was a scam. But I saw legs lengthened in plain sight – or so it appeared. I did notice that those with healed legs still walked with the same pronounced limp as they headed back to their seats. So how did he do this?

Do this experiment. Place someone in a chair and lift their legs straight out. If you shift their legs to the left, the left leg will appear longer than the right. Shift to the right, and the right leg will be longer. Since the hips are held in place by the chair, the legs can be manipulated to appear longer or shorter. So to heal a shorter leg, just make sure that leg is closest to the audience. They will clearly see the soles of the shoes of the longer leg. Then use a motion that masks the fact you are slowly shifting the legs, the audience will see the shoe soles begin to even up with each other as the longer leg is shifted toward the shorter one. Then the 'healer' places the microphone against the now even soles to show there is no difference. There was no healing; just a change in visual perception, but this man made a big show of the healing power we supposedly witnessed.

---

[108] John 12:48

I also discovered that the healer's team gathered information about people's needs from surrounding churches. Now all they had to do was match the need with a name. This was done by friendly people mingling before the services. It was quite a clever ruse. But one that has detrimental consequences. Consequences both spiritually and physically. My friend later died of his aneurism, but he never visited a doctor again since he claimed to be healed.

You may be asking what this has to do with knowing the truth. It very much applies, for all these religious scams distract people from the truth so they miss the real purpose of God's plan, and it turns people away from the Lord. When someone has been scammed, they believe God is a scam.

I had an atheist send me an article with a note, "If you read this, you won't be a Bible believer by the end." I read it, and I'm still a Christian and Bible believer. The article was account after account of people doing atrocities in the name of God, duping people in the name of God, and abusing the scriptures for their own gain.

My response to him was, "How does it disprove the Bible to show a list of people who acted contrary to the Bible?"

The Bible warns us against these very things, and nearly every apostle in the New Testament warned the church that these people were coming. We have been forewarned that people will arise among our own congregations and draw disciples after themselves[109]. Jesus said that many will arise using His name, but they are false teachers and prophets. He even warned that because of these people doing evil in God's name, the way of truth will be spoken against. Sounds to me like this confirms the scriptures rather than disproving them.

Jesus said, "See, I have told you beforehand." We are warned so we are not led away. These will come, pervert the truth, and then lead many into deception. But we have been forewarned that we might be grounded in the truth of scripture and not be deceived. Any Christian that is led astray has ignored the warnings of Jesus.

The Bible uses the term, 'wolf in sheep's clothing' when speaking about the teachers who contradict the scriptures. Think

---

[109] Acts 20:30

about what that means. The deceiver will look like the real thing, talk like the real thing, show many outward signs that they are of God, but inwardly they are ravenous wolves[110]. Yet Jesus said we will know them by their fruits.

Do teachers / preachers / prophets fulfill the mandates of scripture? Do they point to Christ or themselves? Do they call us to fulfill our flesh, or walk in the Spirit? Do they point to the word, or something else? Do they make disciples by teaching them to obey all that has been commanded? Or do their followers remain in the same spiritual condition as before? Do they teach people to love the world, or to seek the Kingdom? Is it a self-centered gospel, or Christ centered?

Many speak in God's name and will give a pretense of honoring the scriptures. But they will use crafty arguments to explain away scriptures that contradict the message they claim is of the Holy Spirit. We are commanded by scripture to *not* believe every spirit, but to test the spirits to see if they are truly from God[111]. Neglecting this command is the first step toward deception.

Deception always requires a willing participant. Manipulation of the truth is how the deceiver tries to persuade you to willingly follow the craftily veiled lie.

The Holy Spirit

The Bible tells us that the scriptures are spiritually discerned and that we have the ability to know the truth by the anointing of the Holy Spirit, which has been given to every believer. This also is a point of confusion for many. Before we move on to look at how we know the truth, let's look at the foundation of that knowledge, the Holy Spirit's guidance within us.

According to the Bible, many false spirits masquerade as the Holy Spirit. The Bible calls these spirits of deception. Some scoff at the idea of demonic spirits, but if we believe in angels, why would we question the Bible's teaching of fallen angels? A demon is

---

[110] Matthew 7:15
[111] 1 John 4:1

nothing more than a fallen angel. We are not to fear them, but rather to be aware of the schemes of the devil that is designed to confuse the truth. We'll get more into this when we look at spiritual warfare in a later chapter. For now, just be aware that the Bible describes the fall of a third of the angels coinciding with the rebellion of Satan and his fall.

This is what is meant when the Bible speaks of spirits of deception. The Bible says that Satan masquerades as an angel of light and his prophets pass themselves off as apostles and prophets of truth[112]. The same holds true for counterfeiting the Holy Spirit. We are commanded to compare those who claim to have the Holy Spirit with what the Bible teaches about the Holy Spirit. I won't spend a lot of time on this, but there are some basic things to look at when being told a work or service is Holy Spirit inspired. Look now at **John 16:13-14**

> [13] "However, when He, the Spirit of truth, has come, He will guide you into all truth; for He will not speak on His own *authority,* but whatever He hears He will speak; and He will tell you things to come.
> [14] "He will glorify Me, for He will take of what is Mine and declare *it* to you.

Add this to Jesus' description of the Holy Spirit above. **John 15:26**
> But when the Helper comes, whom I shall send to you from the Father, the Spirit of truth who proceeds from the Father, He will testify of Me.

When instructing His disciples, Jesus states a few key points. The Holy Spirit will not speak of Himself, but will testify of Jesus' authority, and reveal the teachings of Christ. He will also glorify Christ. The Spirit of God also testifies of Jesus Christ. Are you seeing to purpose of the Holy Spirit? His role is to point to Christ, reveal the scriptures (all of which are of Christ-He is the word made flesh), and to teach believers how to conform to the image of Christ.

---

[112] 2 Corinthians 11:13-15

Romans 12:2, Ephesians 6:17, and Titus 3:5 tell us that the Spirit renews our minds through the word. We are then told that the Holy Spirit pours the love of God into our hearts[113], and produces the fruit of the Spirit[114].

According to scripture, the true evidence of the Holy Spirit is:
- Impart God's love into our hearts (agape).
- A transformed life.
- A renewed mind.
- Conviction and repentance of sin.
- Affirmation of the Word.
- Understanding of the Word.
- Pointing to Christ.
- Glorifying Christ.
- Not testifying of itself.
- The power to crucify the flesh and bring it under subjection to God.
- The equipping of the saints for ministry through gifts that edify the church to glorify Christ.

A false apostle or teacher will instruct you *not* to question or test the spirit, because he doesn't want the truth to expose the deception. No godly leader will instruct you not to test with the word of God. If the spirit being presented doesn't fulfill the roles given by scripture, or worse yet, if it contradicts these basic things, it is not the Holy Spirit.

The Holy Spirit will never contradict the word, but will instruct us in the word. It will not show us a new way that contradicts Christ, but will affirm the teachings of Jesus. The Spirit gives us understanding in the word, and teaches us how it applies to our life in today's world. Our ultimate goal is to conform to the image of Christ so we can inherit the kingdom as God has promised to those who obey His word. The Holy Spirit works to accomplish this in the life of the believer.

---

[113] Romans 5:5
[114] Galatians 5:22-25

Keep these things in mind as you look to the Spirit for guidance, and then trust the Lord to reveal truth through His word by the Spirit.

You shall know the truth

Jesus made the statement, "You shall know the truth, and the truth shall make you free."

Free from what? Free from sin, deception, and the things that entangle our lives. Truth was given to us in the word so that we can know it. Nothing about Bible study is complicated. There are two basic rules. Scripture is to be understood in light of the rest of scripture, and we must diligently study. Unless we know the truth, we can't hope to fully understand it, so diligence is necessary. And if we take portions of scripture out of context, it's easy to misunderstand the intended meaning.

This should be easily understood, if we stop and think for a moment. Anything taken out of context can be twisted into an unintended meaning. That's the nature of language. A politician once gave a speech where he made the comments, "Some people say, 'Abortion is okay because the mother has the right to her own body,' but I disagree."

Several years later, his new opponent wanted to show him in a negative light, so just before the election, his campaign sent out a flyer with the statement, "My opponent said, 'Abortion is okay because the mother has the right to her own body.'"

Technically, he did say those words, but out of context it appears that he's saying something he clearly did not intend. A partial quote became a lie.

Earlier I told the story about how my grandfather enjoyed teasing the ladies. "I can prove that the Bible warns against women driving," he would say. When someone took the bait, he'd pull out his King James Bible (it only works with KJV) and turn to Acts 27. He'd then read, "We let her drive. And so were driven. All hope that we should be saved was then taken away." He'd grin and say, "That's right out of the Bible. Women are dangerous drivers."

Of course we already know that in Acts 27, women are not even the topic being discussed. 'Her' was a ship and the situation was that the people on board were in a fierce storm and lost hope of coming out of it safely.

In good humor my grandfather made the Bible say what he wanted it to say by only pulling out the words that would support his joke, and ignoring the rest. In context there is no way to misinterpret what the Bible is saying, but taken out of context it could be manipulated to make his point.

Whether it's scientific data, political speeches, or the Bible, taking information out of context can mislead. This is not unique to our day, for the apostles warned against this very thing. Look at **2 Peter 3:15-17**

> [15] and consider *that* the longsuffering of our Lord *is* salvation -- as also our beloved brother Paul, according to the wisdom given to him, has written to you,
> [16] as also in all his epistles, speaking in them of these things, in which are some things hard to understand, which untaught and <u>unstable *people* twist to their own destruction, as *they do* also the rest of the Scriptures.</u>
> [17] You therefore, beloved, since you know *this* beforehand, beware lest you also fall from your own steadfastness, being led away with the error of the wicked; (Emphasis added)

In this passage, the Apostle Peter is pointing to a problem the people in the church were already aware of. Those who were not stable in the truth would take the writings of the Apostle Paul (along with the rest of scripture), twist them out of their intended context, and then lead people into error by presenting a lie and calling it the words of scripture. The church is being warned to look at this example and be on guard so they are not also led into error.

This is exactly what we see today. Everyone claims to have truth and many claim to have a secret insight into the knowledge of God. They do so by taking things out of context and making it appear as if the Bible is saying something not intended. People are led astray because they don't know the scriptures and can't recognize the distortion. The only way we know the error is by knowing the truth.

Before technology that detects counterfeit money became available, individuals were trained to find phony money. They learned to detect the forgery by knowing the features of authentic bills. When something falls short of the real thing, it is revealed to be a fake. The same is true with art, antiques, or any other valuable item.

Unless we know the truth, we can't identify the twisted version of it. In fact, as you grow in your own faith and knowledge of the word, you'll discover that many of the things you believe now miss the mark. Scripture gives doctrine, reproof, correction, and instruction. Things I once believed were corrected by scripture when I understood a passage in its proper context. Things I grew up believing and have always assumed to be true turned out to be wrong. It wasn't intentional deception, but it fell short of rightly dividing the word of truth.

I took a five year period of my life and determined to study nothing but the scriptures. No outside influences. No study guides. No books about doctrine. I didn't even use a study Bible. In that period, I read through the Bible more than thirty times. This completely changed my life and gave me a depth to understanding scripture I could have never discovered any other way. I also discovered that many things I once believed were incorrect. The light of scripture upon the rest of scriptures gave me the perspective to see things in context that I previously couldn't see.

Often the errors we believe don't fall to the level of heresy. However, misconceptions cause us to misunderstand the principles that lead us to a deeper understanding of God, and false beliefs prevent us from maturing as we ought. Our salvation may not be at stake from a misconception, but anything that taints our understanding stunts our spiritual growth. When the scriptures correct what is false, we must let misconceptions go and receive the right understanding. This is especially true when our misunderstanding has led to a cherished, but false belief.

Paul said it well when he stated, "When I was a child, I thought as a child, spoke as a child, and understood as a child. When I became a man, I put away childish things.[115]" Most (but not all) of our childish beliefs are based on selfish motives. A child only thinks about what he or she wants. Self-centeredness then becomes the motive for evaluating right and wrong. While in an immature mindset, our thinking is based on what we want. We want, therefore, we believe, then we act. Spiritual maturity changes this.

Maturity teaches us to act based on all factors. I often have to give up what I want because the gratification isn't worth the cost. Or what I want it isn't worth neglecting more important needs. An immature person is willing to step on others to fulfill selfish desires, but the mature learns to consider others before their own desires.

Most doctrinal error is based on feeding the desires of the flesh without considering our relationship with God or each other. As we saw previously, on these two commands hang all the law and the prophets – love God and love our neighbor. Bad doctrine often neglects one or the other – or both. Bad doctrine may also skew our understanding of love so it hides selfish motives.

When someone presents a truth, we must have the ability to discern whether it is consistent with the word. And we can only do this if we know the word. There is another passage that helps clarify this. Look at **2 Peter 1:19-21**

> [19] And so we have the prophetic word confirmed, which you do well to heed as a light that shines in a dark place, until the day dawns and the morning star rises in your hearts;
> [20] knowing this first, that no prophecy of Scripture is of any private interpretation,
> [21] for prophecy never came by the will of man, but holy men of God spoke *as they were* moved by the Holy Spirit.

Prophecy does not mean to foretell the future. Prophecy means to proclaim the truth of God's word. Sometimes God foretells what will happen in certain events, but this is not the only

---

[115] 1 Corinthians 13:11

form of prophecy. Prophecy of scripture is the word of God. It is the word God gave through the Holy Spirit to His prophets and apostles for the purpose of being written down for our learning.

Notice that this passage says that we have the word confirmed. It was confirmed in the same way as was mentioned earlier. The spirit of the prophets was made subject to the prophets. What was being spoken was evaluated against what was known to be true, and proven as the word of God. It was confirmed that it agreed and did not contradict.

Occasionally, I hear Bible critics take issue with the ancient letters that were excluded from the Bible. There are many letters from other early church leaders that are not considered scripture. The letters of Barnabas, who served with Paul come to mind. There are also letters that supposedly came from Paul, but he addresses these as being falsely signed as if from him.[116] There are also the Gnostic Gospels that were presented to the church, claiming to be written by the apostles. These were all rejected because they either could not be confirmed, or they contradicted what was already confirmed. Those who canonized the prophets and letters to the church did so with scriptures that could be confirmed as being Holy Spirit inspired by those the church knew were anointed by God to write scripture.

There were many good teachings to the church in that era that were not considered to be scripture, just as there are good books and teachings today. These draw from scripture, but can never be confirmed as if they were scripture.

What is the purpose of the confirmed word? It is to give understanding in our hearts so the light of truth shines through. We too must confirm what is being spoken today against what we know to be true.

Take note of verse 20 above, "Knowing this first." That phrase speaks volumes. The first thing we must know before proceeding any further is that no prophecy (word of God) is subject to man's private interpretation. What God says through His word is true for all. We may have different levels of understanding, and a passage

---

[116] 2 Thessalonians 2:2

may shed light on another passage to give a greater understanding, but what's true for you has to be true for me. What's true for me has to be true for you. Otherwise my ideas are being treated as scripture, and error will result.

Each time bad doctrine appears, it is always scripture out of context and mixed with ideas of something outside the Bible. Man's philosophy plus scripture equals error. Rather than overlaying our ideas on top of scripture to come up with a doctrine, we must compare our beliefs to scripture and see if they hold up. We draw from the word, not add to the word.

Any time we have to explain away scripture, or add to the scriptures to make doctrine work, we are making ourselves the private interpreter of the word.

Recently, a well-publicized prophecy that the rapture was about to occur became a shameful spectacle when it failed. Both the above elements were present in the failure. They explained away scriptures that clearly contradicted their beliefs, and they added their own ideas to the word, and treated them as scripture.

When confronted with Jesus' clear statement that no man can know the day or the hour, a leader in the group said, "We can't stop there. We must look deeper." Why? If Jesus gave a clear answer to the question, why reject his statement and dig for hidden clues?

They also added a formula created by the group's head. When the rapture failed to appear at the appointed time, a spokesman for the group said, "I can't understand why nothing happened. I did the calculations myself," referring to the formula created by the group's prophet.

There is a problem with that statement. By those very words, he testified that their philosophy was not taught in scripture, but was an outside philosophy added to the scriptures in order to come up with a specific conclusion. The Bible warns that adding to God's word and taking away from the word makes us a liar, and will be reproved by God[117].

There will always be something or someone claiming to have hidden insights into the Bible. But if we must add to, or take away

---

[117] Deuteronomy 4:2, Proverbs 30:6, Revelation 22:18-19

from the word to make it fit, or abandon the clear meaning of scripture, avoid that ideology. The focus of scripture is not to find a hidden meaning, but to equip the saints for ministry and to teach us to become disciples of Christ.

Searching for hidden meanings is nothing more than twisting the scriptures into our own private interpretations. Look at the Bible codes. They promised to reveal the future, but they only produced countless false prophecies. Over the centuries, teachers have risen and claimed divine revelation, but their prophecies failed. In the future, it will happen again. Jesus told us this would be the case. He also showed us how to avoid getting led away with the masses.

The way to interpret scripture is to look for the clear meaning. The Bible is to be our instruction. Searching for hidden mysteries misses the point. The mystery that appears to be hidden is actually in plain sight. The word teaches us how to become like Christ. The truth is only veiled by our limited understanding, but revealed by the Spirit to us when we apply ourselves to the accurate study of the word. The hidden truths are revealed when we understand the basic things necessary to grasp before we can go deeper. In truth, they are not hidden at all. The reason they are not seen is because human understanding is blind to the truth – but our eyes are opened by the Spirit.

A child cannot know algebra until they first understand multiplication and division. They can't understand multiplication and division until they understand adding and subtracting. Children can't comprehend adding and subtracting until they first learn how to count. Each step in the learning process builds on the previous step. Each process in learning is incomprehensible until the previous lessons are understood and fitted into the foundation of their understanding.

It's no different in our quest for spiritual knowledge. Without the Holy Spirit, little can be understood. Before we come to Christ, we understand everything from the human perspective and not the eternal. Then we learn the basics of our faith. With each truth we understand and fit into our lives, we become capable of understanding deeper truths.

It isn't that the deeper things are waiting to be unlocked by some spiritual secret. The deeper things are waiting for you to prepare yourself by first understanding what God is teaching you now. Deeper truths are not hidden, but rather, it's limited by our lack of understanding. As we build knowledge, we are preparing ourselves to new things God has stored up for us to learn. Depth of knowledge is dependent upon willingness to learn and apply the simpler things to our lives in obedience.

I've had people tell me that they want to really get to know God and go deeper. But years roll by and they never mature. They keep searching for that key to understanding, keep praying, keep reading books, and even go to special services that claim to change people's lives. Sometimes they get excited and have a temporary upswing, but when the emotions fade, they find themselves floundering again.

There is no short cut. Just as you can't jump from kindergarten to graduate school, you can't discover the deeper truths until you learn and apply the basic things. The Lord gave us this answer when He spoke in **Isaiah 28:9-10**

> [9] " Whom will he teach knowledge? And whom will he make to understand the message? Those *just* weaned from milk? Those *just* drawn from the breasts?
> [10] For precept *must be* upon precept, precept upon precept, Line upon line, line upon line, Here a little, there a little."

Precept *must* be upon precept. You can't learn the next thing until you learn and understand what comes before it – for they are dependent upon each other. Most Christians never stop nursing on milk because they are unwilling to draw away, and begin seeking the truth through diligent personal study. They remain perpetually dependent upon others feeding them and telling them basic doctrines.

Learning Line Upon Line

Here are the basics for understanding the word. Each person has their own learning style, but certain things are consistent among everyone.

Read the Word.

There is quantity reading and quality reading. We need both. One of the most common excuses is the lack of time. This is exactly what Jesus was warning about when He said many would receive the word among the thorns. The cares of this life and other things crowding in choke the word in our lives so we become unfruitful.

One thing is certain, what you value you will find time to do. It's hard for people to value the word because they can't see the eternal value of it. This is also why we sin. Temptation is right before us, but the promise stands behind the veil of eternity. Only when we are walking by faith can we see the value of the eternal. In the flesh we value what we can see, touch, feel, and experience in our bodies.

Make it your prayer to have a love for the word. Until we see the value, it's hard to persevere. The Bible says, "Where there is no revelation, people cast off restraint.[118]" When God reveals eternity to you, the word will have value and you'll be willing to restrain yourself from allowing activities to crowd out the word.

I struggled with consistency for many years. I would do well for a while, but then let it go by the wayside. I began praying for a desire to know the word and that He would give me a true love for the scriptures. God answered that prayer. If you are like me, you'll struggle to keep the time for the word as a high priority. If you skip a day, it's easy to skip the next. Once the habit is gone, it's hard to motivate ourselves to get back into a good habit.

Discipline yourself to spend regular time in the word. If time is lacking, cut out something that has no real value – such as an hour of TV. Do you remember what your favorite show was about last month? What about last year? Though entertainment may seem like

---

[118] Proverbs 29:18

something of value, what you watch on TV will be quickly forgotten, so what is being really missed when we skip an hour?

If you aren't big on reading, get the Bible on audio. I highly recommend the Alexander Scourby version of the Bible on audio. You can download the entire Bible on MP3 for around thirty dollars. It's the King James Version, but even if you prefer another translation, you'll appreciate Scourby's version. While most audio Bibles just read in monotone, Alexander Scourby makes the scriptures come alive with his passion, inflections, and pace of reading.

When you read, find a time that fits your learning style. If you are a morning person, get up earlier to read in the morning. Night people, turn off the television or find a quiet room. With the audio version, you can listen while driving to work.

One thing I highly recommend is to read the New Testament through three times in a short time frame, such as three months. It's important to do this in a short time frame so you can begin remembering what you read in Matthew while you're reading in Hebrews or Revelation.

Don't neglect the Old Testament. It's rich in truth and necessary to fully understand the New Testament. The writings of the Apostle Paul are focused on the Old Testament. Paul consistently points to the Old Testament Law to help the Jews understand the New Testament teachings of Jesus. There is as much to glean from the time before Christ as there is from the writings after Christ.

Don't be legalistic about reading every word. If you find yourself getting bogged down in the genealogies, look for where it ends and begin reading again. Keep an eye out for tidbits tucked into the genealogies, though. Often a significant event can be found with the name of the person being mentioned.

Find your own reading method and stick to it. If you miss a day, don't feel like you have to read twice as much the next day. Just pick up where you left off and move on. The purpose of discipline is to keep yourself consistent, not to create a new rule.

Journaling.

You will be surprised how much you learn when you journal. It may seem awkward at first, but it won't be long before you find yourself coming alive during your journaling time.

Journaling forces you to have a listening heart. Don't journal during your quantity reading time. Set ten or fifteen minutes aside afterward or at a different time and dedicate it to journaling. You may even want to journal a completely different passage than you are reading during your quantity time.

When journaling, take a passage of scripture, read it, and write down what God is saying to you. Or you can write as though you are explaining it to someone else. Often, other passages will come to mind and you'll discover how God is revealing something to you that you would normally have passed over. Be as detailed or basic as you want. Some days the word will come alive, and other days nothing jumps out to you. That's okay, just be consistent.

Some people like to buy a journal or use a notebook. I use a computer and journal my thoughts into a Word document. Use the resources that fit the way you think and work. One thing is certain, you will discover things about the Bible you didn't know before. When we have a listening heart, God promises to show us great and mighty things we didn't know[119].

What could be more exciting than having God open our eyes to see what we have never been taught, and to see truths that go beyond what we previously understood?

Memorize scripture.

Psalm 119:11

Your word I have hidden in my heart, that I might not sin against You!

Memorizing scripture is a powerful tool for our spiritual development. When you memorize, focus on the context. Some

---

[119] Jeremiah 33:3

short passages are complete thoughts, but most span several verses. You want to understand what is being communicated, so focus on capturing all of what is being said. Find a logical starting place and ending place where a particular thought begins or ends. For example, when I memorized the fruit of the Spirit, I included Galatians 5:22-25. These four verses complete the thought in my opinion, though the other passages around it support the idea being taught. Obviously we would want to study the chapter, but I broke down my memorization to these specific passages.

Afterward I came back and memorized the works of the flesh that was being contrasted with the fruit of the Spirit. That would include Galatians 5:19-21.

When I memorize, I use 3x5 note cards. I place the reference on the back, and the text on the lined side. Since I'm memorizing the thought, I put the entire reference on each notecard – even if I have to use multiple cards. So I put Galatians 5:22-25 on three notecard backs, and spread the text across the three fronts. You might want to have each verse and reference on separate cards. Choose a method that works best for you.

Let me give another word of advice. If you haven't memorized anything in a long time, your mind will have gotten lazy. Don't get discouraged. When you first start, it might seem very difficult to memorize the first card. It won't always be this way. As you exercise your mind, learning will become easier and you'll find yourself absorbing the information much quicker.

When I first started memorizing, it had been decades. I was shocked at how hard it was for me to memorize a simple passage. I felt like nixing the idea. Once the hard shell of my brain broke loose, I started memorizing at an astonishing rate. Before I knew it, I had hundreds of cards memorized.

My method is to spread longer passages over multiple cards. I don't move to the next card until I memorize the first card. Once mastered, I add another card. Then I say the first card along with the second. I always add to what I'm memorizing so that when I remember it, I have a consistent flow from beginning to end.

The next week when I add new passages from other parts of the Bible, I mix in what I've already memorized. That keeps the older ones fresh, plus it's encouraging to have success of reciting old passages while learning the new ones.

After several weeks, I rotate the verses I've mastered to an index card box. I keep the newest passages in my memorization stack, and as one complete passage is fully committed to memory I move it to the box. Each week I add a previously memorized passage to my memorization stack. I rotate previously memorized passages into my current stack by pulling from the front of the box, and adding to the back when I'm ready to return something to the box.

At the beginning of each week, I take my oldest memory cards, place them in the back of the index card box, and take a passage from the front of the box. This way I don't forget what I've already committed to memory. When I return it the next week, I place it in the back and take a new set from the front. This keeps them constantly rotating, so nothing slips from memory.

If you follow these steps, or come up with another process that works for you, and remain consistent, you will develop a solid biblical foundation and have the understanding to discern the truth.

You *can* know the truth. Each time we apply ourselves to studying the word, the Lord honors our obedience and reveals more of His truth to us. Keep in mind that the apostles were untrained and uneducated men. But because of their understanding of the word, others perceived that they had been with Jesus.[120] Each time you dive into the word, you too have been with Jesus, and in time, it will show in your life and in your conversation.

---

[120] Acts 4:13

The Battle of the Mind

The mind is the guardian of the heart. This is why we are commanded to renew our minds daily[121]. We are also instructed to do this by washing and renewing in the Word of God[122]. The Bible speaks much about renewing the mind and not allowing ourselves to be conformed to this world.

The corruption of the world around us is inescapable. It's impossible to live without being exposed to the influences that challenge our walk of faith. Even driving down the highway exposes us through billboards, signs, and even vehicles painted with seductive advertisements. Radio, TV, and everyday life challenges the moral standard of the Christian life. For this reason, we must be active in renewing our spiritual state of mind. Consider the words of Paul in **Romans 7:22-23**

[22] For I delight in the law of God according to the inward man.

[23] But I see another law in my members, warring against the law of my mind, and bringing me into captivity to the law of sin which is in my members.

Don't be surprised when you struggle. Though our soul has been redeemed from sin, we remain in a corrupt body which groans for its day of redemption[123]. Even the apostles, those closest to Christ and who were given the power to lay the foundation of the church, were not exempt from this struggle. They may have had a special calling, but they were no different than you and I. They, too, strove against temptation in their quest for a holy life.

A teacher once claimed that those who reach a certain level of spiritual maturity will no longer be affected by sin. He claimed temptation was like a layer of clouds. Once you rise above it, temptation would now be below you and could no longer affect your life.

---

[121] Romans 12:2
[122] Titus 3:5 and John 15:3
[123] Romans 8:23

How I wish that were true. As is the case with most misconceptions of truth, this teacher was reading a book by someone who claimed to have achieved this level. Anyone who says they are free from sin or temptation is blind and has deceived themselves. If the apostles of Christ, those God used to communicate scriptures to the church, were not immune to temptation and human failure, why would anyone today think they would achieve this level? Those closest to Christ still struggled, so we can expect the same. Peter was rebuked for being caught up by peer pressure and showed great hypocrisy. Paul confessed his own struggles. And these are the two apostles most highly regarded by the church and other apostles.

No one is above temptation and no one can breeze through life without wrestling against the flesh. We all strive to conform to the standard God has empowered us to stand upon. The Apostle Paul expressed the groaning of his soul by acknowledging that his natural tendency was to do what was wrong and neglect what is right. Even more disconcerting is his statement that sin in his flesh wars against his mind, trying to bring him back into the captivity of his old lifestyle. I say disconcerting because it shows how we all can expect this struggle. However, it is also encouraging to know we are not alone in our battle.

The Bible gives a clear solution to this problem. We are commanded to set our minds on the things above – the eternal things of God. Setting our minds on the things above doesn't mean we are gazing into the heavens and waiting for eternity. It means that we focus on godliness and how to live by faith in this present world.

We do this by teaching our minds how to untangle from worldly things and how to remain on the right things. How we think affects who we are, what we believe, and the focus of our life.

Incorruptible Seed.

Let's discuss something that is the cause of confusion among Christians. We just read the Apostle Paul's lamentation of his struggle with sin in his flesh, and how at times it causes him to do what he knows is wrong. In a moment we'll look at the Apostle John's discussion about how the child of God does not sin and cannot sin, because he has been born of God.

Christians look at John's statement and wonder, am I really a child of God? If we cannot sin because we are born of God, then does that mean sin disqualifies my claim of faith?

Absolutely not. The apostles struggled with sin, just as every person who has ever lived. Sin remains in our flesh and wars against our minds, attempting to entangle us back into sin and enslave us in our old passions. It's a life long struggle. The battle will rage until our bodies are redeemed at the coming of Christ.

How then do we reconcile the struggles against the flesh with the promise that we cannot sin? It's the battle of two opposing forces in our lives. Though our old nature of sin was buried with Christ, our bodies of flesh remain susceptible to sin. Even so, we have a new nature, incorruptible and holy. Look at **1 Peter 1:22-23**

22 Since you have purified your souls in obeying the truth through the Spirit in sincere love of the brethren, love one another fervently with a pure heart,

23 having been born again, not of corruptible seed but incorruptible, through the word of God which lives and abides forever,

Take notice of Peter's words in verse twenty-three. We are born again of incorruptible seed. Remember when we discussed the doctrine of being born again? Our old man (old nature) is crucified with Christ. It's crucified, buried, and we are raised as a new creation with eternal life. This new nature is placed within us by God. It is of God and has its life through Christ.

God is incorruptible. What God gives is without corruption or sin. Our inner man is immune from corruption. In the passage above, Peter makes this clear. We don't have a nature that can be corrupted – it's incorruptible. Because our new man (or new nature) is born through the word of God which lives and abides forever, our new man also abides and lives forever. God's word is incorruptible, God is incorruptible, and our nature that is placed within us and sustained through the Holy Spirit is also incorruptible. Now let's bring **1 John 3:9-10** into the picture.

9 Whoever has been born of God does not sin, for His seed remains in him; and he cannot sin, because he has been born of God.

10 In this the children of God and the children of the devil are manifest: Whoever does not practice righteousness is not of God, nor *is* he who does not love his brother.

Righteousness is practiced through the inner man – the incorruptible seed that God has placed within those born into the Spirit. That inner man cannot sin because he has been born of God. Let's apply this understanding to Paul's explanation. After explaining that sin lives in our members (body of flesh), the Apostle Paul also explains how sin in our flesh wars against our minds in an attempt to draw us back into bondage. He then concludes his explanation in **Romans 7:25**

I thank God -- through Jesus Christ our Lord! So then, with the mind I myself serve the law of God, but with the flesh the law of sin.

If we serve our flesh, we are serving the law of sin. Sin is in the body and is acted upon through the flesh. The flesh can corrupt our relationship with God and bring us back into bondage, but it cannot corrupt our inner man. The inner man is the seed of the Holy Spirit, created in Christ Jesus, and what is spiritual cannot be corrupted by the flesh.

The flesh cannot serve God because it is not eternal. Notice how Paul explains his service. Through the body he serves sin, but through the mind he serves God. We serve God as we set our minds on the things of the Spirit and not by works of the flesh. Even our best and most noble efforts of the flesh cannot produce anything but that which is of the flesh – corruption. That's why the Bible says our best righteousness is filthy in God's sight. We sin when we allow our minds to follow our flesh, but we are walking in righteousness when we set our minds on the things of the Spirit. Though we live in a body of flesh, our service is through a mind set upon Christ. We act out based on a mind of the spirit or a mind set upon the flesh.

Unlike Adam who fell from life when he sinned, we are sustained by God through His Holy Spirit. Life is now through God, not through man's ability to live in perfection. The weakness of the law was man, but now the strength of the law of righteousness is Jesus Christ. Thus we are secure in our eternal life from the temptations of sin.

We are indeed held accountable for what is done in our bodies, but it does not corrupt the spirit of our inner man that has life through the Holy Spirit. Our minds can be corrupted, but not the Spirit that is born of God. Paul goes on to explain this in **Romans 8:1**

> *There is* therefore now no condemnation to those who are in Christ Jesus, who do not walk according to the flesh, but according to the Spirit.

Who has no condemnation? Those who are in Christ and walk according to the Spirit. The Bible also explains that if we are led by the Spirit, we are no longer under the law.[124]

If we put it all together, the message is clear. We do indeed struggle with sin, but it no longer has dominion over us because of our freedom in Christ. Sin will continue to war against our minds, attempting to lure us back into the lusts of the flesh so we are again entangled, but we have the power to renew our minds and submit to the leading of the Spirit.

There will be times when we will give in to sin, but because we are born of God, the Spirit continuously draws us toward righteousness and empowers us to rise above the calling of the flesh. Though our body is corrupted by sin, that which is born of God cannot sin. The seed of God, the new man created in Christ, cannot sin because it is of the Holy Spirit.

The challenge is to renew our minds so we are walking according to the Spirit and not living for the flesh.

---

[124] Galatians 5:18

The Battle of the Mind

Next, let's look at a biblical discipline that is rarely taught in the church. Biblical meditation is a spiritual discipline the Bible puts a lot of focus on. But we must understand meditation from a scriptural perspective.

Meditation

For every godly practice, there is an ungodly counterfeit. Just as there is bad doctrine and good doctrine, there is also a biblical form of meditation and an unbiblical meditation. Nearly every religion has a form of meditation, but as Christians, we must take care to not follow the practices of the world. The Bible has a lot to say on meditation; however, many meditation practices that pass themselves off as Christian are not. Many New Age practices are repackaged with Christian terms and then called by various names that sound innocent, but are still based on New Age practices.

I'll point out a few misconceptions along the way, but rather than making the counterfeit practices the focus, we'll look at what the Bible teaches on meditation. When we know the biblically sound way, the unbiblical way will be evident.

Engage your Mind

The Bible never calls us to turn our minds off. Instead of emptying our minds, we are called to fill our minds and think upon the good things God has revealed to us.

The New Age form of meditation is to empty your mind and try to think of nothing. The idea is that a good force will come in and bring enlightenment. The concept is that we must first be empty before our minds can be brought to a higher state. Some try to claim the Bible teaches this practice by quoting phrases out of context. "Be still and know I am God," is often used. But what does it mean to be still? Does quieting our minds mean that we create a vacuum? Does it mean we must stop our minds from thinking?

Certainly not. Even the passage that says "be still," also says, "know that I am God." To know is to think upon something that gives knowledge. We quiet our minds from worldly distractions, but not from thinking.

Jesus told a parable of a sower who planted seeds. The ones that fell on good ground produced good fruit, but many seeds fell on bad soil. Some fell on stony ground and had no depth of faith and fell away when the hearer was offended. Some fell on the wayside, and birds took the seeds away. These are forgetful hearers of the word. Others fell among thorns. This example applies to our discussion.

The seeds among thorns were choked by the weeds and became unfruitful. Jesus explained that the thorns are riches, the cares of this life, and other things coming in. These choke our lives so we cannot grow into spiritual maturity. Other things coming in, and cares that hammer at our thoughts prevent us from seeing the glory God is revealing in us. We must purposefully be still and know He is God.

I encourage you to find a concordance and search for the word 'meditate' in the Bible. I've selected a few passages below. Take note that in each case, meditation is to think upon something God is revealing. We'll use the greatest example of meditation in the Bible – the Psalms written by King David. This man rose from the fields where he kept the sheep to become the greatest king of Israel. God blessed him in every area of his life, promised that his family would keep the throne in Israel, and even was promised that Jesus would come from David's descendants. Why did God bless this man so?

The Bible says that David was a man after God's own heart. What made David's so special in God's eyes? Why did this man have such a desire to pursue God? The love David had for God caused him to strive to know God more. Yet the Bible says that God does not respect one person over another. Therefore, what made David special is not special at all. I say 'not special', but by that I mean that he was not unique. God didn't love David because he was special. David experienced God's love greater because he pursued it.

I have several children. I love each of them with the same love, but not all experience the same amount of love. A child that wants to be held will naturally feel closer than a child that stands aloof. Some of my kids are affectionate, while others are less so.

This also applies to God. The Lord doesn't love the preacher more than the layman. Those who seem strong in faith aren't that way because they are more loved. They pursue the Lord and therefore experience more.

The Bible doesn't say that God was after David's heart. God reaches out to every heart. The thing that set David apart is that he saw God's great love and it caused him to pursue God. He wanted to touch the heart of the Lord who had touched him.

What David had is available to us all. The same principles are for you and I. So the question to answer is, what inspired David to passionately pursue God? One simple word, meditation. The Psalms David wrote were penned from his times of meditation. Let's look at the way he meditated, how it caused him to recognize the value of his relationship with God, and how it taught him to deal with the difficulties of life.

Let's first look at what meditation means. Two passages clue us in on the meaning. Let's start with **Psalm 77:6**

I call to remembrance my song in the night; I meditate within my heart, And my spirit makes diligent search.

Earlier in this Psalm, David begins by saying, "I complained and I was overwhelmed." He is in a difficult time in his life and troubles seem to be swallowing him. Complaining didn't resolve his troubles. It led to feelings of being overwhelmed. He recognized this and turned his focus onto the good things the Lord had done. He meditated on these things and during that time of meditation, he made a diligent search of his memories, and how they reflected the goodness of God.

Rather than emptying his mind, meditation was to diligently seek to remember the goodness of the Lord. As he remembered, he meditated on those things to find encouragement.

This is a strong lesson for us all. Like David, our natural tendency is to look at our problems and complain. Does complaining to ourselves ever resolve problems? No, it adds to our heavy heart and creates feelings of being overwhelmed. Instead of focusing on what we don't like or our troubles, we must force ourselves to focus on the works of the Lord. Remember, this is a process of walking by faith. Once I recognize the hand of the Lord, I can have confidence in Him during my troubles. Troubles shrink in the presence of the Lord; therefore, we must be looking to Him instead of to what bothers us.

Consider the apostle Peter. When Jesus walked to the disciples on the water, Peter called out, "Lord, command me to come to you." Jesus said, "Come," and Peter stepped out onto the water. The disciples had been rowing against the fierce wind for hours and the waves were pounding them. Peter started walking on the water, but then took his eyes off Jesus and focused on the boisterous wind and became afraid. The wind became bigger than his faith in Jesus' call to come, and he began to sink.

It wasn't the wind that defeated Peter. It was that he took his eyes off the Lord and focused on the trouble around him. The wind had been hammering him for hours, but for a moment they were small and insignificant. While he trusted in the Lord and focused on Christ, they had no power over his life. But once he put his faith in what troubled him, trouble became more powerful than his view of God.

Jesus' answer said it all. "O you of little faith. Why did you doubt?"

Every day you are meditating on something. The question is, are you meditating on your problems and the things that bother you, or are you taking time out to meditate on the things God has called you to meditate upon. Let's look at another example from **Psalm 119:27**

Make me understand the way of Your precepts; So shall I meditate on Your wondrous works.

Once again, meditation is not stilling the mind, but stilling ourselves so we can put our focus on something eternal. Meditation is to focus on understanding God's precepts so we can think upon the wonderful works of God.

Most people never see the wonders of God's plan unfolding in their lives. The reason we miss God's plan is because we are focusing on the way we want things to be instead of the works God is doing in us and through us. God takes things away that hinder us so he can give us eternal things that benefit us. But like a child who screams when something harmful is taken, we only focus on what we lost, instead of on the love God has for us.

Consider the grapevine. The Bible often uses this to illustrate God's work in our lives. A grape vine only produces healthy clusters on new growth. An unattended vine will produce a few grapes, but for the most part, it is unfruitful. The vine is spending all its energy maintaining old growth and has little left for fruit.

A vineyard tender will prune the vine back at the end of each year. In the spring, new vines emerge, filled with life and energy. Clusters of grapes appear everywhere and much fruit is produced.

Our lives are much like an old vine, we spend most of our energy keeping up with busyness and things that produce nothing of eternal significance. This is why the Lord says that even those who produce fruit, God will prune that they may produce more fruit.[125] Yet the average Christian is blind to what God is doing. We spend so much time mourning over what was lost during pruning that we cannot apply ourselves to new growth.

This is why meditation is vital. You must set time aside to turn off the outside things crowding your thoughts. Don't think about duties, TV, or other activities. Turn off your inner complainer. Turn off the things that bother you. For a moment, force your troubles out of your focus. Meditate. Think upon the Lord. Quiet your thoughts that are warring to take over your mind. Pluck them out like weeds. When they spring back up, pluck them out again. Find something godly to focus on and search the word and your heart to discover what God is revealing.

It is difficult to accomplish this. We have spent our whole lives surrendering our minds to every whim, thought, and distraction. It's easy to float downstream. Just let go and allow your thoughts to carry you where they will. Unfortunately, our natural man often doesn't carry us to good places. It's part of living in a fallen world.

The law of entropy says that everything in the universe tends toward disorder. Unless something intervenes, breakdown and

---

[125] John 15

decay is the natural result. The Bible teaches how to intervene. Let's take a little time and look at how the Bible instructs us to use the practice of meditation to overcome the flesh that wars against our minds.

Godly Meditation helps resolve anger.

Anger is a part of life. Everyone gets angry. Anger is not a sin, it's an emotion. It is how we deal with it that determines whether it is healthy or not. Consider the meditation of **Psalm 4:3-4**

[3] But know that the LORD has set apart for Himself him who is godly; The LORD will hear when I call to Him.
[4] Be angry, and do not sin. Meditate within your heart on your bed, and be still. Selah

The instruction of scripture is to put anger in its proper place. This begins by putting ourselves in the proper spiritual position. Those who are godly are set apart for God. This means that if we act according to scripture's call, we are in a position to see the goodness of the Lord. We first see His favor in our lives, then we see His hand in our circumstances. A godly perspective is how we must begin when dealing with anger. We don't brood, but rather meditate. There is a difference.

When I'm angry, I must meditate and be still. The same is true for you. First still yourself and push the emotional reactions aside. Meditate upon the things you know about God and godliness, and then put your anger into perspective. Stop and look at what created the anger. Is it anger over not getting our way? Is it petty things that aren't worthy of the emotional energy we put into it? Stress is often the accumulation of little annoyances, but when we take the time to think upon the object of our anger, and put it into a godly perspective, anger and frustration can be diffused.

Not every battle is worth fighting. Not every situation has a resolution. People are blind to the faults they have that frustrate us. And we are blind to our faults as well. Sometimes we have to look at the frustration in light of the entirety of life and the eternal perspective of our Christian walk.

Jesus warned, "Hold fast to what you have that no one takes your crown."[126]

What we have is the gift of God. Not only do we have redemption, but we have God's path He created for us to walk in. The Lord said that He fashioned our days for us before we were born[127]. The same passage also says God has precious thoughts toward us that are greater in number than the sand of the seas. This means that God has already laid out a way for you to experience life to its fullest. This includes our eternal life.

Sadly, we let go of the crown of God's reward so we can cling to anger against people. This is one way we let people take our crown. Some are led away from God through worldly philosophies, but even a theologically sound person can lose perspective and invest their lives in meaningless things at the cost of eternal things. Selfish anger is one of those meaningless things.

Anger isn't always bad. Sometimes anger causes us to act in a good way. When Peter denied Jesus three times, he was defeated and guilt ridden. Afterward, Jesus came to him. "Peter, do you love me more than you love these?" When Peter said yes, Jesus gave him the command to feed his sheep, referring to teaching others how to become disciples of Christ.

Jesus asked Peter again if he loved Him. Again Peter said he did. Then Jesus asked a third time. Peter was grieved that Jesus kept asking the same question, but there was a point. Peter was defeated. His focus was only on himself and he didn't feel worthy to be the apostle Jesus had called him to be. By the third time Jesus asked the question, anger began to light a fire in Peter's heart. He was being forced to take his eyes off his defeat and put them on his calling. God used anger to stir Peter back to life.

Selfish anger never produces righteousness. We try to make our anger appear righteous, but the truth is, if I'm focused on myself, it's selfish anger. When people become angry at how they've been treated, their emotions become destructive. But let someone

---

[126] Revelation 3:11
[127] Psalm 139:16

get angry at the neglect of the poor and what happens? They set out to change the part of the world within their power.

A man recently passed away named David Wilkerson. He was a struggling pastor until an event angered him into action. In his book, The Cross and the Switchblade, David describes the event that changed his life. A gang of youth were being tried for murder. When he saw the picture in the paper, he saw children. Kids not yet in high school were committing murder. These forgotten children were being left without guidance on the cruel city streets of New York. It angered him and he set out to touch their lives. Though he never had the opportunity to meet the kids he went to see, God used that anger as a turning point and a call to action to reach the youth of New York's streets.

When we feel anger, it's a call to search our hearts while looking toward godliness. Is it my wrong that makes me angry and creates selfish indignation? Or is it a call toward a need. Maybe that need begins with dealing with my own selfishness.

Most people get angry and react, but never meditate. We go day to day reacting to what bothers us while anger builds up pressure and erodes away godliness. Jesus became angry on several occasions. But not once did He show anger for wrongs done to Him. He saw the poor being fleeced in the temple and he became angry and put a stop to the business of buying and selling. What happened when people called Him demon possessed, a drunkard, a sinner, and a deceiver? He explained the truth but never defended Himself out of pride.

Be still and think upon your walk of faith. How does anger reveal what needs to be changed in the world around you? How does selfish anger reveal what needs to be changed in your life? How can you turn a brooding heart into a meditating heart?

Meditation teaches us how to trust the Lord.

When we cease to meditate, our focus shifts from trusting in God's leading hand and toward reacting to circumstances. Circumstances should not be the driving force in our lives.

Sometimes difficult situations arise that push us into a different direction, but there is always a reason behind it.

Proverbs 16:7 tells us, "When a man's ways please the Lord, He makes even his enemies to be at peace with him."

God uses enemies to force us toward a better way, and prevent us from going the wrong way. The same goes for difficult situations. Problems are enemies to our peace, but sometimes God sacrifices our peace to bring about our good. That's why the Bible says not to think it strange when we find ourselves in the midst of a fiery trial as though something strange has happened to us[128]. We are told not to lament our trials, but to rejoice in what God is doing.

Easier said than done. That's why I must meditate and seek understanding and not just look for a way out of the situation that bothers me.

The truth is that I can't see the future. Nor can you. I make decisions based on what I think is best with the information at hand. Sometimes the things that look like a good decision turn out bad in the end. Was it foolishness? If I knowingly made a foolish decision, yes. But sometimes the direction I want to go looks like a wise decision when it is not. I can see the beginning of a course of action, and I can anticipate where I'm going based on life experiences. But when unforeseen circumstances await, I'm blindsided by problems I couldn't have anticipated.

Our spiritual walk is much like that. However, the Bible tells us that God planned our life from the beginning of the world, so He knows the end result of every path. Even if I'm walking with godly motives, I still can make a choice that does not lead where God wants to take me. The true benefit is often on a path I would never have taken. In this situation, my ways do not please the Lord. He has eternity in mind and will guide me to the right way. And sometimes God will force me to the right way. Often God raises up enemies to force us into a way that may not look right but is the way of blessing.

Joseph is a good example of this. In the book of Genesis, God reveals a dream to Joseph that one day the sun, moon, and stars will

---

[128] 1 Peter 4:12

bow down to him. He didn't know it at the time, but the sun and moon referred to the religions of Egypt and his family would look to him for protection.

The young man, Joseph, had it good. His father loved him and gave him a special coat. Work was easy. Checking up on his brothers was Joseph's only real responsibility. There was no rebellion in his life, nor any evidence of a sinful lifestyle that would displease God. But Joseph wasn't mature, nor was he the type of person to be a great leader. A life of blessing was all he had. Though his life would prove that God was his focus, his life wasn't heading in the direction of God's best for him.

God raised up enemies within his own house. His brothers grew to hate him and conspired to kill him. God's plan will not be thwarted, so the murder plot dissipated when a band of traders passed by. They sold Joseph into slavery, and he ended up in Egypt as a house slave in a governor's home.

The governor's wife tried to seduce him, and when he refused her advances, she accused him of attempted rape. For three years Joseph was in a prison, forgotten by the world. In prison Joseph gained a reputation for accurately interpreting the dreams God gave the servants of Pharaoh's court. One of the prisoners was released and served Pharaoh again, and for a time, forgot all about Joseph.

After many years, God used Pharaoh's nightmares to remind the ex-prisoner of Joseph and he was called before the king. Through Joseph's interpretation of the dream, he was promoted to the second highest authority in Egypt and he was able to prepare for a coming famine. When Joseph's family came to seek food, God completed his plan in Joseph's life and he was not only honored by his family (including the brothers who once hated him), but God used him to deliver both Egypt and Israel.

Joseph's words to his brothers summarize it best, "You meant it for evil, but God meant it for good."

This is how we must think upon our hardships. Whether it is an enemy rising up, or a hardship turning our life upside down, God is behind it. On the surface it may appear evil, but if you belong to Christ, God is working good. That's why the Bible says that all things work together for the good of those who love God and are called according to His purpose[129]. If you are walking in His purpose, no circumstance will fall short of God's goodness. Those who remain faithful will see the end of God's mercy and will soon thank God for His perfect will.

This also is how David encouraged himself in difficult times. Look at his meditation in **Psalm 63:6-7**

[6] When I remember You on my bed, I meditate on You in the *night* watches.

[7] Because You have been my help, Therefore in the shadow of Your wings I will rejoice.

We first remember, then we consider what God is doing, then we rejoice. If biblical meditation is part of our life, we will already be aware of God's goodness. We remember our salvation and how God intervened in our lives. We remember the hand of God we have seen in the past when He revealed his goodness in other situations.

Since we know He is our help, and we know we are covered by the shadow of His wings, we can rejoice in the midst of any situation. Though pain may not create joy, the knowledge of God's goodness does. We rejoice knowing He is truly looking for our good. And this life isn't the only good. This present life is a speck in eternity. To miss out on something here to gain something better for eternity is not a sacrifice.

Meditation teaches thankfulness

Thanksgiving is vital for the spiritual health of believers. An unthankful heart is a faithless heart, but a thankful heart is living and able to see what others cannot. First look at the command of **1 Thessalonians 5:18**

In everything give thanks; for this is the will of God in Christ Jesus for you.

---

[129] Romans 8:48

What is meant by 'everything'? It's easy to be thankful for the good, but what about the things that cause discomfort or pain? The truth is, if you are walking in God's plan, everything is good. Mankind measures good by our comfort and feelings, but God measures good based on eternal value and significance.

It's easy to be thankful when I get a new car. Or house. Or job. Is it easy to be thankful when a storm comes through and destroys my car and house? Or layoffs take my job? It's not easy. In fact, it's impossible to be thankful unless we can see beyond the circumstances and into God's loving kindness.

An unthankful heart destroys faith, joy, and the ability to walk in God's promises. Look at **Romans 1:21**

Although they knew God, they did not glorify *Him* as God, nor were thankful, but became futile in their thoughts, and their foolish hearts were darkened.

This passage is speaking of those who have rejected salvation, but the sad truth is that it also applies to you and I. We know God, but do we glorify Him as God? Do we rest in the truth that He guides our lives and has the right to give, take, and lead as He sees fit? We, who are called by His name, can become unthankful and futile in our thoughts. Then our heart becomes darkened and foolish.

Just think about the results of thanklessness. When someone becomes angry at God, what happens in their lives? They rebel, adopt destructive behaviors, become bitter, and crumble as a person. Have you ever seen a bitter person bubbling with life? No, they slowly implode and become lifeless and more bitter.

It's interesting that being unthankful is at the center of those experiencing darkness in their lives. When we're thankful, everything about our outlook is bright and vibrant. When we're unthankful, all of our thoughts are futile, vain, and worthless. An unthankful person thinks negatively about everything. They can't see the good because they are focused on the bad. An unthankful person can't enjoy the scores of good things surrounding them because they can only see what doesn't fit their expectations.

When our thoughts become futile, relationships suffer, our heart suffers, and everything in life suffers. It becomes a heavy burden that we carry needlessly. The more weight we carry, the more frustrated we become, and the more weight we add to our load.

Unload the burden. It isn't yours to carry. Every defeated Christian lives in a self-imposed prison. Bitterness is the material that we use to construct our own prison. Then everything in life falls short of God's glory. This is why the Bible warns that one root of bitterness springing up can defile many[130]. A Christian cannot thrive without thankfulness. Every unthankful Christian will fall short and miss out on God's plan. Fortunately, the Bible tells us how to maintain a thankful heart. Meditation. Look at **Psalm 77:11-12**

> [11] I will remember the works of the LORD; Surely I will remember Your wonders of old.
> [12] I will also meditate on all Your work, And talk of Your deeds.

I love the way the Psalmist explains meditating on God's works. He first speaks about thinking upon the wonders of old. What have we seen about God's goodness and ability to fulfill His good will through the examples we have in scripture? Or examples in the history we've read from those who trusted Him? Asaph, who wrote this psalm, progresses up to his own life. Then he meditates on all of God's works. His heart overflows with gratitude so that instead of complaints, he feels the need to talk about the wonders of God's works.

Meditation teaches us how to live in the word.

Psalm 119 is one of the richest collections of advice of any chapter in the Bible. In it we get a glimpse of the value of meditating upon the scriptures. I've quoted a number of verses to capture the

---

[130] Hebrews 12:15

context. Take note of how many times David places his focus on the word. **Psalm 119:9-17, 148**

[9] How can a young man cleanse his way? By taking heed according to Your word.

[10] With my whole heart I have sought You; Oh, let me not wander from Your commandments!

[11] Your word I have hidden in my heart, That I might not sin against You!

[12] Blessed *are* You, O LORD! Teach me Your statutes!

[13] With my lips I have declared All the judgments of Your mouth.

[14] I have rejoiced in the way of Your testimonies, As *much as* in all riches.

[15] I will meditate on Your precepts, And contemplate Your ways.

[16] I will delight myself in Your statutes; I will not forget Your word.

[17] Deal bountifully with Your servant, *That* I may live and keep Your word.

...

[148] My eyes are awake through the *night* watches, That I may meditate on Your word.

Whether he says your word, precepts, statutes, or commands, he keeps the focus upon the word of God. This is an important practice of meditation. When we meditate on the word, it is not focusing on syllables, sounds, or letters. It is to focus upon knowing God's commandments to understand and live by them.

There are some who teach and practice that we meditate on a single word or sound, but this is merely a form of Eastern meditation and is contrary to the Bible's teaching. The focus of meditation is to cleanse our lives through the word by taking heed to its commandments, statutes, and principles, so we do not stray from the truth. We meditate to be taught. We meditate to discover understanding. We meditate so we know how to live and abide in God's will.

Jesus often referred to the Psalms and perhaps He intended this chapter to be taken into consideration when He said, "You are already clean because the word I have spoken to you." The focus of the word is always to find understanding of God's ways so we can walk in close fellowship with Him. This isn't only taught in the Old Testament, but the same practice is taught in the New Testament as well. Look at **1 Timothy 4:15-16**

[15] Meditate on these things; give yourself entirely to them, that your progress may be evident to all.

[16] Take heed to yourself and to the doctrine. Continue in them, for in doing this you will save both yourself and those who hear you.

Once again, the word is the focus. Good doctrine is explored as we meditate on the truth of scripture. Whenever we see the word 'doctrine', it simply means 'the teachings of scripture'. Don't think of this as a theologically complicated practice. We take a passage of scripture, think upon it, and give ourselves wholly to obeying the word and teaching others to do the same.

Memorization plays a role in meditating upon scripture, but memorizing alone is not meditation. We think upon the meaning of the scriptures, how it applies to our lives, how it testifies to the majesty of the Lord, and how it directs us into God's perfect plan.

Any meditation practice that doesn't fit what is taught in scripture misses the mark and can lead us down the wrong path. However, biblical meditation is a valuable practice in the Christian's life.

Meditation is often neglected. For this reason, our minds get crowded with the weeds and thorns of life, and our godly perspective becomes choked out and unfruitful. Yet those who meditate on the things of God find understanding. God delights in revealing His goodness to His disciples.

Finding God's peace and guarding our heart.

Everyone deals with anxiety and few know how to handle it in a healthy way. When a difficulty arises, people often say something like, "Don't let yourself worry."

Unfortunately, we can't just decide not to think about something, our mind needs to be focused. Do this experiment. Think about nothing. Most people think about blackness, but blackness is something. Empty space is something. Anything that represents nothing to us is something. This is what we are expecting when we say, "Don't worry." Thinking about not worrying keeps the focus on what we are trying to avoid.

It doesn't work does it? I have yet to see someone stop worrying when told to do so. Often times, when sermons are preached or advice is given on worry, it only creates more worry. At first we worried about a problem, now we worry that we don't have enough faith to stop worrying. When someone says that worry is a lack of faith, we become concerned about our spiritual condition on top of the problem we were already struggling with.

The Bible gives the answer. It is not to just stop and create a vacuum in our minds, but to have a shift of focus. Look at **Philippians 4:6-8**

[6] Be anxious for nothing, but in everything by prayer and supplication, with thanksgiving, let your requests be made known to God;

[7] and the peace of God, which surpasses all understanding, will guard your hearts and minds through Christ Jesus.

[8] Finally, brethren, whatever things are true, whatever things *are* noble, whatever things *are* just, whatever things *are* pure, whatever things *are* lovely, whatever things *are* of good report, if *there is* any virtue and if *there is* anything praiseworthy -- meditate on these things.

This passage doesn't merely say not to be anxious, but to overcome our anxiety by following practical steps. Steps that we know how to do if living biblically is already part of our lives.

The Battle of the Mind

The passage above gives us clear direction. Best of all, the results are not dependent upon us. It doesn't say that we should guard our hearts and minds against worry / anxiety. It says that if we do these things, God will give us peace beyond human understanding as He guards our hearts and minds through Christ. How can we have peace in the storms of life? It's impossible by human standards, but God has the power to give us a peace that goes beyond our human understanding.

Let's look at the steps. First, we focus on prayer. Not just a prayer of, "God get me out of this," but a prayer established upon thanksgiving. Remember David's testimony in Psalms? When he complained, grief overwhelmed him, but when he meditated on the works of the Lord and the goodness of God's hand in his life, he found comfort. His problems were still present, but how he faced them changed.

The Bible promises that the believer has the privilege of coming confidently before the throne of God in our time of need[131]. Prayer is how we come before the throne of God. Prayer is talking to God. You don't need to sound holy and spiritual, just pour your heart out before Him. That is what supplication means – to entreat the Lord, ask, or present a need before Him. But notice that we are entreating the Lord for our needs with thanksgiving. This is a very important part of praying for our needs or the needs of others.

A faithless prayer is, "Why are you letting this happen? Get me out of this mess." There is no thankfulness. There is no focus on the end result or the eternal perspective.

A thankful heart reveals our true focus. A thankful heart stops and thinks upon the goodness of the Lord, and considers the truth that God seeks our eternal good through every situation. God will sacrifice your good in this life to keep you in the goodness of the eternal life to come. The thankless can't see this clearly. But if we are living a surrendered and thankful life, we will have removed our greatest barrier to God's goodness over us.

A stubborn person has to endure much more pain than a submissive one. There are people who go through life with both fists

---

[131] Hebrews 4:16

balled. They are usually those who think life is unfair. It's unfair because life doesn't stay within the boundaries of what they believe is right and wrong.

The truth is that God sees the plan of eternity and how you fit into that plan. Sometimes life doesn't make sense, but one thing is certain, the one who clings to faith always finds the goodness of God's plan. The ones who buck against the Lord often miss it. Or can't see it before them.

When I present my petition to God with thanksgiving, I am acknowledging His wisdom and my trust that His word is true – He really is out for my good. Sorrow is not a lack of faith. Acknowledging pain and frustration isn't a lack of faith. Demanding that God change His plan is a lack of faith. Demanding that God conform to our will is also a lack of faith.

Freely acknowledge your struggles, hurts, worries, and feelings. And do so with thanksgiving. This will help you trust what God is doing rather than trying to escape it. Be thankful for what He has done and is doing. Meditate on His wondrous works. Search your heart to find reasons to be thankful. It will change your attitude. Over time, it will transform your heart into one that seeks the Lord. And it places you squarely in the promise that when you do so, He will guard your heart and mind, and give you His incomprehensible peace.

God's word remains untried in the life of most Christians. It sounds good in theory, but because it goes against human nature, we abandon it when we need it the most.

It's no accident that the passage above concludes with an instruction on meditation. We can't meditate with a tumultuous mind; therefore, we pour out our hearts, set our minds on thanksgiving, and afterward, we follow God's plan of bringing the focus of our minds to where it should be.

Most of us brood. We may force out a meager praise and make a prayer, but afterward we pick up the burden again through our brooding. The troubles we supposedly gave to the Lord remain the focus of our thoughts and we again dwell upon our problems. Anxiety remains and we fall into self-pity. Or we pick up our anger and frustrations and brood upon these and cultivate bitterness, frustration, and hatred.

The method God has given us is to end our prayers with meditation. Think upon these things – whatever is true, lovely, pure, honest, just, things of good report, praiseworthy, or virtuous, etc.

This goes completely against human nature. A bad report hits our tongues and is spread at lightning speed. We like to talk about bad things, and we naturally dwell on negative thoughts. There must be an intentional effort to set our minds on the things that are godly so we remain in the peace of God and cultivate a thankful heart. It's the only way to fully experience the peace of God and grow into spiritual maturity. To neglect these things stunts our growth and keeps us in the circle of frustration.

True biblical meditation is difficult to put into practice. It's not difficult to understand, but it goes against human nature. Knowing what God has taught means nothing until we learn to put these things into practice. Each moment you spend in thought, you are either training your mind toward negative habits, or positive. Negativism is a strain on the mind, while meditating on the godly things strengthens the mind and heals emotions.

Consider the plain truth before us. What causes someone to have a nervous breakdown? There are exceptions, but the vast majority of the time it is prolonged stress. Each stressful thought adds to the burden and the pressure builds. When the mind reaches the breaking point, a total collapse occurs, and the person is incapable of dealing with anything.

While we cannot control many of the situations that cause stress, we can learn to deal with it in a healthy way, and we can unload our mental burdens through the principles we have discussed here. We have the power to overcome these thoughts. Look at **2 Corinthians 10:4-5**

[4] For the weapons of our warfare *are* not carnal but mighty in God for pulling down strongholds,

[5] casting down arguments and every high thing that exalts itself against the knowledge of God, bringing every thought into captivity to the obedience of Christ,

We naturally want to confront the flesh through the flesh; however, God presents a different way. Our spiritual minds are mighty in God and He empowers us. Or should I say that He has already empowered us. It's called walking in the Spirit. We'll discuss walking in the Spirit in the next chapter, but for now be aware that our goal is not to muscle our minds into submission, but to turn from the flesh and walk in the Spirit where victory has already been given.

You and I have the power to take every thought captive and into obedience to godliness. When we catch ourselves dwelling on unhealthy thoughts or brooding, we must put God's ways into action. The offending thought should be arrested and taken out of the way.

When angry, your first inclination will be to brood and give stress free reign over your mind. You will not have the desire to take that thought captive because our flesh enjoys its indulgences. You and I have to willfully submit ourselves under God's direction and give ourselves wholly to the word of God. And I assure you that you won't feel like it until after you've stepped into faith. Then you'll discover the world of victory and wonder why it was so difficult. Yet the next time you'll have the same battle.

As we develop spiritual disciplines, it gets easier, but not necessarily easy. Each time we must willfully choose to surrender to God's ways before we overcome. The good news is that as you do these things God has commanded, you'll be training your mind to dwell on godly things and it will change your attitude, outlook on life, and drive you toward spiritual maturity.

The Bible says that we must constantly put ourselves and others in remembrance of these things. You will forget. This goes for every spiritually good thing. We naturally tend to drift toward old patterns and the easy way of thinking. Any dead fish can float down stream. In the same way, it takes no life and no effort to allow ourselves to drift toward our old ways of thinking. We must swim against the current and remind others of these principles so they can be refreshed in the Lord, too.

When we read the Old Testament account where the Jewish people murmured against God, it's easy to wonder how they could be so blind. Yet we face the same scenario each day. The Lord has given me the answers to living a focused life. These principles teach me how to have a good attitude, see the loving hand of God, and be encouraged in any circumstance. If I refuse to apply these things in my own life, I'm no different than those who refused to see the miracles and the strong hand of the Lord, and instead said, "Has God brought us into the wilderness to die?"

The same God who led a faithless group of people out of bondage and to the edge of the promise, also leads you and I. They couldn't inherit the promise because they couldn't see past their problems to see the blessing. Can we? We can if we apply our hearts to the wisdom of God's teaching.

Wisdom is the Spirit of God instructing us through His word. In scripture, wisdom cries out, "Turn at my rebuke; Surely I will pour out my spirit on you; I will make my words known to you.[132]" Not only does the word rebuke my bad attitude, it shows me how to change it. The same voice of wisdom also warns that if I refuse the instruction of God's wisdom, I will eat the fruit of my own ways and suffer the calamity of my actions. Then if I call for deliverance, I will not be rescued from the consequences of refusing God's instruction of wisdom[133].

We have the answer before us. As Jesus said, these words are spirit and they are life. It isn't easy to turn from our own ways, but we must do so in order to find the joy of God's peace, life, and deliverance from the ways of the flesh.

Do you want to be a man or woman after God's own heart? Meditate on these things. Cultivate a thankful heart. Think upon the word, God's works, and then trust Him enough to let go of anything that prevents you from submitting wholly to the Lord. It will change your life.

---

[132] Proverbs 1:23
[133] Proverbs 1:24-33

Walking in the Spirit

One passage in scripture lays the groundwork for the benefits of walking in the Spirit. Look at **Galatians 5:16**
> I say then: Walk in the Spirit, and you shall not fulfill the lust of the flesh.

The average Christian takes an approach to faith that is counter to God's ways. We attempt to overcome our weaknesses by strengthening our flesh. Many times I've said to myself, "If I can just try harder," or "resist more," or "put forth more effort, then I can overcome and be more spiritual."

There are disciplines in the Christian life as we saw earlier, but harder work and more effort is not what makes us better Christians. It also is not how we overcome sin in our lives. When the Galatian church attempted to make themselves more spiritual by human efforts, they were rebuked. In their case, they thought they had to keep a certain portion of the law in order to complete their salvation.

Paul's answer to them equally applies to us. "Are you so foolish? Having begun in the Spirit, are you now being made perfect by the flesh?"[134]

The same question echoes through time to our day. Are we foolish enough to think that we can perfect ourselves through the efforts of the flesh? Whether that perfection be an attempt to make ourselves more righteous, or an attempt to overcome our weaknesses, the same principle applies. The Bible says that the weakness of the law is the flesh. Our human nature is the weak link. It's foolish to use the weakness of the flesh to attempt to strengthen the spirit.

Before Jesus was arrested, He withdrew with three of His disciples to pray. When the disciples didn't realize the seriousness of what they would soon face, Jesus said, "Watch and pray, lest you enter into temptation. The spirit indeed is willing but the flesh is

---

[134] Galatians 3:3

weak." Human effort is weak and incapable of accomplishing spiritual victory. Resisting in the flesh doesn't overcome our flesh. Let me give an illustration.

When I was young and athletic, I'd hit the weight room with my friends to get in better shape. One of our more painful exercises was also the most effective. To build endurance, we'd lie on a bench and put a small amount of weight on a barbell, then hold it halfway up. When beginning the exercise, holding the weight was easy, but it wasn't long before fatigue set in.

Regardless of our strength, not one of us could hold that weight in this position for more than a few minutes. Eventually, the weight that seemed easy to lift became so heavy our arms were unable to hold it up. Regardless of our willingness and determination, once the flesh hit its limit, it was powerless to overcome even the lightest of tasks.

This is what the flesh does when we attempt to overcome in the flesh. Why do great men fall to temptation? Why do people we know that are Christians sometimes do things that shock us? I've known godly men who fell into terrible sin. When a high profile Christian falls, we hear about it on the news, but the truth is that we are all vulnerable. Unless we understand the war between the flesh and the Spirit, we are ill-equipped in the battle. We equip ourselves by understanding the challenge of the flesh and what it means to walk in the Spirit.

Each believer must learn how to walk in the victory as the Bible promises, and we do this through the Spirit, and not through human effort. Otherwise we're in a losing battle. Since the flesh is the weakness that prevents us from fulfilling the law, it stands to reason that when we stand in the flesh, we are weak in all spiritual matters. The law is spiritual. So is the new life God has given us. What we could not do through the law, Christ accomplished for us, and then gave us the spiritual life that was once hidden behind the law. This passage explains it well. Look at **Romans 8:3-9**

[3] For what the law could not do in that it was weak through the flesh, God *did* by sending His own Son in the likeness of sinful flesh, on account of sin: He condemned sin in the

flesh,

[4] that the righteous requirement of the law might be fulfilled in us who do not walk according to the flesh but according to the Spirit.

[5] For those who live according to the flesh set their minds on the things of the flesh, but those *who live* according to the Spirit, the things of the Spirit.

[6] For to be carnally minded *is* death, but to be spiritually minded *is* life and peace.

[7] Because the carnal mind *is* enmity against God; for it is not subject to the law of God, nor indeed can be.

[8] So then, those who are in the flesh cannot please God.

[9] But you are not in the flesh but in the Spirit, if indeed the Spirit of God dwells in you. Now if anyone does not have the Spirit of Christ, he is not His.

The flesh cannot be subject to the law of God. Our flesh is at war with God and cannot accomplish anything but to produce death. Christ has given us life, but we can still submit ourselves under the curse of the flesh by being carnally minded. The word 'carnal' means, sensual nature, animal cravings, or of the flesh.

Take special note of the warning, those who set their minds on the flesh live in the flesh. And vice versa. Life is to those who set their minds on the things of the Spirit. Through your flesh – human efforts – you cannot please God. Jesus expressed this same thought when He warned the religious people of His day, "The flesh profits you nothing. The words I speak to you are spirit and they are life."[135]

A Christian is defeated in the flesh. This is true whether they are pursuing sinful desires, or attempting to live out their faith by human effort. We come to Christ by faith and are born into the Spirit. And that is exactly how we live out our faith. We begin in the Spirit and therefore, must walk in the Spirit. We don't begin by faith and then walk by human effort.

We are told to flee temptation. Whether that temptation is sensuality, or the desire to become our own source of

---

[135] John 6:63

righteousness, we are called to flee, or remove ourselves from the things that draw us into the flesh. To stand and resist is like holding a weight out with our arms. Eventually we all get tired and if we remain under the burden, it will overcome us.

Proverbs tells us that a proud spirit comes before a fall. Pride is why people attempt to make themselves righteous by human effort. We want to accomplish something, look back, and say, "Look what I did for the Lord." But the Bible says that God resists the proud and gives grace to the humble. God also makes it clear that no flesh will glory in His presence.

Anything that brings glory to the flesh is rejected by God. The Apostle Peter found this out the hard way. Throughout his time with Jesus, Peter showed himself to be strong by his own personality. He was always the first to speak out and he was the first to get into trouble.

The night Jesus was arrested, Jesus foretold of the events and said, "You will all be offended because of me this night, and you'll leave me alone."

Peter said that even if everyone forsook Jesus, he would never forsake Him. He claimed that he would willingly go to prison or even to death. After Jesus said, "Before the rooster crows twice, you will deny Me three times," Peter continued to insist that he would never fall.

He did fall. And hard.

In that culture, women had little influence. Even their testimonies held little weight. After fleeing with the rest of the disciples, Peter followed the arresting party from a distance and slipped unnoticed into the palace area where Jesus was being tried. A servant girl, probably the lowest class of citizen in that culture, began the accusation. She pointed to Peter and said, "Aren't you one of His disciples?" Peter denied even knowing who Jesus was. He cowered under the accusation of a girl whose testimony wouldn't have even been allowed in that ancient culture.

As the girl incited others, Peter's problems mounted. He denied even to the point to where he called down curses upon himself to prove he didn't know Jesus.

Standing upon his own strength, Peter was powerless to overcome temptation. It rolled over him like an avalanche. After the resurrection, Jesus came to get Peter and restore him. His life was never the same. No longer did Peter depend on his own strength. He discovered what God also revealed to the Apostle Paul: God's strength is made perfect in our weakness[136].

In other words, when we stand in the flesh, the flesh is all we have. It's weakness is our weakness. However, when we recognize our inability to stand strong in the flesh, we learn to be strong in the Lord and then we have the power of His might[137].

Peter, who cowered before a servant girl and denied Christ, later stood before those who condemned Jesus and boldly proclaimed their guilt, and then explained God's forgiveness offered to them.

This is what walking in the Spirit is all about. It is removing our dependence on the flesh so the Spirit of God can reign unhindered in our lives. Standing firm in the flesh is an eventual defeat, but walking in the Spirit is certain victory. If you walk in the Spirit, you will not fulfill the lusts of the flesh.

The flesh verses the Spirit.

You may be like me. For years I had no idea what it meant to walk in the Spirit. In fact, I wasn't sure what it meant to be in the flesh or the Spirit. Let's take a moment to clarify what these things mean, and then will look at how the Bible teaches us to walk in the Spirit.

The flesh is our bodies and the sinful nature that corrupts it. The Bible uses a few terms to describe this, such as the natural man, carnal man, old man, and the flesh. Before coming to Christ, the Bible describes us as being the natural (or carnal) man. Unless gender is specifically addressed, when the Bible uses 'man', it refers to mankind. So whether you're a man or a woman, these things apply.

---

[136] 2 Corinthians 12:9-10
[137] Ephesians 6:10

As we looked at earlier, we are born into a sinful nature. The Bible teaches that we are freed from the power of the flesh when our old man was crucified with Christ. Look at **Romans 6:6-7**

> [6] Knowing this, that our old man was crucified with *Him,* that the body of sin might be done away with, that we should no longer be slaves of sin.
>
> [7] For he who has died has been freed from sin.

The Bible says that we should not walk in our former conduct since we have put off the old man with his deeds[138]. If we are in Christ, we are a new creation and have a new man – that inner being that was born through the Spirit, and is not corrupted by sin or the fall.

Even though we have a new nature, we still have the influences of our old selves because sin remains in our physical bodies. We've already discussed this, but it bears repeating. We know that sin in our flesh wars against our minds and seeks to bring us back into captivity to sin. That is the flesh. It's what we have to deal with every day of our lives. Given the chance, sin in our flesh, will again dominate our lives.

Walking in the Spirit is to walk in fellowship with the Lord through the word, renewing our minds, and putting the focus of our minds on things that are of the Spirit. The flesh lives for the world, the Spirit strives for eternity. In order for the Spirit to reign in our lives, the flesh has to be crucified and taken out of the way.

Crucify the flesh.

Crucifying the flesh is a message that isn't well received in today's church culture. It seems too sacrificial until you put it into practice. Most are taught that we add Jesus to our lives in order to gain fulfillment. But the Bible teaches that we lay down our lives in this world in order to find eternal life. When someone wants Jesus and their own ways, a conflict is inevitable. Christianity then

---

[138] Ephesians 4:22, Colossians 3:9

becomes a quest to justify our choices instead of walking in the Spirit. Consider the words of Jesus in **Luke 9:23-24**

^{23} Then He said to *them* all, "If anyone desires to come after Me, let him deny himself, and take up his cross daily, and follow Me.

^{24} "For whoever desires to save his life will lose it, but whoever loses his life for My sake will save it.

The ways of Jesus were not the ways of the culture around Him. When people followed for the wrong reasons, He offended them with hard choices. Christ was more concerned about making disciples than gaining followers. If someone follows for the wrong reason, God will make them choose in order to show what kind of faith they really have.

When Jesus uttered the words above, the masses were following Him. To make it clear that this wasn't a motivational seminar, Jesus identified what a true follower looked like. Unless we fulfill this instruction, we aren't truly following Jesus. This draws the line between a pretentious faith and the real thing.

Discipleship requires that we deny ourselves. I want temptation. If I didn't, it wouldn't be tempting. Sometimes denial is setting aside a good thing because it hinders our walk. Hobbies, sports, television, recreation, careers, and other activities are not necessarily wrong, but they can choke the word in our lives and hinder our walk. Several apostles compared this to being entangled. We are not to allow ourselves to be entangled in the cares of this life, or the temptations that once ensnared us. Otherwise, we are casting off the eternal for something that is temporary and will be passing away. The things we naturally value in this life are worthless after our physical deaths.

Things we consider as good can be an entanglement if they prevent us from fulfilling our calling. That is why it's called denying ourselves. Something I may like, that isn't necessarily wrong, if it hinders my spiritual life, should be set aside. It might be television. Even wholesome programming can crowd out our time with the Lord. It boils down to what we value. Do I value what is eternal over the things that are passing away? If so, I'll be willing to deny these things an undo place of prominence in my life.

Jesus also said to take up our cross. I've heard many explanations of what this means, but the Biblical meaning is clear. Taking up our cross does not mean to suffer – though we might be put into a position to suffer. Some teach that we have to have something in our lives that cause suffering. Personal suffering does not serve as a penal substitute. Nor does it make us more Christ-like, though it can turn our hearts to seek Him deeper. Many with infirmities suffer and are bitter. Atheists suffer, but it doesn't make them Christ-like.

Taking up the cross means the death of the flesh. It means to be crucified with Christ. This is spoken in context to what Jesus was to accomplish on the cross. He is our example. He did not love His own life, but laid down his life to accomplish the will of the Father and to put sin to death.

In every context where the cross or crucifying the flesh is mentioned, it is always to put off our selfish will, so we can take up the new life God has given. The Bible says that Jesus was put to death in the flesh but made alive by the Spirit[139]. Paul stated that he died that he might live in Christ[140]. You can't follow Christ while carrying the burden of the life centered around the flesh. Walking in the Spirit takes our hearts and minds where the flesh cannot go.

The cross is the death of the flesh and the death of the will that seeks to follow our own ways. When people were exploring Jesus' call to repentance, He warned them to count the cost before beginning. There is a cost. We are being called to give up our lives in this life so we can gain the life to come. We're being asked to give up a temporary life in the flesh to gain an eternal life in the Spirit. 'Just try Jesus' doesn't work. Unless someone lays down their life, they cannot experience life in the Spirit. Nibbling on spirituality doesn't reveal the true things of God. Read this passage from **Romans 12:1-2**

---

[139] 1 Peter 3:18
[140] Galatians 2:19-20

Walking in the Spirit

¹ I beseech you therefore, brethren, by the mercies of God, that you present your bodies a living sacrifice, holy, acceptable to God, *which is* your reasonable service. ² And do not be conformed to this world, but be transformed by the renewing of your mind, that you may prove what *is* that good and acceptable and perfect will of God.

Take note of what is being taught in this passage. We first present our bodies as a living sacrifice. It's a reasonable request because Christ first gave Himself for us. Only then do we have the power to fulfill the second verse – not to conform to this world. We have first yielded ourselves to God, and then we turn from the world and its lusts by renewing our minds. In doing so, we discover the perfect will of God.

This idea takes us back to the illustration of the weight. To say, don't conform to the world, isn't enough. Looking at temptation and resisting it is a losing battle. Resisting what our minds are focusing on is like asking someone to hold up a weight forever.

We must resist the lust of the flesh by turning from the flesh, and toward the Spirit. We cease from conforming to the world because our renewed minds become focused on the word and godliness. We renew our minds by the word, prayer, meditating on the Lord, and all the things God gives for us to grow in our faith.

Misunderstanding this basic principle is why people struggle needlessly with their weaknesses. Some misquote scripture and say, "Resist the devil and he will flee from you." Not so. People try to believe this, but then wonder why temptation continues to hammer at them. There is much more than mere resistance, so let's look at the passage where this quote originates in its context. **James 4:7-8**

⁷ Therefore submit to God. Resist the devil and he will flee from you.
⁸ Draw near to God and He will draw near to you. Cleanse *your* hands, *you* sinners; and purify *your* hearts, *you* double-minded.

What comes before resistance? Submission to God. We turn from temptation by turning to the Lord and submitting to His will. When we draw near to God, He draws near to us. But we first must answer His call for submission. Then He overcomes our weaknesses by drawing us out of the flesh and close to Himself. While submitted to the flesh, it is impossible to draw near to God. There must first be a yielding to His will.

This is made evident through our example of Jesus Christ. He learned obedience by surrendering His will. Look at **Hebrews 5:8**

Though He was a Son, *yet* He learned obedience by the things which He suffered.

To understand what this passage is saying, let's look at the event where Jesus learned obedience. Look now at **Luke 22:41-43**

[41] And He was withdrawn from them about a stone's throw, and He knelt down and prayed,

[42] saying, "Father, if it is Your will, take this cup away from Me; nevertheless not My will, but Yours, be done."

[43] Then an angel appeared to Him from heaven, strengthening Him.

Jesus is our High Priest and is able to identify with our weaknesses because He had to endure all things like us[141]. Yet He did so without sin. Jesus learned obedience without rebellion. In the garden where He prayed, Jesus agonized over the coming crucifixion. He pled that if there were any other way that this cup of suffering would pass from Him. But there wasn't another way. By His own testimony, this was the reason He came into the world.

In His suffering, Jesus shifted His focus from the suffering, to the will of God. You can see His progression toward obedience through each prayer. Three times He asked to escape the cross, but each time the focus becomes more on 'your will be done' and less on, 'let this cup pass away.'

---

[141] Hebrews 4:15

This is a lesson for us. Jesus didn't force His will to align with the Fathers. He said, "Not my will, but yours." Obedience was dying to His own will and submitting to the will of the Father.

In the same way, your goal is not to make your will align with God's will. Often times they will be opposed – especially when your will draws from the flesh. According to scripture, the flesh and the Spirit are at war with each other and will never agree. Many times your will and God's will won't be in agreement, but you overcome by saying, "Not my will, but Yours."

Like Jesus, who longed for a way of escape, we also will long to fulfill our desires over the Lord's call. Having a will that opposes God's will is not a sin. Choosing our will over God's will is where sin is found. Rather than trying to force our will to conform, we must do as Christ did – pray and surrender our will while following the Father's will.

When Jesus surrendered His will, an angel from heaven renewed His strength. We also have this promise. According to the Bible, angels are ministering spirits sent to minister to those who will inherit salvation[142]. You may not see God ministering with human eyes, but when you are surrendered to His will and walking in obedience, heaven is sent to strengthen you.

It's okay to acknowledge that God's ways are not what we desire. It's okay to pray for God to make another way. Wrestling with ourselves as we press toward obedience is not a lack of faith. It is only a lack of faith when we believe our will is greater than the Lord's.

When we have to put down our cross and follow our own ways, we have turned away from the Spirit. And there will be times when we don't understand God's will or what choice is right. We resolve this by prayer, seeking the Lord, renewing our minds, and at times, fasting.

It's okay that you will have times of struggling. Don't think you are spiritually immature or that you have failed in some way. Sometimes we have to wrestle free of the grip of the flesh.

---

[142] Hebrews 1:14

When I put off my will and take up the will of God, I am crucifying the flesh and walking in the Spirit. Putting off my will may be the process of changing my conversations, putting off certain behaviors, or simply refusing to live for my own desires. It must be an active choice. Just as Paul said, "I die daily," we must daily take an active role in putting off our flesh and taking up the cross. Look at **Ephesians 4:22-24**

> [22] that you put off, concerning your former conduct, the old man which grows corrupt according to the deceitful lusts,
> [23] and be renewed in the spirit of your mind,
> [24] and that you put on the new man which was created according to God, in true righteousness and holiness.

The call of God is to put off our flesh (crucify it and take up the cross) and put on the new man (our incorruptible spirit given to us). Remember that Jesus said to take up the cross and follow Him daily. It's not a one-time act. Each day we wrestle against our flesh as we put off our former conduct and put on the new ways of God. Putting off the conduct is taking up the cross. Putting on the new man is to follow Christ.

False religion is trying to do something to earn God's favor, but true obedience is putting off what hinders our faith. Our call of God is to crucify the flesh so the light of truth can shine. According to Romans 8:13, it is through the Spirit we crucify our flesh. By submitting to God, we find the power to bring our flesh under subjection and find righteousness. Righteous works comes from God, but our work is to put off the hindrances so He will work through us. The Bible gives a great illustration of this in the life of Gideon.

Gideon was a young teen, hiding in a wine vat and threshing wheat[143]. He was hiding because the enemies of Israel, the Midianites, oppressed the nation to the point of complete poverty. If they saw an Israelite with wheat or another crop, they came in with raiders and stole it. God came to this ill equipped young man and declared he would be the leader of Israel's armies and

---

[143] Judges 6:11

proclaimed that God would deliver Israel from the Midianites through Gideon.

Gideon raised up an army and prepared for war. To keep the people from trusting in their own abilities, God sent every soldier away except three hundred men. The Midianite army responded by joining with other nations to bring together an army in excess of a hundred-thousand warriors. Gideon was afraid, but God strengthened him as the young man obeyed.

God then gave the instruction to take torches, insert them into clay pots, and then gather around the massive army by night. When the signal was given, each of the men shattered the clay pot and shouted. Without human effort, the army was defeated because God sent the soldiers into confusion, and they began killing each other.

The deeper truth of this account is usually missed by most Christians. Gideon's victory is a picture of the Christian walk of faith. It is a visual image of walking in the Spirit. The torch is symbolic of the light of Christ placed in our hearts when we are born again. The clay pot is the flesh of our bodies. This is affirmed when the Bible says, "We have this treasure in earthen vessels that the power may be of God and not us."[144]

Victory isn't found by great feats of strength or human effort. We simply break the flesh so the work of God can shine through. Like Gideon, we proclaim the victory and see the work God is doing. The battle is not in accomplishing the work of God, but in breaking the flesh. We remove the flesh (the earthen vessel) so the treasure of God's power can work in our lives.

God could do this by force, but He does not. He calls us to remove the flesh and gives the promise that He will do His work. While the flesh stands in the way, God remains silent. I'm sure Gideon and his men thought the attack plan was absurd. How can breaking a clay pot give three hundred men victory over such a strong obstacle as this mass of seasoned warriors? It can't. Breaking the pitchers didn't do anything to the army. But God honored their obedience and He defeated the enemy before their eyes.

---

[144] 2 Corinthians 4:7

This might help you see why the Christian life appears so foolish from the outside. What we do can't accomplish anything. Our acts of faith simply release our strongholds and the strongholds of the flesh so we can see the promise of God stepping into our lives to do as He has promised.

You too must obey the call of the Lord. Crucifying the flesh doesn't accomplish the will of God. But it does put you in obedience, removes the barrier, and lets the light of God's spirit shine. It simply removes what hinders so God's promise can shine through. The victory is His. The work is His. Success is His. But obedience is yours, and so is the reward.

We remove the flesh by renewing our minds while crucifying the flesh. Without renewal, our minds become influenced by the world around us. The more we are in the world, the more desensitized to sin we become and the less we care about the eternal things of God. Renewing changes this. It must be a daily choice. You can't thrive on yesterday's spiritual renewal.

Renewing in the Spirit.

In the Old Testament, God used manna as a picture of spiritual food. In the New Testament, Jesus called Himself the manna from heaven and then called His words (teachings) the source of life.

The Old Testament is valuable in understanding the New Testament. Israel was led out of bondage and toward the Promised Land. This is a picture of the Christian's journey. Just as the Children of Israel were enslaved to Pharaoh, we were enslaved to sin. God defeated Pharaoh and delivered His people from bondage. We were in bondage to sin, but Christ defeated Satan on the cross and led us out of sin. God led the Israelites across the desert and toward the Promise. We also are wandering in the desert of this world as we journey toward our promise.

In the desert, there was no food to sustain God's people, so He sent manna from heaven. Each day, the people had to go out and gather the manna for that day's nutrition. They were forbidden to gather more than a day's worth at a time. Manna would not keep until the next day.

There is no nutrition for our souls in this world, so we also are called to gather the day's nutrients from the manna from heaven. According to Jesus, that is Him, who is the Word of Life. Those who make a practice of daily digging into the word grow and have stronger spiritual health. Those who neglect are starving their spiritual lives. Famished Christians faint along the way, and often abandon the journey.

This was given to us in scripture as an example of how we ought to live. Daily we grow in the word as we study to renew our minds by the word and by the cleansing of the Spirit.

The Israelites who lost focus on the destination began to desire what they left behind. They became unsatisfied with the manna, unsatisfied with the ways of God, and even tried to establish their own leadership. For this, God judged them. Those who rebelled never found the promise.

In our church culture, we see this same scenario played out. People forget where they are going and begin to look back. This is why Jesus said, "No one, having put his hand to the plow, and looking back, is fit for the kingdom of God.[145]"

This doesn't mean we can't repent and start going forward, for God's hand is always drawing His children back to fellowship. This person has his hands on the kingdom but he is looking back to the world. His (or her) heart is still upon what they are leaving behind. Every one of us will look back if we forget to look ahead to where we are going. The solution is found in **Hebrews 12:1-3**

[1] Therefore we also, since we are surrounded by so great a cloud of witnesses, let us lay aside every weight, and the sin which so easily ensnares *us,* and let us run with endurance the race that is set before us,

[2] looking unto Jesus, the author and finisher of *our* faith, who for the joy that was set before Him endured the cross, despising the shame, and has sat down at the right hand of the throne of God.

---

[145] Luke 9:62

[3] For consider Him who endured such hostility from sinners against Himself, lest you become weary and discouraged in your souls.

Jesus is not only the Author of our faith, but also the Finisher. He's the finish line we are racing toward. The sin that ensnares us can be anything that draws our eyes off of where we are going. Considering His sacrifice for us and love toward us becomes an encouragement when we're discouraged.

Jesus endured the cross while despising its shame. Think about the weight of that statement for a moment. The cross was the highest form of shame. The crucified prisoner would be stripped of clothing, nailed by their hands and feet, and then raised up on a hill near the city for everyone to see. It was not only intended for maximum pain, but also to be a shameful public spectacle.

Crowds gathered while insults were hurled toward Jesus. While the masses gawked and taunted, Jesus was forced to push down on His pierced feet in order to release enough tension on His chest to grab a breath of air. It was a slow and excruciating death.

Yet Jesus found the joy to endure. The joy wasn't in the cross. He despised the cross. He begged for another way, knowing what He was about to endure. Endurance came in the form of joy. The joy set before Him provided the endurance. For Christ, the joy before Him was your reconciliation. He looked beyond the cross to the joy – our redemption and eternal life.

For us, we endure our troubles the same way. We look ahead to the joy set before us. That joy is the finish line. Our eyes remain on the kingdom of God, and the Lord who redeemed us. He is our strength and we stand upon the promise that He is with us, and the promise of inheriting the kingdom with our Lord.

When we lose sight of this, we are distracted by other things and where our eyes are looking, our lives will soon follow. When we realize we are looking elsewhere, repentance is in order. Repentance isn't groveling in misery, but correcting our way. Because we belong to God, His Spirit is always working in our life to guide us into His perfect will. Repentance is a God-empowered choice to turn from the wrong way toward the right way. For some, it is a 180 degree turn around. For others, it is a course correction. Everyone drifts, and when we realize it, we return our focus onto the kingdom and begin heading in the right way again.

When you fail, stop acting as though God is ready to lash out at you in anger. Rather than cowering from God, recognize that the Lord acknowledges our weakness of the flesh, and turn to Him for the power to break free from the bondage of the flesh. Don't substitute the bondage of the flesh with the bondage of religion and legalistic thinking. We don't have to miss anything God has in store. Nor is it necessary for us to flounder without direction. God shows us how to avoid the things that entangle us and distract us. And He shows us how to focus on the joy set before us.

The Lord loves to show Himself strong on our behalf. The Bible says that the eyes of the Lord search throughout the earth to show Himself strong in those whose hearts are completely His[146]. Our hearts are either wandering into the prideful flesh, or it's completely His. To be completely God's, we must first lay down our lives. We must lay aside our human strength before we can stand upon His. Peter found this out when he fell. Paul discovered this when he felt vulnerable because of what he called, a thorn in his flesh. A messenger of Satan pounded him constantly and he begged God three times for deliverance.

God's answer was, 'no'. Because Paul was the source of many revelations of scripture, God blessed him with weakness. To keep the apostle from being lifted up with pride, a physical ailment was given, and a messenger of Satan buffeted him. To buffet is to strike with violent force. This was a source of pain and grief to Paul, but God's answer was, "My strength is made perfect in weakness."

Paul's flesh and human efforts were reduced to a state of weakness so God could show Himself strong on Paul's behalf. Once he realized the benefit, Paul said, "I glory in my weakness, for when I am weak, then I am strong."

This is not only echoed throughout the New Testament, but it's beautifully explained in **Isaiah 40:29-31**

---

[146] 2 Chronicles 16:9

[29] He gives power to the weak, And to *those who have* no might He increases strength.

[30] Even the youths shall faint and be weary, And the young men shall utterly fall,

[31] But those who wait on the LORD Shall renew *their* strength; They shall mount up with wings like eagles, They shall run and not be weary, They shall walk and not faint.

Notice, it isn't the strength of the individual. The strength of men fail and the vibrant youth will faint in their weakness of human effort. The strength is only to those whose renewal is in the Lord – those who depend on God's strength.

Are you struggling? The answer is not to find strength within yourself. It's not to become a better you. Embrace the truth that the flesh is weak and surrender it to God, and depend wholly on His strength. The strength of God is to the weak. Only the weak learn what it means to walk in the Spirit, for they have crucified the flesh, laid it aside so they no longer depend upon it, and they place their trust completely in the Lord.

Are there things you don't like about yourself? Almost everyone has things they don't like. It could be something we think is ugly, weak, inabilities, speech problems, or any number of challenges that hinder man. In the world's eyes, beauty and strength gain the highest praise, but in the Christian's life, shortcomings are a blessing. They turn our hearts to depend on God.

Like with other hardships, some allow it to cultivate bitterness, but to those who glory in weakness so they can experience God, these find true confidence and strength. True strength comes from the Lord. Nothing gives more confidence than knowing God is our designer, sustainer, and the one who gives us the strength and the ability to do His will.

When your heart is completely His, God will show Himself strong through you. This is what it means to walk in the Spirit. If you belong to Christ, you have the Spirit of God within you and have the power to walk in the Spirit. That power is God's hand in your life.

Victory is found through submission, not commitment. It's not through commitment, but surrender.

Your strength will fail, but to those who are strong in the Lord, they have the promise of the power of God's might.[147]

---

[147] Ephesians 6:10

Spiritual Warfare

Few topics have more varying beliefs than that of spiritual warfare. Some deny the existence of any supernatural opponent, while others exalt Satan into a rival god. And you'll find anything in between these two extremes. These variations are nothing new. Even in Jesus' day, not only did the people have varying superstitions, but there were also groups like the Sadducees, who denied the supernatural. The Sadducees were religious leaders along with the Pharisees, but they denied the resurrection, afterlife, and denied the existence of angels[148].

The only way to deny the spiritual world is to discredit the entire Bible. This includes denying the teachings and resurrection of Jesus. Christ made it clear that each of these exists. This includes Satan.

Unfortunately, people add personal beliefs to the scriptures, take the spiritual world, and create something that does not exist. There is a tendency to make Satan into something more powerful than he is. Once I listened to a sermon on the radio where the preacher said, "Satan is a being of incredible power and we should be afraid of him."

That isn't exactly what the Bible says about Satan. Let's take a peek at the end of all things and see how the 'mighty' Satan is bound. **Revelation 20:1-3**

[1] Then I saw an angel coming down from heaven, having the key to the bottomless pit and a great chain in his hand.

[2] He laid hold of the dragon, that serpent of old, who is *the* Devil and Satan, and bound him for a thousand years;

[3] and he cast him into the bottomless pit, and shut him up, and set a seal on him, so that he should deceive the nations no more till the thousand years were finished. But after these things he must be released for a little while.

---

[148] Acts 23:6

There is an interesting fact in this passage that most people overlook. When God is doing something great, He sends a high ranking angel. When God sent an angel to the prophet Daniel, it was Gabriel. The nation of Israel had been defeated as part of their judgment, but when Daniel began praying for the nation and interceding for them to confess their sins and ask for forgiveness, God declared their future hope.

Gabriel was sent to reveal that Jerusalem and the temple would be rebuilt, and that when the command goes out to rebuild, their Messiah would come 490 years later. This, of course, was fulfilled in Christ. Four hundred and ninety years later, Jesus rode into Jerusalem on a donkey to proclaim Himself as their king.

When the birth of Jesus was announced, Gabriel was again dispatched to proclaim the news to Mary. Most people have also heard of Michael the Archangel. He stands against Satan and is heaven's warrior. He also blows the trumpet to call the church home.

Who is sent to collect Satan? We don't know. And I believe that is the point. I have a theory. When the time comes to end Satan's reign (for he is called the ruler of this world), God will pick out the lowest ranking angel, give him a chain, and say, "Go get him." No battle. No war. No struggle. The Bible says an angel – a single angel – waltzes into Satan's domain, binds him, and casts him into a pit to reserve him until man's final testing in Revelation 20. Let's look at another passage that speaks of Satan after he is bound. Look at **Isaiah 14:10-17**

¹⁰ They all shall speak and say to you: 'Have you also become as weak as we? Have you become like us?

¹¹ Your pomp is brought down to Sheol, *And* the sound of your stringed instruments; The maggot is spread under you, And worms cover you.'

¹² " How you are fallen from heaven, O Lucifer, son of the morning! *How* you are cut down to the ground, You who weakened the nations!

¹³ For you have said in your heart: 'I will ascend into heaven, I will exalt my throne above the stars of God; I will

also sit on the mount of the congregation On the farthest sides of the north;
[14] I will ascend above the heights of the clouds, I will be like the Most High.'
[15] Yet you shall be brought down to Sheol, To the lowest depths of the Pit.
[16] "Those who see you will gaze at you, *And* consider you, *saying:* '*Is* this the man who made the earth tremble, Who shook kingdoms,
[17] Who made the world as a wilderness And destroyed its cities, *Who* did not open the house of his prisoners?'

To some, it may seem odd that Lucifer is identified as a man. Angels are often shown in appearance as men – and Lucifer is a fallen angel. This occurs several places in the scripture. A good example is Daniel 9:21, where the angel Gabriel is referred to as, 'the man Gabriel.' Daniel also says that he saw Gabriel fly swiftly, so don't mistake the physical description as though it were actually a human.

Both Gabriel and Michael are referred to as having an appearance like a man, but both are shown to also put men in fear when they arrive due to their spiritual power. In Daniel 10:7, the men who were with Daniel fled out of fear, even though they never saw the angel that was sent to him. Fear also overwhelmed Daniel when he saw Michael. He had no strength to stand until 'the one having the likeness of a man' touched him and gave him strength[149]. Though the appearance was like a man, the spiritual presence of these strong angels put mere men into fear. Often they lost strength and fell face down. The manlike appearance doesn't downgrade the spiritual nature of angels.

I say all of this so we have a realistic view of Satan. When stripped of his authority, people look upon him and are amazed that this could actually be the same Lucifer that disrupted the whole earth. He looks powerless, and indeed he is.

---

[149] Daniel 10:18

The next logical question is, if this is how people will see Satan, how did he get his power?

According to scripture, Satan was the highest ranking angel in heaven. He was also the light bearer, hence the name Lucifer, son of the morning. According to scripture, until he is stripped of his power, he still is able to transform himself into an angel of light and deceive those who don't hold to the word of God.[150]

As explained in the passage above in Isaiah, Satan fell when he determined to exalt himself above the Most High – God. According to God's description of Satan in Ezekiel 28, he was perfect in every way until pride was found in his heart. He was the picture of beauty and the bearer of light. God calls Lucifer the King of Tyre – a city once thought to be undefeatable, and filled with riches and beauty.

Jesus describes the fall of Satan as lightning flashing from heaven[151], banished to the earth[152], and he took a third of the angels (stars) with him[153].

According to the Bible, Satan will be one of the ways God tries man. Those who love the lie and love darkness will follow after the spirit of deception. Everyone claims to love God, but when put to the test, man's heart is revealed. To fully understand this, consider what we read previously in Revelation. The angel will bind Satan for a thousand years. Afterwards he is released for a short time.

After Satan is bound, the Bible describes the thousand year reign of Christ on this earth. Those on the earth are not only Christians, but anyone who survived the time of tribulation. The book of Daniel describes this time in great detail. Daniel 7:9-14 and Revelation 19:19-20 describe the same event. Christ overthrows the nations and sets up His kingdom.

Daniel adds an interesting comment. Christ calls the kings of the earth, 'beasts', strips them of power, but allows them to remain. Calling these people 'beasts' is referring to man's savage nature without redemption. The kingdoms were taken away, but the beasts

---

[150] 2 Corinthians 11:14
[151] Luke 10:18
[152] Revelation 12:12
[153] Revelation 12:4

were allowed to remain for a time. That time is during the thousand year reign.

These are also the nations and families mentioned in Zechariah 14:16-17. Those who remain on the earth are required to worship Christ once a year during the thousand year reign. Those who refuse to come during the Feast of Tabernacles and worship Christ will not receive rain for the coming year. The redeemed are in the city, but any who remain but do not accept Christ are not permitted inside the city gates.[154]

So we can see that during the millennial reign, both believers and unbelievers will remain on earth. This is significant, for it shows how man's heart will be proven.

For a thousand years, mankind will have no influence by Satan or demonic forces. They will see God in His glory, and see the perfection of earth without evil. Yet what set's apart those who love God and those who do not? It's the same thing that caused Satan to rebel from the beginning – pride. Some see the value of God and cherish His mercies. They also acknowledge that He created all things, has the right to be Lord over His creation, and because He is God, He's also worthy to be worshipped as Lord of all.

The heart of pride says, "I will not have Him rule over me." It's the desire to be like the Most High. The lie that deceived Adam and Eve was the promise, "You will be like God."

When Satan is released, we see the proving of mankind's heart. After the thousand years, the devil is released, and he will assemble the largest army the earth has ever seen. All those born during that thousand years will either surrender to Christ, or join the effort to dethrone Him. An army of the kindreds of the earth will encamp around the city and prepare for war. (See Revelation 20:7-10)

Let me give a secular illustration that seems to fit this scene that will one day unfold. There's a book called *The Scarlet Pimpernel*. The villain spends his life trying to capture his nemesis, the one who sneaks into prisons and sets prisoners free. At the end of the book, the villain thinks he has succeeded when he captures

---

[154] Revelation 21:24-27

the Scarlet Pimpernel, and he sends his soldiers out to execute his enemy. With satisfaction he stands guard over his enemy's wife while the muskets fire. Victory is spoiled though. He turns around and there is Sir Percy, the Pimpernel. It turns out that Percy's men arrived beforehand and took the soldiers prisoner and then staged the execution.

With disgust Percy's enemy walks up and says, "Why this big charade," referring to the mock execution.

Percy raises his brows and says, "My dear friend. I wouldn't think of depriving you of your moment of glory. But alas, a moment is all I can spare."

This seems to be a good picture of the final battle of Satan. Look at **Revelation 20:9**

> They went up on the breadth of the earth and surrounded the camp of the saints and the beloved city. And fire came down from God out of heaven and devoured them.

Now that's a disappointing finish for the devil. God allows him to gather the masses from the earth, prepare for battle, but alas, that's all the time He can spare. In a flash, it's over. And Satan didn't even get a shot off.

The point of the war is not to prove God's power over Satan. That has already been established. It's to prove man's heart. Even in the presence of paradise, man in his natural state cannot be satisfied. He is unwilling to submit to God, and therefore, Satan in all his wickedness is considered a better option than abiding with God. Heaven is like hell to those who do not love God. But it is the thrill of eternity to those who do.

Separating Warfare from Superstition

Not one time in the scriptures are we told to fear Satan. In fact, we are told the opposite. Look at the words of Jesus in **Matthew 10:28**

> And do not fear those who kill the body but cannot kill the soul. But rather fear Him who is able to destroy both soul and body in hell.

We should only fear the one who has power over our body and soul, and that is God alone. People are often needlessly afraid, but there is nothing to fear. Perfect love casts out all fear.[155] If your love for the Lord is solid, fear has no place to take root.

Even so, many unbiblical beliefs abound. A few years back, a man claiming to be an ex-warlock provided free videos that would supposedly teach us how to be protected against demonic forces. Of course, he's willing to accept donations to help him fight this spiritual battle.

On the tape he warned us about how witches and warlocks place curses on objects in order to get demons into the houses of Christians. Supposedly, these objects were the cause of many of our problems: rebellious teenagers, sickness, financial problems, and all sorts of other woes. This man taught that we should go through our houses and locate anything that could be cursed, and get it out of the house. He even claimed that allergies were the result of demonic forces. If that's true, I've discovered that Flonaise has the power to repel demons.

Let's think for a moment about this claim. Are we so faithless that we think God's promises can be overthrown by a witch or cursed object? Can Satan inhabit objects? Of course not! The Bible says an idol is nothing. If anything should be cursed, it would be an idol. Look at **1 Corinthians 8:4-6**

⁴ Therefore concerning the eating of things offered to idols, we know that an idol *is* nothing in the world, and that *there is* no other God but one.

⁵ For even if there are so-called gods, whether in heaven or on earth (as there are many gods and many lords),

⁶ yet for us *there is* one God, the Father, of whom *are* all things, and we for Him; and one Lord Jesus Christ, through whom *are* all things, and through whom we *live.* -

The Corinthian church lived in a pagan culture. The Romans had many religions and idolatry was a common practice. Many

---

[155] 1 John 4:16

people in the church had come out of idolatry. The specific problem Paul is addressing is the question of meat offered to idols. Meat used in pagan rituals was sold at a discount after being offered to idols. Some within the church were buying this meat, but others took offense at the idea that a Christian would eat something offered in a pagan sacrifice.

Paul gives two instructions. First, he addresses the Christians he calls 'weaker in faith'. An idol is nothing. The meat offered to pagan gods was just meat and there was nothing to fear. If they didn't feel right about eating this meat, they should abstain and not violate their own conscience.

To those who were eating this meat Paul instructed them to care for those who were weak in faith. He didn't tell them not to eat it, but to not eat it around those who considered it evil. The only danger was the violation of the individual's conscience. The idol was a piece of wood, stone, or metal. It isn't evil. It isn't good. It is an inanimate object. The meat was not evil or good, but we must always consider those whose faith will be challenged by our liberty in Christ.

A similar question arises on the issue of Christmas trees. I've seen this mentioned and it was brought out in the video I spoke of a moment ago. In Jeremiah 10, God is condemning those who go in the woods, cut down a tree, fasten it with nails, and decorate it with gold and silver. The man on the video said, "This is a Christmas tree," and if we have trees, we are under God's condemnation.

Of course, if you keep reading in Jeremiah, the Bible calls it an idol. It isn't a tree, it's a craftsman who cuts down a tree with his own hands, shapes it into the likeness of a man or animal, layers it with gold, and then bows down to it. God is pointing out an absurdity. The idol couldn't exist unless it was first crafted into an image, and then it can't move without being carried. How can anyone be so foolish as to worship their own craft? Look at how God describes these things in **Jeremiah 10:5**

> Do not be afraid of them, For they cannot do evil, Nor can they do any good."

Those who teach superstitious spiritual warfare are teaching others to fear these things, but God said specifically, don't be afraid of them. They can't do evil or good. They aren't a demonic force, nor are they a good force. The same is true for a rabbit's foot, lucky coin, horse shoe, penny laying face up, lucky shirt, or any other thing we attribute as the source of good or luck. It's just another form of idolatry, and a denial of the providence of God. The object itself has no power.

When I was about ten, I found a box my father brought back from Japan when he was in service. It was seven or so Japanese gods. To my dad, they were souvenirs. To some in that Japanese culture, these were objects of worship. For a ten year old boy, they were toys. I played with them until they were all broken. To the propagators of superstition, I was playing with cursed objects and bringing demonic forces into my life. But the truth is, they could not do evil, nor could they do good.

The power of the idol is the faith of a person. It isn't a demonic force attached to the object; it's a tool by which a man or woman tries to communicate with what they think are gods. Some claim that drums call up demons because pagan religions use them in their worship. It isn't the drum that calls up demons, it's the person submitting themselves to the devil through the drums. It makes no difference what the object is. If someone is reaching out to demons, they will find what they're looking for. It could be a drum, flute, idol, crystals, New Age meditation music, or a hole in the wall. Paul explains this in **1 Corinthians 10:19-20**

[19] What am I saying then? That an idol is anything, or what is offered to idols is anything?

[20] Rather, that the things which the Gentiles sacrifice they sacrifice to demons and not to God, and I do not want you to have fellowship with demons.

The Apostle Paul first explains that idols are nothing and any object offered as a sacrifice to the idol is as harmless as the idol itself. However, after making this clear, Paul then goes on to warn Christians not to participate in these idolatrous practices. When someone tries to reach any god or spiritual force through an idol or ritual, they are actually reaching out to demons.

The only difference between an idol and a toy is the way the person is using it. The same is true for a figurine, souvenir, or any artifact. It has no power; however, you can use it to submit to demons. Whether someone thinks they are communicating with spirits, or touching God, the result is the same. This is idolatry and it is always demonic.

However, if a Christian has an object that has been used for any ritual, it is just an object. It can't do good, nor can it do evil. Nor can demons hitch a ride on the object. If someone struggles because of a lack of faith, they should avoid these things for their own conscience sake. But be aware that Satan doesn't have the power to overcome God's will with any object or curse. Demons don't sneak into our houses through objects, but through temptation to sin. We reap what we sow – whether it's sin leading to death, or obedience leading to righteousness.[156]

The curse is not something that comes from without, it is something that comes from our own hearts. Let's take a moment to explore what the Bible says about curses.

Curses, foiled again!

I've seen people petrified with fear over the idea of curses. One man once explained a near miss at a local drug store. He bought something and paid with a ten. His change was $6.66. The man refused his change and bought something else. "That's the sign of the devil," he said.

The number 666 means nothing in our lives. This number comes from Revelation 13:18. The irony is, the Bible calls this the number of man, not the number of the devil.[157] It's referring to a man declaring himself to be God. A number can't curse you. Even in the curse of Revelation where this is mentioned, the curse is to those who choose to swear allegiance to the new human religion and deny God.

---

[156] Galatians 6:7-8, Romans 6:16
[157] Revelation 13:18

Do you realize that there is only one who can curse? Nowhere in the Bible do you see God's people cursed – or anyone cursed, without the Lord. The real curse is found in **Deuteronomy 11:26-28**

> [26] " Behold, I set before you today a blessing and a curse:
> [27] "the blessing, if you obey the commandments of the LORD your God which I command you today;
> [28] "and the curse, if you do not obey the commandments of the LORD your God, but turn aside from the way which I command you today, to go after other gods which you have not known.

This hasn't changed. Those who are in Christ are under the blessing. Those who choose other gods – including themselves – are under the curse. Those who put their trust in anything but the Lord are already under the curse.[158] Sin is a curse and it has consequences. If someone steals and then is condemned to prison, did God curse them? In a sense, yes. He warned that to disobey is to choose the curse.

People want a 'precious promises God', but the truth is that God's promises are found in obedience. If you obey, you are blessed. I can claim every promise in the Bible, but if I am walking contrary to the Lord, my words mean nothing. The same holds true for curses. If I'm walking in obedience, a curse from the mouth of an enemy means nothing. If every witch, Satan worshiper, and pagan priest on earth gathered together to pelt my life with curses, it means nothing. A preacher can't curse me. A pagan can't curse me. Consider the promise of **Psalm 128:1-4**

> [1] Blessed *is* every one who fears the LORD, Who walks in His ways.
> [2] When you eat the labor of your hands, You *shall be* happy, and *it shall be* well with you.
> [3] Your wife *shall be* like a fruitful vine In the very heart of your house, Your children like olive plants All around your table.

---

[158] Jeremiah 17:5-8

[4] Behold, thus shall the man be blessed Who fears the LORD.

This is the word of the Lord. It's a promise. Is Satan more powerful than God? Absolutely not! How then can we think that this promise can be nullified by an object or curse? If I fear the Lord and walk in His ways, but then Satan can send a pagan to curse me, it would make the word of God null and void. Have faith in God. If you obey and walk with God, not one promise will fall short and no force on earth can stand against the Lord's blessing.

Consider the attempted curse of Balaam. When Israel was heading toward the Promised Land, Balak, the King of Moab was afraid of them and considered Israel to be a threat to his kingdom. When his priests couldn't curse Israel, he thought the only hope of doing so would be the words of a prophet of God.

Keep in mind that before scripture was written, a prophet was the way God communicated His word to the people. One requirement of a prophet in the scriptures is that they must be 100% accurate. Anything short of that would create confusion and make it impossible to know what word was true and what was false. Balak's reasoning was that if a prophet of God cursed Israel, it would have to come to pass. Being a superstitious pagan, he thought the power was in the words themselves.

The king of Moab sent messengers to Balaam to hire him for the job. As he journeyed to the land of Moab, God sent an angel with a drawn sword to stand before the prophet. This is where we see the story of Balaam and the angel speaking through his donkey.

The donkey he rode suddenly stopped and refused to go forward. He began beating his donkey as his rage grew and the angel first spoke through his donkey, and then opened his eyes. When the angel was revealed, Balaam saw him standing on the path where the donkey wouldn't walk. A sword was drawn and pointed at the rebellious prophet. The message was loud and clear. If Balaam attempted to speak anything other than what God spoke to him, the prophet would be struck down before the words left his mouth.

The reason wasn't that Balaams words meant anything. It was because a false prophecy would cast doubt on the previous words spoken through the prophet.

Three times the king of Moab took the prophet to a place in the mountain where he could see and curse the people of God. Three times the Lord put a blessing in the mouth of the prophet. Enraged, King Balak said, "I would have given you all these treasures, but you keep blessing my enemy and not cursing them."

Balaam answered, "The Lord has blessed them, and I cannot reverse it."

The same is true for you. If the Lord has blessed you, not a force on earth can reverse it. The only thing Satan can do is lure you out of God's will and tempt you into sin. But that requires your willing participation.

Our Spiritual Battle

We are called warriors, but not against people. We battle against spiritual wickedness in high places. Many times the Bible uses soldiers as a word picture of the Christian striving to overcome in this life. Some misunderstand this to mean that Christians are called to be militant; however, the Bible explains it differently. Look at **2 Corinthians 10:3-6**

3 For though we walk in the flesh, we do not war according to the flesh.

4 For the weapons of our warfare *are* not carnal but mighty in God for pulling down strongholds,

5 casting down arguments and every high thing that exalts itself against the knowledge of God, bringing every thought into captivity to the obedience of Christ,

6 and being ready to punish all disobedience when your obedience is fulfilled.

Our battle is not against carnal things (things of the flesh), but against spiritual wickedness. Occasionally, someone will make the news by committing an act of violence in the name of God. Someone will take a phrase from scripture and use it as justification for their actions. The Bible warns us that the heart of man is deceitful and desperately wicked, and that only God can search the hearts, try our motives, and reveal to us the right ways.[159]

Everything in spiritual warfare and being a soldier of Christ is founded upon the statement, "Our weapons are not carnal / physical." We are also called pilgrims and sojourners, traveling through a land that is not our own as we journey toward our eternal home. It is not the Christian's job to set up God's kingdom in the world. We are not called to transform the world, but to be transformed out of the world.

Our shining light will have an impact on the culture. We are called salt and light. Salt adds flavor and preserves, and light dispels darkness. When the church is faithful to God's call, the Bible promises that He will raise up leaders and He will heal our land. We are not called to force the gospel down the throats of the culture. Nor are we called to take up arms and force others to conform to the standard of the gospel. We are called out of the world and then sent to call others out of the world. This is where the battle rages. We will be attacked when we take our light into a dark culture, but our light will also have a dramatic effect on the culture around us.

Each time we see this battle explained, it is always to endure and remain separate. According to Jesus, the world will not turn to Christ. Our battle is to go behind enemy lines and lead those being called by God out of the world and into the church. This is what evangelism is all about.

Some falsely believe that Jesus can't return until we reclaim the world for the Kingdom of God – as though God were dependent upon man. However, according to scripture, Jesus returns after there is first a falling away from the faith, and then the man of sin is revealed.[160]

We shouldn't expect the culture to conform to the gospel. We should expect the culture to battle against the gospel as we draw individuals out of the darkness. Consider the words of Jesus in **John 15:18-21**

---

[159] Jeremiah 17:9-10
[160] 2 Thessalonians 2:3-4

[18] If the world hates you, you know that it hated Me before *it hated* you.
[19] "If you were of the world, the world would love its own. Yet because you are not of the world, but I chose you out of the world, therefore the world hates you.
[20] "Remember the word that I said to you, 'A servant is not greater than his master.' If they persecuted Me, they will also persecute you. If they kept My word, they will keep yours also.
[21] "But all these things they will do to you for My name's sake, because they do not know Him who sent Me.

Notice Jesus' words, "I called you out of the world." He later explains, "I am sending you into the world as sheep among wolves." Just as Jesus called His disciples out of the world, He also sends us, His disciples, into the world to issue that same call. And here is the call in **Matthew 7:13-14**
> [13] " Enter by the narrow gate; for wide *is* the gate and broad *is* the way that leads to destruction, and there are many who go in by it.
> [14] "Because narrow *is* the gate and difficult *is* the way which leads to life, and there are few who find it.

And **John 14:6**
> Jesus said to him, "I am the way, the truth, and the life. No one comes to the Father except through Me.

Jesus also said that he is the door and any who enter through Him will be saved and feed on the goodness of God.[161]

It's important to understand all of this so we can have the right foundation to understand spiritual warfare. Our goal is not to force the world to conform to the gospel. It is not to prepare the world for the coming of Christ. He is not dependent upon us; we are dependent upon Him. Since Jesus made it clear that the world cannot love Him, and the Bible says that the Day of the Lord will not come until there is first a falling away and the revelation of the man

---

[161] John 10:9

of sin, it is clear that our focus must be on something other than conquering the world for Jesus.

Spiritual warfare has two main focuses: standing firm, and walking in God's will. Let's first look at the stand. This is explained in detail in **Ephesians 6:11-18**

[11] Put on the whole armor of God, that you may be able to stand against the wiles of the devil.

[12] For we do not wrestle against flesh and blood, but against principalities, against powers, against the rulers of the darkness of this age, against spiritual *hosts* of wickedness in the heavenly *places.*

[13] Therefore take up the whole armor of God, that you may be able to withstand in the evil day, and having done all, to stand.

[14] Stand therefore, having girded your waist with truth, having put on the breastplate of righteousness,

[15] and having shod your feet with the preparation of the gospel of peace;

[16] above all, taking the shield of faith with which you will be able to quench all the fiery darts of the wicked one.

[17] And take the helmet of salvation, and the sword of the Spirit, which is the word of God;

[18] praying always with all prayer and supplication in the Spirit, being watchful to this end with all perseverance and supplication for all the saints --

Once again, it is reiterated that we don't wrestle against flesh and blood, physical things, but against spiritual forces that oppose God in our lives. There is spiritual wickedness, and it reigns in the lives of those who submit themselves wholly to the flesh. Even your enemies are not your focus. Everyone sees with human eyes, but only the Christian can see beyond the flesh and to the war for the hearts of man.

Let's stop for a moment and consider the rules of engagement. Most people have the idea that Satan and demons are running free without restraint and able to do great evil in the world. The truth is, their strength is played out through man's desires.

This is even true among those who claim to be followers of God. People do evil in the name of God all the time. Some religions condone violence. And who are drawn to those religions that claim God promotes killing and pillaging? Violent men are drawn to it because it gives them a license to sin and live for the desires of their hearts.

Part of spiritual warfare is identifying the deceptions that ensnare men's souls. Whether deception wraps itself in Christian sounding terms, calls itself by another religion, or claims to be anti-religious, it is still deception.

The devil can't force you do anything. You must be a willing participant. He appeals to human nature and the desires of the flesh. This is why the Christian is called to crucify the flesh with its passions and desires. Is there any example of man doing evil in the name of God without violating scripture? As we saw in an earlier chapter, taking a phrase or passage out of context doesn't reflect upon the Bible – it reflects on man's desire to justify himself. If anything, the evil that man does in the name of God or in the name of humanism proves the Bible's claim, "The heart of man is deceitful above all things and desperately wicked[162]."

Not only does Satan's deception require a willing participant, but his actions require the authority of God. Read the Old Testament book of Job. In it you see God putting Job to the test. Several times Satan came back in failure but said, "If you will remove your hedge around him, I can make Job curse you to your face."

This is important to understand. First, Satan and demonic forces have boundaries. They are completely subject to God. They reign freely within the domain God has provided, but they are *not* in rebellion against God's authority. Rebellion against God's ways, yes, but authority, no. The reason is that any spirit who opposes God will receive immediate judgment. They may hate God's authority, but they cannot rebel against it. Look at **2 Peter 2:4**

---

[162] Jeremiah 17:9-10

Spiritual Warfare

> For if God did not spare the angels who sinned, but cast *them* down to hell and delivered *them* into chains of darkness, to be reserved for judgment;

We know that all fallen angels are not chained. The Bible refers to them often and as we'll see in a moment, Jesus dealt with demons during His ministry. Remember how he gave His disciples authority? And they returned rejoicing and said, "Even the demons are subject to us in your name."

The passage in 2 Peter above is referring to an event at the fall of Satan. When a third of the angels fell, some were in rebellion against God's authority. These are already bound and awaiting judgment. The rest are unbound, but know that judgment is coming. Consider Jesus' encounter with two demon possessed men in **Matthew 8:28-29**

> [28] When He had come to the other side, to the country of the Gergesenes, there met Him two demon-possessed *men,* coming out of the tombs, exceedingly fierce, so that no one could pass that way.
>
> [29] And suddenly they cried out, saying, "What have we to do with You, Jesus, You Son of God? Have You come here to torment us before the time?"

These spirits recognized Christ, and take note of their comment, "Have You come here to torment us before the time?" If you read the rest of the account, these demons were subject to the word of Christ. They were not at all in rebellion. In fact, they begged Him to direct them toward a heard of swine rather than to be cast into the abyss.

I say all of this to point out that we should not fear evil. We should fear the consequences of submitting ourselves to evil. If we willfully sin, we are subjecting ourselves back into slavery to sin and have given Satan an advantage over us. But demons have no power over the Christian unless it is given to Satan from God. And there are only two reasons why God would give that authority. First, to test and refine us. Second, to judge our willful sins and turn us back to the eternal path.

An example of this is found in the life of a man within the Corinthian church who was having an incestuous relationship with his mother. Paul explains the role of Satan in this situation in **1 Corinthians 5:5**

> Deliver such a one to Satan for the destruction of the flesh, that his spirit may be saved in the day of the Lord Jesus.

Whether God is trying us, or judging our sins, in each case the goal is our good.

Preparing to Stand.

Let's go back to **Ephesians 6:13-17**

[13] Therefore take up the whole armor of God, that you may be able to withstand in the evil day, and having done all, to stand.

[14] Stand therefore, having girded your waist with truth, having put on the breastplate of righteousness,

[15] and having shod your feet with the preparation of the gospel of peace;

[16] above all, taking the shield of faith with which you will be able to quench all the fiery darts of the wicked one.

[17] And take the helmet of salvation, and the sword of the Spirit, which is the word of God;

Spiritual warfare requires preparation. The goal of putting on the armor is to stand. The evil day is the day of trial or temptation. It could be persecution, or hardship, or a strong temptation, or anything that would normally send us into a tailspin.

The problem with spiritual warfare in the lives of most Christians is that they wait until trouble arises to look for answers. If a soldier sat idly or did his own thing until the enemy attacked, he would lose the battle. Can you imagine a frontline battalion falling under attack and then scrambling for their weapons, armor, boots, and battle plans? It would be a sure defeat. And this is why so many Christians are defeated in their lives and attitudes.

Let's look at the armor for a moment. When Paul wrote this, he was a prisoner in Rome after being arrested for his faith. Paul looked at the Roman soldier and realized their uniforms were a perfect illustration for the Christian.

The Romans revolutionized warfare. They successfully conquered nearly every nation they encountered, and their uniforms provided a battlefield advantage in every battle. It was light, allowed free movement, and adequate defense.

Belt of Truth. The belt held everything firmly in place. It was the centerpiece of the uniform and without it, nothing would remain in its proper position. Truth is the belt of the Christian's armor. If we don't understand truth and have it firmly established, nothing else will remain secure. Someone who doesn't understand truth is vulnerable in every area.

Breastplate of righteousness. Without righteousness, a believer's heart is under attack. Just as the Romans guarded their heart with a breastplate, we too must guard our hearts. The Bible says, guard your heart with all diligence, for out of it spring the issues of life.[163] We guard our hearts with righteousness, and righteousness begins with the mind. If we allow our thoughts to entertain sin, we are taking it into our hearts. We entertain thoughts of revenge, bitterness, lust, greed, covetousness, or anything else that finds its roots in the flesh. When we dwell on these things, we are taking them into our heart. Where our eyes look, our heart will follow. Where our heart looks, our lives will follow.

Have your feet shod with the preparation of the gospel of peace. The Romans broke every former rule when it came to footwear. Most armies of that era wore heavy leather boots or metal plating to protect their feet. It was a protection based on fear. Soldiers were afraid that if their feet were wounded, they wouldn't be able to run or fight.

---

[163] Proverbs 4:23

The Roman's philosophy was that if they were swift and powerful, the enemy would be on their heels and not in a position to attack their vulnerable feet. The foot was mostly exposed except for a strap that held the sole in place and wrapped around the ankle and up to the calf. It was held firmly in place and wouldn't slide off the foot.

The bottom was ribbed leather, and some had spikes like cleats protruding. This gave them extra traction. In a battle, they would have a sure footing, and this gave them a superior advantage against their enemies. It's hard to push back someone whose feat won't slide, and it's hard to outmaneuver someone who is faster on their feet.

A Christian prepared in the gospel won't slide because they have a sure footing.

Shield of Faith. The Roman soldier also carried a small wooden shield, instead of the traditional heavy metal shield. In an attempt to use the wooden shields against them, opposing forces would shoot flaming arrows at the Romans. If the wood caught fire, they would have to discard it. The Romans solved this problem by soaking their shields in water before battles. Then the flaming arrows would be quenched and no harm done.

We have a shield of faith that also quenches the fiery darts of the devil. He shoots everything in his arsenal at the believer. Rather than being discouraged by his attacks, if we have taken up the shield of faith, the fire is quenched.

When someone stands upon faith, it's hard to get past that shield. People say discouraging words, and if our confidence is dependent upon praise or affirmation, we are wounded. But if we are secure in the Lord, we remain focused on our calling. Consider the words of scripture in **John 2:23-25**

23 Now when He was in Jerusalem at the Passover, during the feast, many believed in His name when they saw the signs which He did.

24 But Jesus did not commit Himself to them, because He knew all *men,*

^{25} and had no need that anyone should testify of man, for He knew what was in man.

This was Jesus' response to those who believed on Him. Even though they believed, Jesus still did not allow His sense of value to come from man. People are volatile. One misunderstanding or miscommunication and friends can become foes. There have been people I thought were gentle in spirit but turned out to be very vindictive. Of course the opposite is also true. Sometimes compassion comes from unexpected sources.

The point above is that Jesus knows the weakness of man. Though these believed on Him, human nature can get the best of people. And this can be a fiery dart at our lives. Those who remain focused on the Lord stand upon faith. This is true if the discouragement comes from people, jobs, health, or any other hardship.

Faith in God absorbs the blow and keeps us standing firm. When I believe the promise that God works all things for my good, I can stand firm even when I can't see the good that has yet to be revealed. If faith is in our circumstances, we will fall with anything that attacks the foundation we have built our lives upon. Christ is the only sure foundation. Anything else is vulnerable to attack.

The helmet of salvation. Without salvation, our mind and confidence is wide open to attack. The head is the most vulnerable place to attack. A good blow to the head ends the battle. Without salvation, we have no protection.

Sword of the Spirit. Finally, our only offensive weapon – the word of God. When Satan tempted Jesus in the wilderness, He defeated the trials with the word of God. "It is written," Jesus kept saying. When it comes to putting on the armor of God, the word is the way we confront problems and deception. Notice, it is called the Sword of the Spirit.

It's the work of the Spirit to accomplish the results of God's word going out. We are not beating people over the head with the Bible, but using the word to guide others toward the truth. We also use the word to parry off the deceptions that would normally mislead us into temptation. We are taking up the Bible for the purpose of the Spirit using the word of God to accomplish His will in our lives, and the lives of others.

Walking in the Battle.

The church is a collective body of believers who have become what the Bible calls, the body of Christ. Don't mistake 'a church' with 'the church.' If you are a disciple of Christ, you and I belong to the church. It isn't denominational. Nor does it require joining a membership. We join a local church in order to connect with like-minded believers. However, we are of the same body, regardless of which denomination or organization we belong to. Our only concern with local churches is that we find one that truly honors the word of God as the scripture teaches.

The church is an army of sojourners passing through a world that is not their own and toward a city, whose builder is God. We must understand two things when it comes to our personal battles in spiritual warfare. The battle is against your soul, and the battle is against your ministry.

Each person is a minister of Christ. That ministry is fulfilled by first taking our position in the body of Christ (the church) and then walking into our circle of influence in the world. Remember what we read in scriptures earlier? We are saved for good works which God prepared beforehand that we should walk in them[164].

When you are walking in the works God has equipped you to do, and called you to fulfill, expect warfare. I've been involved in many ministries over the years and I can always tell who is following God's call and who is in it for the wrong motives. When the road becomes difficult, any selfish motive will be made clear because people either fall away, or attempt to gain personal glory. A discouraged man or woman who is certain of their call will seek strength on their knees, but remain true to the calling.

When the early church was threatened, it was a great concern. The people making the threats had the ability to arrest the

---

[164] Ephesians 2:10

Christians, publicly beat them as punishment, and even put them to death. The church was warned severely not to speak in the name of Jesus or they would sufferer the consequences. Look at their response in **Acts 4:24-29**

[24] So when they heard that, they raised their voice to God with one accord and said: "Lord, You *are* God, who made heaven and earth and the sea, and all that is in them,

...

[29] "Now, Lord, look on their threats, and grant to Your servants that with all boldness they may speak Your word,

They pressed ahead with the knowledge of the consequences, but they did so under the power of God through prayer. This is what divides the called from those who's emotions stir them to action. If you know God has called you, there will be the confidence in spite of adversity. After all, we have the promise that if God is for us, who can be against us? No one.

The spirit of deception may stir up adversaries, but they cannot stand against the Lord. The church stands today in spite of the most powerful kingdom that has ever been on earth using its military to attempt to wipe Christianity from the Roman Empire. In the end, the empire was gone and the church stood. And the church did not fight back with swords and violence. They committed themselves to the will of God, come what may.

The same holds true for your personal walk of faith. Everyone has faith when things are going well, but let a struggle begin and our faith is revealed. Is our faith in our circumstances so that we are dependent upon things going our way, or are we dependent upon the Lord who is our strong foundation? Consider **1 Peter 2:11-12**

[11] Beloved, I beg *you* as sojourners and pilgrims, abstain from fleshly lusts which war against the soul,

[12] having your conduct honorable among the Gentiles, that when they speak against you as evildoers, they may, by *your* good works which they observe, glorify God in the day of visitation.

Temptation is part of that war. When we are trying to live a godly life, Satan will throw things our way. Many of these attacks will come wrapped as gifts. Some will strike right at our sinful desires. The goal of the devil is to either lead you off the path of righteousness, or drive you off that path. He will do so with personal discouragement, people, hardships, and even physical problems. The Bible's instructions are designed to keep you from falling for these traps. As Paul said, "We are not ignorant of his devices." Yet we are often overcome because we stand on the wrong foundation. It's impossible to stand without the empowerment of the Spirit of God and following His leading.

Don't be surprised when the world calls you evil. Jesus was called a deceiver and His apostles were called all manner of things. All were punished for the perceived threat against the people. Yet, on the day of visitation, God revealed truth to the very ones who persecuted them.

When I served in Germany, I met a Bible smuggler who worked throughout the Soviet bloc countries. This was in the 1980s, before the fall of the Soviet Union. He frequently met with underground churches and saw firsthand many of those who had been persecuted for Christ. One church was led in worship by a piano player with gnarled fingers. In an attempt to thwart worship, her interrogators broke all her fingers. But they couldn't break her heart of worship.

The pastor was also arrested several times. In an attempt to solve 'the problem', the preacher was put into a cell with two men deemed to be the worst of the criminal population. When the guard brought in the two violent offenders, he said, "Have your way with him. No questions asked."

The next morning the two men were listening intently to the pastor as he taught the two new Christians. Never try to guess what God is doing, and never underestimate His ability to use our faithfulness in the most impossible circumstances. Whether in persecution or in victory, look toward the finish line, where our calling ends and eternal life begins.

God is calling us to go where no man can go, and to accomplish what no man can accomplish. Yet we can do all these things through Christ who strengthens us.

The Bible says, "I can do all things through Christ who strengthens me," but many misunderstand this passage. It is not saying that Christ goes through me to give strength to do my own thing. I am going through Christ to find strength. I must be going where Christ is going, not asking Him to go where I'm going. There is a difference.

We are called to endure hardships as a soldier. Part of endurance is staying on the path of God's calling. When we step out of God's will, we are often entangled. These are deceptions with the underlying goal to war against our soul and recapture our minds. If our soul is led out of righteousness, the battle is over. That is, until we repent, reach up for God to rescue us from the mire, and set us back onto our secure foundation.

Spiritual warfare is not running from shadows and being afraid of curses, objects, and the devil. Nor do we look for demons behind every tree. In fact, the focus is not on the enemy at all. Our focus must be on the goal.

We don't prepare for the war by studying demons or false religions. We prepare by studying the truth and preparing ourselves with the things God has given us. We strive to be established in the faith, bind truth around our lives, walk in righteousness, be prepared with the gospel, and have a firm hold on the sword of the Spirit – God's word.

The goal of the enemy is to disarm us by luring us away from the armor, and dabbling in things that will bind us. Sometimes in competition, an opponent tries to get an advantage by provoking the other to anger. The goal is to distract them from the game plan so they lose their cool and make a mistake.

The enemy will do anything to lure you out of your firm stance and away from the path of victory. This takes us back to the renewing of our minds. Life is filled with frustrations and temptations. In time, these things will wear us down and make us vulnerable. But those who are renewed in the Lord are the ones who find new strength and rise like eagles over the sins that once easily ensnared them.

This won't just happen. You must follow the scripture's instructions. The battle is not won during the time when we wrestle, but it's won now. It's the time of preparation and renewal that you put on the armor and do all to stand.

When we feel unchallenged, we tend to become idle and forget to seek the Lord. But make it a discipline in your life to seek even when the passion seems to be absent. The enemy waits to attack, and like any formidable opponent, he won't strike when you're hunkered down, but instead will hit when you aren't expecting it.

Though it may seem like people are the problem, the truth is that people are tools in the hand of the enemy. Even you and I can be a tool of discouragement if we don't guard against it. Most of the time it's unintentional, and we don't even realize we have offended. Misconceptions can be just as destructive as an assault.

The real enemy isn't seen with human eyes. We wrestle not against flesh and blood, but against spiritual powers in high places. Human nature is putty in Satan's hands. Therefore, we must not allow ourselves to be manipulated by lusts that war against the soul. That includes anger, bitterness, temptations, or anything that appeals to the flesh.

Don't fear Satan, but be aware of his devices. Don't focus on the devil or evil, but focus on first fulfilling obedience in your own life and *only then* will you be able to avenge disobedience.

Avenging disobedience doesn't mean retaliating. The first principle in Spiritual warfare is always to evaluate our focus. The war is not in the flesh, but in the Spirit. The flesh can't be overcome by fighting against the flesh. We avenge disobedience by following our calling into enemy territory, and leading others out of disobedience and into truth.

There's no greater blow to the enemy than to set one of his prisoners free.

When you hear the topic come up about spiritual warfare, victory over the enemy should be your first thought. We don't fear the enemy because we stand upon the promise, "Greater is He who is in you than he that is in the world. "[165] Victory is in submission and the battle is the Lord's. The Bible tells us that deliverance is of the Lord, not by the strength of our weapons, and His name is the strong tower where we run to find safety.

Only the righteous has the promise that God prepares a table before us in the presence of our enemies.[166] God has the power to refresh us and provide rest in any circumstance. Only He has the peace that goes beyond human comprehension.

Never fear evil. Be on guard, be diligent, be prepared, but do not be afraid. Satan has no power over the life of those who belong to God. No man can curse you. No object can bring evil into your life without your submission to it. Only sin in your life can take you out of God's perfect will. Let's conclude with this passage from **Proverbs 3:33**

The curse of the LORD *is* on the house of the wicked, But He blesses the home of the just.

No man, ritual, or spiritual power can change this truth. The curse is of the Lord and rests upon the wicked. The same call that went out to the people of Moses' day goes out today. "I set before you a blessing or a curse. Choose righteousness and live." If you live in God's justice, His favor cannot be overthrown by Satan.

---

[165] 1 John 4:4
[166] Psalm 23:5

Power of Words

In most New Age and Eastern religions, there is an emphasis on the power of words. It has also been a part of pagan religions for thousands of years. However, as Christians, we must take care to discover truth from the scriptures rather than overlaying worldly philosophies or even our own ideas on top of scripture. Misconceptions become commonly held beliefs when our ideas are mingled with the word of God.

The word is pure. Mixing anything with purity creates impurity. For this reason, we must carefully examine what we believe or what we are being taught to see if an idea is drawn from scripture, or if the idea is presented with scripter and cleverly crafted with an explanation that implies it is a scriptural teaching. Even a sincere Christian can present a clever but false belief, if that is what they have been taught and believe it to be true. This very much applies to the teachings on our words.

Occasionally, Eastern philosophies will seep into the church and be mixed with Christian sounding terms, and will even take certain passages out of context to support the claim that the Bible teaches these things.

As we have seen, the Bible warns us to test the spirits to see if they are from God, for many false prophets have gone out. A false prophet is someone who claims to speak on God's behalf. A book that was introduced in several local churches in my area has the following statement:

God created the universe by speaking it into existence. Seven times He said, "Let there be..." and there was! This *ability to speak things into existence is how we are like God.*

How does this match up with passages like **1 Corinthians 4:20**? For the kingdom of God *is* not in word but in power.

Does God give us, the individual Christian, the power to create? Are we like God? If we master the spoken word will we be able to speak things into existence and be like the Most High? The lie that deceived Adam and Eve was the promise, "You will be like God." The fall of Satan came through the confession of his mouth, "I will be like the Most High." When man tries to usurp power or authority that belongs only to God, consequences follow.

The Bible gives us unmistakably clear instructions on how we use words, what power words carry and how we apply this understanding to our individual lives. Words are very significant and we'll look at how the Bible addresses this later in this section. But first, let's look at the meaning of words.

Do Words Contain Power?

A doctrine that is rapidly growing in popularity is that words are containers that we either fill with positive energy through speaking positively or words carry negative energy that will fulfill our negative confessions. This has been taught in New Age and mystical circles for thousands of years, but recently has been modified to make it palatable to Christians. Instead of using 'positive energy' or similar terms, New Age beliefs in the church substitute in the words like 'faith', 'fear', and 'doubt' as the substances that fill word containers.

Misconceptions of the power of words have led many people into the realm of superstition and fear. Many people live in fear thinking that they have created negative circumstances by a slip of the tongue. Others have bought into the original lie Satan used to tempt Eve into rebellion by claiming, 'You will be like God'.

There are scriptures that address the power of our words, which we will look into as we go through this chapter, but first we will look at the misconceptions about the power of words that find their origins in religions that are contrary to scripture. Not one passage of scripture teaches or implies that words are containers. Nor does the Bible teach that our words change reality. On the other hand, there are many scriptures that refute this concept expressly. One of the clearest examples is found in **1 Thessalonians 5:3-4**

> [3] For when they say, "Peace and safety!" then sudden destruction comes upon them, as labor pains upon a

pregnant woman. And they shall not escape.

[4] But you, brethren, are not in darkness, so that this Day should overtake you as a thief.

Notice the confession of their mouths, "Peace and safety", but what was created? Nothing, for sudden destruction came upon them. This scripture is speaking of the end times when the church has departed from the Lord, and the Day of Judgment has come. The false prophets will be speaking good words and comforting those who are in rebellion against God. As we saw earlier, we are blessed if we obey, and cursed if we disobey the commandments of God – regardless of the words we speak. We can say all the positive words we want, but if we are living contrary to God's word, our positive words mean nothing.

The proclamation of peace, safety, and prosperity does not bring these things. Blessings come from the Lord as a fulfillment of His promises to those who obey Him. Misconceptions arise because people forget that all things come from the hand of God. We can't look out to the universe for power, nor our own words. Both are forms of idolatry for they are replacing God with something created.

Let's take a few moments to look at some examples that are wrongly used to teach that the Bible promotes the belief in the power of our spoken words. You may encounter these misunderstood examples, so it's important to know what is actually being taught in scripture.

The Blessing of Balaam.

The story of Balaam is found in Numbers chapter 22. In the last chapter we touched on this story. It's the time when the King of Moab hired Balaam to curse Israel, hoping they could be defeated. Three times the prophet blessed the nation he was hired to curse.

It is sometimes taught that this is proof that our words have power; however, there is much more to this than the power of Balaam's words. Failed prophecies only prove that a man has spoken presumptuously in the name of the Lord. God strongly condemns that prophet, and warns the people not to listen to any of his words. For this reason, God could not allow Balaam to make a false proclamation over Israel. A curse could not come to pass; therefore, God protected His previously spoken words through Balaam by sending an angel to warn him not to speak anything but what God commanded.

His lying words would have thrown confusion on what God previously said through this prophet. The curse would have done nothing to Israel, for it would have been a lie. But it would have polluted the words God had already given the prophet.

Balaam had no power to curse for God had already blessed. When King Balak was enraged because Balaam could not curse, the old prophet explains why in **Numbers 23:**

> [20] Behold, I have received *a command* to bless; He has blessed, and I cannot reverse it.

God has blessed and Balaam could not reverse it. This should give the Christian great confidence, for no man, spirit or even Satan himself can curse you if God has blessed. God has indeed blessed us as long as we stand in agreement with God's word. The same was true for Israel. They were blessed in their obedience but cursed when they disobeyed. Both the blessing and the curse are seen in this account. First consider **Numbers 24:10**

> Then Balak's anger was aroused against Balaam, and he struck his hands together; and Balak said to Balaam, "I called you to curse my enemies, and look, you have bountifully blessed *them* these three times!

Let's follow the chain of events here to gain an understanding of this subject. God first blessed Israel as He sent them to enter into the Promised Land. Balak was unable to curse them so he hired Balaam to curse them in the name of the Lord. God put a blessing in the mouth of Balaam and he pronounced three blessings upon Israel.

Since the doctrine of 'power words' or 'word of faith' claims that what we say must be fulfilled, the next thing that should have happened to Israel should be for them to inherit the blessing – right? Wrong. Immediately after Balaam blessed Israel, the very next verse unfolds a dramatic turn of events. Look at **Numbers 25:1-3**

> [1] Now Israel remained in Acacia Grove, and the people began to commit harlotry with the women of Moab.
>
> [2] They invited the people to the sacrifices of their gods, and the people ate and bowed down to their gods.
>
> [3] So Israel was joined to Baal of Peor, and the anger of the LORD was aroused against Israel.

Baal of Peor was the idol the Moabites worshiped. King Balak sent his most beautiful women to seduce the men of Israel and invite them to the sacrifices of their gods – statues created by their own hands.

If words create reality, or blessings come by the profession of man's lips, Israel should have been blessed after the three blessings that came directly from the word of the Lord, but this is not what happened. A plague was sent into the camp and 24,000 people died because of the judgment of the Lord. The plague was not removed until those who sinned were judged and slain for their idolatry, and the people repented and returned to the Lord.

So you can see that the blessing was not created by the words of Balaam, but by the obedience of God's people, for God said from the beginning that they would be blessed if they obeyed all that God commanded and cursed if they disobeyed.

Balaam could not curse the people but he showed King Balak how to make the people curse themselves – by sinning against God[167]. Balaam taught Balak that if he seduced the people with the Moabite women so that they were drawn out of God's will, they would no longer be walking in God's blessing. The power of the blessing or curse is not in the power of words, but in our obedience to God which puts us in His will so that we inherit His promises.

The message hasn't changed since the beginning; if we walk in obedience, we will inherit the promises and God's blessings, but if we rebel against God's command we are cursed by our own sins.

---

[167] Revelation 2:14

The Blessing of Zedekiah.

In the previous example, we looked at a blessing that was overthrown by sin. Now let's look at an example of four-hundred prophets, led by Zedekiah, proclaiming prosperity.

Let me give a little background. Ahab, the King of Israel, was a very wicked ruler. He refused to turn from his sins and even had his neighbor murdered so he could possess his property.

Ahab decided to go to war with a neighboring nation that had taken some land during a previous war, and try to reclaim it. He joined forces with the king of Judah and prepared for battle. As was the tradition, the two kings called prophets together to inquire of the Lord to see if they would be blessed in their war efforts. Four hundred prophets proclaimed prosperity in the name of the Lord, but the king of Israel recognized that none were truly prophets of God. He requested that a reputable prophet be called, so they sent for Micaiah. This is where we are picking up on the story. It's a lengthy passage, but a very interesting read. Look at this account in **1 Kings 22:10-28**

> [10] The king of Israel and Jehoshaphat the king of Judah, having put on *their* robes, sat each on his throne, at a threshing floor at the entrance of the gate of Samaria; and all the prophets prophesied before them.
>
> [11] Now Zedekiah the son of Chenaanah had made horns of iron for himself; and he said, "Thus says the LORD: 'With these you shall gore the Syrians until they are destroyed.' "
>
> [12] And all the prophets prophesied so, saying, "Go up to Ramoth Gilead and prosper, for the LORD will deliver *it* into the king's hand."
>
> [13] Then the messenger who had gone to call Micaiah spoke to him, saying, "Now listen, the words of the prophets with one accord encourage the king. Please, let your word be like the word of one of them, and speak encouragement."
>
> [14] And Micaiah said, "*As* the LORD lives, whatever the LORD says to me, that I will speak."
>
> ...
>
> [19] Then *Micaiah* said, "Therefore hear the word of the

LORD: I saw the LORD sitting on His throne, and all the host of heaven standing by, on His right hand and on His left.

[20] "And the LORD said, 'Who will persuade Ahab to go up, that he may fall at Ramoth Gilead?' So one spoke in this manner, and another spoke in that manner.

[21] "Then a spirit came forward and stood before the LORD, and said, 'I will persuade him.'

[22] "The LORD said to him, 'In what way?' So he said, 'I will go out and be a lying spirit in the mouth of all his prophets.' And the LORD said, 'You shall persuade *him,* and also prevail. Go out and do so.'

[23] "Therefore look! The LORD has put a lying spirit in the mouth of all these prophets of yours, and the LORD has declared disaster against you."

[24] Now Zedekiah the son of Chenaanah went near and struck Micaiah on the cheek, and said, "Which way did the spirit from the LORD go from me to speak to you?"

[25] And Micaiah said, "Indeed, you shall see on that day when you go into an inner chamber to hide!"

[26] So the king of Israel said, "Take Micaiah, and return him to Amon the governor of the city and to Joash the king's son;

[27] "and say, 'Thus says the king: "Put this *fellow* in prison, and feed him with bread of affliction and water of affliction, until I come in peace." ' "

[28] But Micaiah said, "If you ever return in peace, the LORD has not spoken by me." And he said, "Take heed, all you people!"

Whose word prevailed? The four-hundred prophets proclaiming in one accord: peace, safety and success? Did the unity of the prophets prevail by their positive confession and faith filled words? No, the word of the Lord spoken by one man proved to be true.

How could one man's word overcome the positive confessions of four-hundred? It couldn't. It does not matter what we proclaim to be true; it only matters what God proclaims to be true. Like any other form of idolatry, positive, faith filled words cannot prevail to produce good or bad. These words are merely the creation of man.

Ahab was judged because of his wickedness, and even the encouragement of the masses speaking in the name of the Lord could not change the judgment against him. He was cursed because he disobeyed God and even the blessings of four-hundred 'prophets' could not change the curse into a blessing. So you can see that when God blesses, no one can curse and when God curses, no one can bless.

God's word will stand and He has already revealed how we are blessed – the one who fears the Lord and walks in His ways will be blessed.

The Blessing of Hananiah.

I want to use one more example before we move on. This example is unique because a true prophet, Jeremiah, agreed with the words of a false prophet, but it did not make the words true.

Israel had continued in its descent away from the Lord. God warned the remaining cities of Israel that they must turn away from their idols or God would remove them from the land. Even until the end, God continued to promise that He would deliver Israel from the hand of Nebuchadnezzar if they would turn from their sins and return to the Lord. The people continued to turn to both Baal and the Queen of Heaven[168] for deliverance until finally God removed His protection and sent the armies of Babylon to overthrow the nation.

By this point in history, all of Israel has been captured and taken captive except the region of Judah. God proclaimed that He would overthrow the city and send them as captives to Babylon and as the cities around them fell, the people greatly feared. God sent Jeremiah to prophesy to the people, and God had him put a yoke around his neck to represent the bondage and servitude the people would experience when Babylon overthrew the city if they didn't

---

[168] Jeremiah 7:18-19, Jeremiah 44:17-30

answer His call to repent from idolatry. Soon those claiming to be prophets began to proclaim positive confessions for Israel. One of the strongest examples is found in **Jeremiah 28:1-4, 6**

> [1] And it happened in the same year, at the beginning of the reign of Zedekiah king of Judah, in the fourth year *and* in the fifth month, *that* Hananiah the son of Azur the prophet, who *was* from Gibeon, spoke to me in the house of the LORD in the presence of the priests and of all the people, saying,
>
> [2] "Thus speaks the LORD of hosts, the God of Israel, saying: 'I have broken the yoke of the king of Babylon.
>
> [3] 'Within two full years I will bring back to this place all the vessels of the LORD's house, that Nebuchadnezzar king of Babylon took away from this place and carried to Babylon.
>
> [4] 'And I will bring back to this place Jeconiah the son of Jehoiakim, king of Judah, with all the captives of Judah who went to Babylon,' says the LORD, 'for I will break the yoke of the king of Babylon.' "
>
> ...
>
> [6] and the prophet Jeremiah said, "Amen! The LORD do so; the LORD perform your words which you have prophesied, to bring back the vessels of the LORD's house and all who were carried away captive, from Babylon to this place.

Take notice that Zedekiah in this passage is not the same person in 1 Kings we just read. This is a common name and the Zedekiah in Kings is the son of Josiah. In this passage, Zedekiah, is the son of Chenaanah. Not the same person.

Here we see another prophet proclaims good news and deliverance, but is he contradicting the Lord?. Hananiah even went as far as to remove the yoke that God had commanded Jeremiah to wear. He broke it in pieces as he announced that the Lord had proclaimed deliverance from Babylon. Hananiah even went as far as to claim that all the people already taken captive would be freed, and all the gold and silver taken would be returned. The people rejoiced at this word and even Jeremiah said, "Amen" – or may it be so. Yet this contradicted the true word of the Lord. Look at **Jeremiah 28:12-17**

> [12] Now the word of the LORD came to Jeremiah, after Hananiah the prophet had broken the yoke from the neck of the prophet Jeremiah, saying,
>
> [13] "Go and tell Hananiah, saying, 'Thus says the LORD: "You have broken the yokes of wood, but you have made in their place yokes of iron."
> ...
>
> [15] Then the prophet Jeremiah said to Hananiah the prophet, "Hear now, Hananiah, the LORD has not sent you, but you make this people trust in a lie.
>
> [16] "Therefore thus says the LORD: 'Behold, I will cast you from the face of the earth. This year you shall die, because you have taught rebellion against the LORD.' "
>
> [17] So Hananiah the prophet died the same year in the seventh month.

In the book of Jeremiah there were countless prophets in Judah proclaiming good news, but they were all false proclamations. When God speaks, what has been said will come to pass. Two months after God foretold of Hananiah's death as judgment, he died. All the prophets and the people proclaimed peace, safety and prosperity, but none of their positive confessions changed the course of the future – Babylon still came.

Jeremiah wanted to believe this word to be true, because he wanted to see Israel return to the safety of God's protection, but his agreement didn't change the word of the Lord. In that culture, when someone said something you agreed with, you proclaimed, "Amen," which means, "May it be so." It's like saying, "I agree and hope your words are fulfilled."

There indeed was a way to escape judgment. God promised deliverance if the people would return to His word. Instead they chose to trust in their own ways, in the false prophets, and in the gods of the pagan culture around them.

Why trusting in words contradicts God.

Here is the problem with the positive confession doctrine. What is being taught is that our words can create a blessing, regardless of our obedience or spiritual condition. This dangerous doctrine teaches people that they can rebel against the commandments of God and live according to their own self-centered desires, and still be blessed if they proclaim good news and believe their own words. They become their own prophets and their own god. The same is true for the similar doctrine of so-called 'seeds of faith'.

I listened to a religious radio station that promised that seeds of faith planted into their 'ministry' would produce results in the donor's life. I listened to people call in and make donations so that God would give their children the supernatural ability to pass final exams; husbands and wives 'sowed' financial donations to improve their marriages; donations were given to gain success in business, and the promises go on and on.

Students are given false hope that they can pass a test without studying if they give God money through a radio station? Can a marriage be built by a financial donation without making any changes in their behaviors? Can we buy God off buy a donation regardless of our spiritual condition or obedience to His word? There is an example in the scriptures where the words 'money' and 'the gift of God' is used in the same statement. Look at **Acts 8:20-22**

> [20] But Peter said to him, "Your money perish with you, because you thought that the gift of God could be purchased with money!
> [21] "You have neither part nor portion in this matter, for your heart is not right in the sight of God.
> [22] "Repent therefore of this your wickedness, and pray God if perhaps the thought of your heart may be forgiven you.

The blessings of God cannot be bought with money or spoken into existence by our own mouths. Nothing spiritual can be created by human effort. Look again at Jesus' statement in **John 3:6**

> That which is born of the flesh is flesh, and that which is
> born of the Spirit is spirit.

Anything that has its origin in the flesh is flesh and cannot be of the Spirit. The flesh cannot produce the things of the Spirit. This is true for your words and for your works. Speaking words of faith cannot make God act, nor can sowing seeds by human works make God respond to our man-produced faith. This passage shows the results of the so-called seeds of faith sown by the superstitious belief that God must obey our will if a request / demand is made with money:

> **Galatians 6:8** For he who sows to his flesh will of the flesh
> reap corruption, but he who sows to the Spirit will of the
> Spirit reap everlasting life.

This passage is not telling us to sow money or possessions. Sowing in the Spirit is to invest your life in the Spirit. Jesus said that unless a grain of wheat falls into the ground and dies, it remains alone. But if it dies, it produces fruit.[169] Jesus then went on to say that when we love our life we lose it. Sowing in the Spirit is dying to yourself and living for the Lord.

Giving should be an act of surrender and trust. When I trust God with my finances, I will be willing to let go of money instead of hording it. Faithful giving is a reflection on my spiritual maturity – not something that produces spiritual maturity. We give because we see the value in funding ministries or meeting needs. Giving out of guilt or obligation, or as an attempt to manipulate God into giving us something in return, is an act of the flesh.

Fruit and the results of our efforts are not physical, but eternal things. Giving comes from the heart of a life surrendered to Christ. It is not how we become obedient to Christ. God may indeed give us good things in life, but these are not our reward. If they were, we would be shortchanged in heaven.

The true blessing is obeying through dying to the flesh and by walking in the Spirit. Anyone who walks in obedience by faith will be

---

[169] John 12:24

blessed even if the world curses. We obey out of faith – trusting God and believing His promises.

The Spirit of God works within us to draw us into obedience by faith, and we either obey and inherit the promises of God, or trust in the flesh and are outside of God's promises. Words do indeed have a role and in the next few sections we will examine the passages that teach us the real power of words.

The Power of the Word is the One Speaking.

While pagan beliefs trust in the power of the word itself, the Bible teaches that power is in the one speaking the word. The words themselves only have the power to convey meaning, but the authority behind the one speaking determines how, and if those words are carried out. Here is a wonderful example of this principle in **Matthew 8:5-10**

> [5] Now when Jesus had entered Capernaum, a centurion came to Him, pleading with Him,
>
> [6] saying, "Lord, my servant is lying at home paralyzed, dreadfully tormented."
>
> [7] And Jesus said to him, "I will come and heal him."
>
> [8] The centurion answered and said, "Lord, I am not worthy that You should come under my roof. But only speak a word, and my servant will be healed.
>
> [9] "For I also am a man under authority, having soldiers under me. And I say to this *one,* 'Go,' and he goes; and to another, 'Come,' and he comes; and to my servant, 'Do this,' and he does *it."*
>
> [10] When Jesus heard *it,* He marveled, and said to those who followed, "Assuredly, I say to you, I have not found such great faith, not even in Israel!

Jesus praised the centurion for his faith because he understood that Jesus had the power and the authority over all things. Jesus' authority gave Him the power to just give the command and it would be done. To explain his faith in Jesus' power, the centurion used the example of his own chain of command that gave him authority. He was a soldier under the Roman military, and his position gave him the authority to just say the word and those under him would do as he stated.

Since Jesus had the authority over everything, all Jesus had to do is say 'be healed' and it would be done. It was not the words themselves, but the power and authority of the one saying the words. The centurion's words 'go', 'come', and 'do this' did not make things happened through the mystical power of the word itself, but rather the authority of the man caused what was spoken to be done. His servant could say the exact same words and nothing would happen because he lacks the authority.

If it was the words themselves, the centurion could have just spoken the words with his own faith and healed his own servant. By Jesus' testimony, this man had more faith than any in Israel. Yet that faith didn't give power to the centurion.

The true authority was in Jesus and the centurion explained his complete faith in Christ. By Jesus' affirmation, no one had yet shown this much faith in Israel. This includes the disciples who had been given much authority already and had done wonders in Christ's name. The disciples succeeded because Jesus gave them the authority to do what He sent them to do. This centurion knew he had the authority to fulfill his role as a high ranking soldier, but didn't have the authority to heal. But he also knew Jesus did.

We can see how authority works in everyday life. Sometimes I hear my children bickering. One will order the other to do something, and she will say, "You can't tell me what to do." But if I say to go do something, they do it. I have the authority to instruct my kids, but they do not possess authority over each other – unless I give it to them. Even when I give the older children authority over the younger ones, I am the one who enforces that authority.

In the same way, we can say the exact same words as God and it has no power at all for we do not have the authority to back up our words. We can proclaim His authoritative word, but not our own. When people rebel, it is against His word, not our power. Consider this passage from **Luke 4:33-36**

³³ Now in the synagogue there was a man who had a spirit of an unclean demon. And he cried out with a loud voice,
³⁴ saying, "Let *us* alone! What have we to do with You, Jesus of Nazareth? Did You come to destroy us? I know who You are -- the Holy One of God!"
³⁵ But Jesus rebuked him, saying, "Be quiet, and come out of him!" And when the demon had thrown him in *their* midst, it came out of him and did not hurt him.
³⁶ Then they were all amazed and spoke among themselves, saying, "What a word this *is!* For with authority and power He commands the unclean spirits, and they come out."

Was it the words that had power according to this passage? No. Jesus spoke the word with authority and power. The apostles had the power given to them by God through the Holy Spirit to command demons to come out of those afflicted but when the Jews who did not have the God given power tried to do the same, they were unsuccessful.

Acts 19 tells the account of seven Jewish exorcists that tried to cast out a demon in the name of Jesus. They commanded the demon to come out in the name of Jesus, but the spirit mocked them by saying "Who are you?" The spirit then overcame them when the possessed man arose and beat these exorcists, so that they fled from the house naked and wounded.

Words themselves have no power; it is the authority of the one speaking that gives power to the word. Look at the source of the power of words as described in **Hebrews 1:1-3**

¹ God, who at various times and in various ways spoke in time past to the fathers by the prophets,
² has in these last days spoken to us by *His* Son, whom He has appointed heir of all things, through whom also He made the worlds;
³ who being the brightness of *His* glory and the express image of His person, and upholding all things by <u>the word of His power</u>, when He had by Himself purged our sins, sat down at the right hand of the Majesty on high,

It is not the word that holds the power to create the world and continue to uphold all things – it is His power. The word of Jesus' power is what has made all things and keeps them in order. If you take His power out of the word then the word has no power by itself. You can try to speak anything into existence, and nothing will happen. Even if you believe with all your heart, you could use the exact same words that God used in Genesis and nothing takes place.

We can have all the faith in the world and speak 'faith filled words' and nothing will happen because the power of your words cannot prosper without the word of His power. If the power is not in you, you cannot have the word of your power. Look at this passage from **Ecclesiastes 8:4**

Where the word of a king *is, there is* power; And who may say to him, "What are you doing?"

It doesn't say, 'where the word is, there is power'. The focus is on the king, for his word has authority behind it. Let a king speak the word and his subjects scramble. But let a subject speak the word under their own authority and see what happens. Without power, words mean nothing.

There is only one source of 'power words' that can be spoken. The word is God's **alone**. This can be given to the man appointed by God to proclaim God's word, but the authority still comes from the Lord. The power to create belongs to God alone. The word of His power is just that – His power. You will never have power like God; you will never be like God; you will never be a creator.

God has plainly stated that beside Him there is no other gods that have been formed nor will there be any after (Isaiah 43:10). Anyone who claims to be a god or even follows those claiming to be gods are called abominations to God (Isaiah 41:23-24). God alone has the word of power. In fact, all power and authority belongs to God. Consider these passages:

Psalm 62:11 God has spoken once, Twice I have heard this: That power *belongs* to God.

Romans 13:1 Let every soul be subject to the governing authorities. For there is no authority except from God, and the authorities that exist are appointed by God.

Matthew 28:18 And Jesus came and spoke to them, saying, "All authority has been given to Me in heaven and on earth.

The word of power belongs to God alone, but the authority that gives words their power belongs to God, and anyone God chooses to grant authority to. Even the Antichrist is given authority from God (Revelation 13:7).

The authority of the apostles were given by God for the purpose of building up the church (2 Corinthians 13:10), and the authority of the believer is given to us by Jesus Christ for the purpose of making disciples (Matthew 28:18-20). My words have power to accomplish what I say when I am in a position of authority that can back up those words.

There are many scriptures that reference the words of our mouths but not once do we see the Bible giving us the power of God with our words. We are never given the power to create or prophesy our own will into existence. Words have meaning, and the power to communicate is the only strength behind the word itself. Beyond that, we must have the authority to back up our command.

Let's take a few minutes to look at what our words accomplish.

Words Build or Destroy.

The real power of words is twofold. Words affect the hearts of the hearer, and words become the confession of our own heart. Let's first look at how it affects others.

Proverbs 18:21
Death and life *are* in the power of the tongue, And those who love it will eat its fruit.

This passage is frequently used by those who teach that we have the power to create with our words; however, this passage doesn't remotely imply that we are creating anything or speaking anything into existence. Let's look at this in light of **Proverbs 15:4**

A wholesome tongue *is* a tree of life, But perverseness in it breaks the spirit.

Let's also tie this into **Proverbs 12:18-19**

[18] There is one who speaks like the piercings of a sword, But the tongue of the wise *promotes* health.

[19] The truthful lip shall be established forever, But a lying tongue *is* but for a moment.

The message being communicated is that the words we say will either build up or tear down. Words cannot create prosperity or curses, other than the meaning behind the words. If I say harsh words or speak cutting words that wound those around me, my words destroy. Kids who grow up under parents that belittle or insult them, grow up with emotional wounds. These scars are carried into and throughout adulthood. Many adults struggle with damage caused by words which assaulted them in childhood.

Children also wound each other with cutting words as they mock those who are overweight, unattractive, or have a physical problem. These words cut deeply and cause others to die inside. Each of us should be diligent to guard our words, and then speak out when we see others being wounded with words. The old saying, "Sticks and stones may break my bones, but words will never hurt me," is false. A broken bone heals, but the wounds **from words** sometimes last a lifetime.

Words that encourage and build up another person gives new life and vigor to them. A seminary professor told the story of a classroom experiment that illustrates this well. Two students were scheduled to deliver a fifteen minute message for the class to evaluate. Unknown to the two students, the class had been instructed to give encouragement to the first student and discouragement to the second, in order to illustrate how we can affect others by our non-verbal communication.

The first student delivered his message and the class smiled, nodded, took notes, said, "amen", and showed him great support. By the end of his message he was fired up and preaching with great confidence. When the second preached, they frowned, looked at their watches, drifted to sleep and looked either annoyed or bored. The second student struggled to deliver his message and then stepped down from the podium in shame. The young man fought back tears as he scurried to his desk. Only then was he informed about the experiment.

Our actions are unspoken words, and can also be just as harmful. A roll of the eyes, angry stare, and even a look that says, "You're so stupid," can cause just as much damage as words. These also break down or give life. The truth is that the experiment above will have consequences. Even after finding out the scene was staged, the scorned student will fight through insecurities until he finds enough success to overcome the failure.

What's true for body language is true for words – and even more so. If we say cruel or harsh words, we break the spirit of others with the words of death from our tongue. If we build up another with words of encouragement, our tongue is a tree of life to that person. Consider this passage from **Matthew 5:22**

But I say to you that whoever is angry with his brother without a cause shall be in danger of the judgment. And whoever says to his brother, 'Raca!' shall be in danger of the council. But whoever says, 'You fool!' shall be in danger of hell fire.

Let's consider what is being taught through this illustration Jesus gave. It is not identifying someone's action as foolish that is being condemned, for Jesus often referred to those who disobeyed the truth as fools. It is not the word fool that puts us in danger of judgment. Look at the entire message of this verse. The word 'Raca' means, "You are an empty headed person, or someone without sense". So when we look at the three problems being addressed here it is clear that this is the process of tearing someone down.

To be angry without a cause is to degrade someone and to despise them as we imply their lack of human value. We've all seen this. Someone just doesn't like another person, and they show anger without any real reason.

Having a critical spirit toward someone is also being angry without a cause. To call someone Raca, or a fool, is to devalue that person. To mock someone, make fun of them, use bitter sarcasm, or express a critical spirit toward another is also devaluing and I believe falls under the condemnation of this passage.

We often do this to our spouses and other family members and do not recognize the harm we are causing that person, and the displeasure God has expressed against our behavior. None of the things stated in this passage are addressing someone's misbehavior or foolish choices, but instead is devaluing someone as you tear them down. You can be in danger of God's warning of judgment without using the word 'fool' if you are wounding someone's spirit with other words that communicate the same meaning.

To criticize for the purpose of correcting and building up in the right way is not condemned. Though it can be if our criticism is bitter and degrading. It is the destruction of another that God is judging. This is explained further in these two passages from 1 John:

1 John 3:14-15

[14] We know that we have passed from death to life, because we love the brethren. He who does not love *his* brother abides in death.

[15] Whoever hates his brother is a murderer, and you know that no murderer has eternal life abiding in him.

1 John 4:20-21

[20] If someone says, "I love God," and hates his brother, he is a liar; for he who does not love his brother whom he has seen, how can he love God whom he has not seen?

[21] And this commandment we have from Him: that he who loves God *must* love his brother also.

Our tongue reveals whether we are in life or death, just as Proverbs states. If we tear down those around us, we are not walking in the love of God, and indeed can't claim to be in the love of God. The power of the tongue is to build up or destroy others.

We are commanded to build up and are also commanded not to destroy. This holds true for our spouse, children, church members, and anyone we encounter in life. If we do not bring our words under guard, we are the cause of our own woes, as well as being responsible for how our words affect others. This is explained in **Proverbs 21:23**

Whoever guards his mouth and tongue keeps his soul from troubles.

The words of our mouth are tools to build up and tear down. These also produce what we sow. There is a produce of our words, but it isn't what we are creating, it is what we are nurturing and bringing to maturity in us. In Galatians 6:7-9, the Bible says that our sins or good works will produce fruit of either righteousness or death. This also applies to our words. They are the works of righteousness or the sins of the flesh. How we live out our life through our words determines what fruit we bear.

The Fruit of our Lips.

Before leaving the topic of the power of words, I would like to look at one more passage that is misunderstood and some use mistakenly to teach that we create with our words. Look at **Proverbs 18:20**

A man's stomach shall be satisfied from the fruit of his mouth, *From* the produce of his lips he shall be filled.

Again take note of the fact that this passage does not claim that you are creating anything with the words you speak. So what is the produce of our lips? When you are interviewing for a job, what is the first thing the interviewer evaluates about you? It is your communication skills.

Each year when companies are surveyed by recruiters to find out what they like and dislike about potential employees, the number one issue for almost every company is communication skills. Lacking in these skills has been a complaint about the up and coming workforce for some time. High school and college students have been steadily losing the ability to communicate effectively for decades.

The book of Proverbs is filled with both spiritual advice and practical advice for daily living. What you speak with your mouth reveals both what is in your heart and what is in your mind. With your mouth you build up relationships or tear down the channels of communication. Those who express themselves wisely will benefit from the words of their mouth. This is explained further in these passages in Proverbs:

Proverbs 22:11
He who loves purity of heart *And has* grace on his lips, The king *will be* his friend.

Proverbs 20:15
There is gold and a multitude of rubies, But the lips of knowledge *are* a precious jewel.

The spiritual condition of your heart will come out in your mouth. If you are walking in God's wisdom, this will affect the way you live and the way you speak. Through wisdom, God has promised to bless, honor, and prosper our lives. If you have wisdom, it will always come out in your speech, and those who live by the wisdom of scripture will be rewarded with the promises of God. Those who truly have godly wisdom will speak what is right and will eat the fruit of their words that are based on wisdom.

As is the case with every spiritual gift, this comes directly from God and not from our intellect or human understanding. This is beautifully explained in **Proverbs 2:6-9**

⁶ For the LORD gives wisdom; From His mouth *come* knowledge and understanding;
⁷ He stores up sound wisdom for the upright; *He is* a shield to those who walk uprightly;

^{8} He guards the paths of justice, And preserves the way of His saints.
^{9} Then you will understand righteousness and justice, Equity *and* every good path.

When we discuss wisdom, it is the wisdom God gives to us. It is a gift of God that we must receive and live by. I encourage you to read the entire chapter of Proverbs 2. It begins with receiving God's word, treasuring it in our heart, and then seeking to understand it by crying out to the Lord for the power to discern the truth – as we continue to seek it.

Once again, it isn't you attaining a higher level, but it is you humbling yourself in obedience knowing that God will answer. He steps into your life of faithfulness and imparts His wisdom, understanding, and knowledge of holy things into your heart.

The tongue of the wise uses knowledge rightly, but the mouth of fools pours out foolishness.[170] Whenever the Bible speaks of being 'wise' or 'having wisdom', it is always in reference to the wisdom of God. There is a worldly wisdom that is foolishness with God, but the wisdom we are talking about is the wisdom given by the Spirit of God through the instruction of scripture.

As you can see, when the Bible speaks of the fruit of your lips, it isn't your power to create or alter reality. It is a call to measure your words carefully, for you will eat the produce of your words, both good and bad. Your words testify to the focus of your life and the types of works ruling your heart.

Words justify or words condemn.

As mentioned earlier, words are the confession of our heart. Words communicate our understanding of truth, and testify for or against us. Consider this passage from **Matthew 12:36-37**
^{36} "But I say to you that for every idle word men may speak, they will give account of it in the day of judgment.

---

[170] Proverbs 15:2

Power of Words

³⁷ "For by your words you will be justified, and by your words you will be condemned."

According to Jesus, the words we speak will be brought into account when we all stand before the judgment seat of Christ, for our words reveal what is in our heart. Our words testify to our knowledge of right and wrong, but they also testify to our faith. Consider this passage from **Romans 10:9-11**

⁹ If you confess with your mouth the Lord Jesus and believe in your heart that God has raised Him from the dead, you will be saved.

¹⁰ For with the heart one believes unto righteousness, and with the mouth confession is made unto salvation.

¹¹ For the Scripture says, "Whoever believes on Him will not be put to shame."

Do the words we say save us? No, this passage doesn't say this. We believe and then confess with our mouth. Not just mere belief as in head knowledge, but belief unto righteousness. It's a transforming faith that we then confess with our mouth. It's the testimony that we believe on Jesus Christ, and the message of the gospel. Saying a prayer does not save anyone, for if we don't believe, it is not a confession.

Anyone can say a sinner's prayer but their life is not changed until someone first believes in their heart, repents of their sins and then confesses Jesus as Lord as a profession of their submission to God's call to their heart.

I said a sinner's prayer when I was a child because I was told that if I said it, I would go to heaven. It wasn't until I heard the message of the gospel many years later that I recognized the truth, heard God's call, and then answered that call. As a child, my words did nothing to change my life, for there was no call of God, and no surrender of my heart. Fellowship with God came many years later when the call was of God and I wasn't being manipulated into making my own confession.

An emotional message can stir a response, but until it's God's call in our hearts, any response remains the work of our own flesh and cannot redeem our souls. The words of our mouth justify only when our words testify that we have indeed surrendered to Jesus as Lord as an answer to His drawing. According to Jesus, no one can come to Him unless he is first drawn by the Father.[171] The Spirit proceeds from the Father to call into our hearts, draw us to Him, convict us of sin, and then transform us into a new creation.[172]

The power of salvation is not in the words of our mouth, but in Christ. The word of God calls us to salvation, and then we confess what God has revealed in our hearts through hearing the word.[173] We then confess in agreement with God, believing His word that Christ redeemed us from sin and salvation has come. My words are dependent upon the power of Christ. His Spirit calls me to salvation, proclaims my deliverance, and then I believe His word, knowing He has the authority to perform what He has promised. My confession is a testimony of faith, not the power to save myself through words.

Misunderstanding this is what causes people to fret over words, and believe that they must say the right prayer. Don't trust in the words, trust in Christ. Putting our trust in anything else is also idolatry. We don't put our faith in words, but in God.

To confess our sins is to agree with the word of God that our actions are wrong and that His word is right. Just as you cannot confess Christ without believing in His salvation and agreeing that He is Lord, you cannot confess your sins without agreeing that God's word is true and that you are forsaking your sins and turning away from them as you turn toward Him. Confessing always involves repentance – answering God's call to turn away from your ways. Look at **Psalm 12:3-4**

³ May the LORD cut off all flattering lips, *And* the tongue that speaks proud things,

---

[171] John 6:44
[172] John 15:26, Galatians 4:6, John 16:8, John 3:3-7, 2 Corinthians 5:17, 1 John 3:9
[173] Romans 10:17

[4] Who have said, "With our tongue we will prevail; Our lips *are* our own; Who *is* lord over us?"

Why does God criticize those who believe that the power of their words will cause them to prevail? Simply put, God resists the proud and gives grace to the humble. Wanting to create with the power of our own lips is rooted in the heart of pride. Human nature desires to be like God. And even over God. A proud heart says, "I have the power to prosper my own way," but the humble acknowledge their need. The humble look toward God for their deliverance and He blesses. Here is the truth about how we prevail: **Psalm 34:7-10**

[7] The angel of the LORD encamps all around those who fear Him, And delivers them.
[8] Oh, taste and see that the LORD *is* good; Blessed *is* the man *who* trusts in Him!
[9] Oh, fear the LORD, you His saints! *There is* no want to those who fear Him.
[10] The young lions lack and suffer hunger; But those who seek the LORD shall not lack any good *thing.*

Good doesn't come from our words, but from the hand of the Lord, to those who walk in His ways. True prosperity is found in surrender to God's will as we trust in His goodness.

How we walk in simple faith.

No book, tape series, or teaching can change your life. Any who claim their words have life-changing power are overstepping their role in teaching. An author or teacher can present the life-changing principles of the scripture, but readers and hearers must apply their hearts to the word, or it has no positive effect on them.

When the disciples came to Jesus to understand the deeper truths, he said, "Those who are on the outside have these things hidden from them, but to you who are within, these things are revealed."[174]

The only difference between those outside and those in the inner circle is the response of the individual's heart. Most people heard the message and walked away. They may have been inspired, intrigued, and even believed. But they walked away without seeking the meaning and how it applies to their life. The word is life-changing, but only when it is received by faith. Take **Hebrews 4:2** to heart:

> For indeed the gospel was preached to us as well as to them; but the word which they heard did not profit them, not being mixed with faith in those who heard *it.*

The word is applied by faith. Those who hear the word and then return to their everyday lives do not profit from the word. But those who receive it, take it to heart, and seek a deeper understanding so it can be applied to their lives, do indeed profit from the word.

You and I make the same choice each time we see or hear the word taught. Or when we read our own Bibles. We either walk away and go back to our status quo lives, or we seek a deeper understanding so we can live by the word and abide in Christ. There are many who spend their entire lives in church and hear the word each week, but never mature out of spiritual infancy. Most of us have been there, but none of us have to stay there. One of the

---

[174] Matthew 4:11-12

clearest pathways to spiritual maturity is found in **Proverbs 2:1-9.** We touched on this in the last chapter, but I want to take a moment to look at this in a fuller context:

> [1] My son, if you receive my words, And treasure my commands within you,
>
> [2] So that you incline your ear to wisdom, *And* apply your heart to understanding;
>
> [3] Yes, if you cry out for discernment, *And* lift up your voice for understanding,
>
> [4] If you seek her as silver, And search for her as *for* hidden treasures;
>
> [5] Then you will understand the fear of the LORD, And find the knowledge of God.
>
> [6] For the LORD gives wisdom; From His mouth *come* knowledge and understanding;
>
> [7] He stores up sound wisdom for the upright; *He is* a shield to those who walk uprightly;
>
> [8] He guards the paths of justice, And preserves the way of His saints.
>
> [9] Then you will understand righteousness and justice, Equity *and* every good path.

It begins with receiving the word, but it doesn't end there. Those who search and make it their life's effort to dig the treasures of truth from the word will find it. It doesn't take a seminary degree or theological training. These treasures are already yours and are awaiting you to dig deep enough to uncover them. Understanding comes from the Lord and is given to any who seek it as taught above. We seek in faith knowing the promise awaits, "Then you will understand righteousness, justice, equity, and every good path." Every good path. This isn't a superficial understanding, but a deep knowledge of God, His word, and His ways.

All the wisdom of the Lord is stored within the pages of scripture. God has hidden these treasures for the purpose of being found. Now you must go out and search for it as you cry out to God to reveal these things and provide discernment. God will answer.

This is the role of the Holy Spirit. The truths of the word are spiritually discerned and the Bible promises that the Holy Spirit will guide us into all truth[175]. Look at the amazing promise of **Psalm 119:98-100**

> [98] You, through Your commandments, make me wiser than my enemies; For they *are* ever with me.
> [99] I have more understanding than all my teachers, For Your testimonies *are* my meditation.
> [100] I understand more than the ancients, Because I keep Your precepts.

Though the Bible appoints teachers in the church for the purpose of equipping the saints for ministry,[176] we are not dependent upon a teacher to understand truth. Nor does our understanding stop with the lesson taught. Some teach that a believer can't grow beyond the level of a spiritual leader, but this is not what the Bible teaches. Teachers are gifted by God to equip the saints so they too can learn to walk on their own spiritual feet. Every teacher's goal should be to make a disciple non-dependent.

This passage affirms this truth. If you and I follow the commands of scripture, our understanding will exceed that of our teachers. The reason is because the Spirit teaches through the word, and any who dedicate themselves to the word will find understanding. Teachers are limited in understanding; the Holy Spirit is not. If spiritual leaders are our source, we are limited to their understanding. If we look to the Spirit, God's understanding is inexhaustible, and so is the depths of what He desires to reveal to you.

It's not just studying the word. Look at the secret of King David's success. He applied the commandments of scripture and found wisdom above his enemies. He was king during a time when Israel was struggling to become a nation. Many adversaries sought to overthrow David, but none succeeded, for the Lord was his keeper.

---

[175] John 16:13, 1 Corinthians 2:14
[176] Ephesians 4:11-16

How we walk in simple faith

He understood more than the ancients – those who passed down the word and were used by God to proclaim the word. How did David gain more understanding than his teachers? He meditated on the word and sought understanding. King David didn't just read the word or hear it and walk away. He didn't stop at a morning devotional. This man sought understanding and meditated on the word. After reading, he rolled it over in his mind, studied it, sought for understanding, and then applied what he learned to his life. Therefore, God gave him great wisdom and understanding.

The gift of teaching plays an important role in the church. God intended this gift to be for equipping the saints for ministry.[177] Part of that ministry is discipleship. Each of us should be equipping fellow believers so that they learn how to seek the Lord. We don't seek the teacher's understanding. We glean from it, learn from it, grow from it. But there must be a time when we cease from thinking as a child and begin maturing in the faith. We never stop benefitting from what God reveals to our fellow believers, but we are also learning directly from scriptures and sharing what God is revealing to us.

No one should be an island, but neither should we be dependent upon being spoon fed the gospel. God's desire is for each of us to grow and share what we are learning from our own walk of faith.

Why God didn't give us a checklist.

Most people look for a list of rules, but Christianity is not based on just keeping a holy checklist. It's about seeking understanding. There are many things that are not sins that we deny ourselves. Not because it is a rule, but because we see a value greater than the pleasure of a distraction. And we have liberty where God has not given specific commandments. If something isn't a distraction, and is not a sin, we have liberty to enjoy many things in life.

All things are gifts from God. We don't live for pleasure, but we are given good things to enjoy. Keeping the commandments

---

[177] Ephesians 4

should be a joy. Making a list and forcing ourselves to do what we don't want to do, or struggling to not do what we shouldn't do isn't a joy. God could have given a list of things to do, and things to not do, but this misses the whole point. Consider **Romans 2:14-15**

> [14] For when Gentiles, who do not have the law, by nature do the things in the law, these, although not having the law, are a law to themselves,
>
> [15] who show the work of the law written in their hearts, their conscience also bearing witness, and between themselves *their* thoughts accusing or else excusing *them)*

As mentioned earlier, a Gentile is anyone who isn't a Jew. The Jews, or people of Israel, lived by the Law given through Moses in the Old Testament. The first Christians were Jews, for Christ came through Israel, but the gospel included Jews and Gentiles alike. A Gentile would not have known the Law of Moses since he or she would not have been raised in that environment, yet they were somehow practicing the heart of the law. Their lifestyle showed that the Spirit of God had written the law in their hearts.

Some mistakenly believe the above passage means that commandments are no longer relevant, but this scripture says so much more than this. Notice, the Gentiles did not have the law, but somehow kept the things in the law. This is the key to understanding what the Bible is teaching here. Being a law in themselves isn't saying they make their own rules; it's saying they are enforcing the law in themselves. And they are doing so without even knowing the rules of the law. It's the Holy Spirit within them guiding them into all truth.

Without a list of rules and laws, the unlearned Gentiles were keeping the commandments of God by nature. It's not by human nature, for this is in rebellion against God. It's the new spiritual nature given to those who are transformed by the Holy Spirit and have become a new creation.

As they sought God and lived out their faith, something within them created the desire to follow the things of the Spirit and please

God. Thus, they fulfilled the law without having to be instructed through the law.

Instead of being a rule follower and forcing themselves to do what they don't want to do, Gentiles followed the new nature to do the things they wanted to do, which was also where God was leading. Through following the faith shared to them through the gospel, they accomplished the same things the law followers attempted to do. Yet if you study the results, those who sought righteousness by the law failed to find it. They never pleased God and never fulfilled the law. Those who followed obedience out of a love for God found both righteousness, and fulfilled the law.

Today the same holds true in our churches. Rule followers become bound by legalism. Legalism causes people to try to justify themselves by keeping rules. Legalism binds people under a burden that cannot be carried. There is no joy, for the only focus is on dos and don'ts. Add to that, the person who has their burden lifted by Christ has an appreciation for grace and a deeper love for God. The one who attempts to lift his own burden through rules does not.

A legalist never finds freedom, for every mistake is followed by the perception of God's anger. There is no room for error, and the human weakness prevents us from living error-free. The one who walks by faith and the one who walks in legalism both attempt to please God, and both fall short. But faith calls us to reach out and allow God to pull us from the mire of failure, while the legalist feels God's rejection. His works are rejected, but he is not. But because rules are the pathway to acceptance, anything short of success creates feelings of God's perceived anger and rejection.

It's a burden too hard to carry. It's also a burden we were not intended to carry. Jesus said, "My yoke is easy and my burden is light."

Is your burden light and easy to carry? It will be if you are yoked to Christ. A yoke is something that connected two oxen so they could plow in unison. The great benefit of being yoked to Christ is that when the burden is heavy, He bears it, not us. Legalism and to-do lists put the burden solely upon our own necks. That's why joy and peace are stripped from the lives of those bound to legalistic thinking. They can boast of their success, but this is nothing compared to what Christ can do, and will do to those who depend upon His yoke.

The Journey of Faith.

Life is so much more than a ticket to heaven. Those who view Christianity as an escape from judgment or a free pass to heaven are missing the true meaning of faith. The Bible says, "Blessed is the man whose strength is in you, whose heart is on a pilgrimage."[178]

Life is a pilgrimage – a journey to a destination – our true home. Along the way, we are striving to become the man or woman that will resemble a citizen of heaven. Our purpose is to glorify God, and our mission is to conform to the image of Christ. All the rewards of heaven are promised to those who overcome their flesh in this life as they conform to the person they were created to be.

Few things give greater joy than first seeing the revelation of God through His word, and then seeing it change our lives as we put it into practice. Add to this the teaching of Jesus, "Where your treasure is, there your heart will be also.[179]" Treasure is stored by overcoming. And overcoming is a lifelong process.

Scripture teaches that a wise man will fall, but will keep getting up again. You will fail and fall flat on your face. Some look only at the failure and then grovel in defeat. Others fall, get up, set their eyes on the finish line and the hope set before them, and then begin the journey again.

God doesn't condemn us for falling. He calls us to get up again and then lifts us out of despair. We feel defeated, but the Lord is looking at the end result. The Bible says that God sees the end from the beginning. God doesn't deal with you based on who you are, but who you will be when you stand before Him completed in Christ.

No matter how many times we fall, defeat is thwarted unless we give up and abandon the journey. Consider **Psalm 37:23-24**

> [23] The steps of a *good* man are ordered by the LORD, And He delights in his way.

---

[178] Psalm 84:5
[179] Matthew 6:21

How we walk in simple faith

[24] Though he fall, he shall not be utterly cast down; For the LORD upholds *him with* His hand.

Who is the good man? This also applies to women, for it is referring to man in the general sense such as mankind. The good is not the one who is perfected. The perfect person wouldn't fall. The good man / woman is the one who is declared righteous by God.

Each step of your journey is directed. God isn't a passive observer, but He's there every step of the way, directing you, showing you the right way, and guiding you down the path He created beforehand that you should walk in it. But we can't see the path and sometimes step in the wrong direction. It could be well intentioned mistakes, or it could be sinful choices. When we step where God isn't directing, we often fall.

Verse twenty-four should give us great encouragement. When we fall, God doesn't cast us down. In a moment of defeat, we may feel like the Lord is angry and casting us off, but the truth is that we are experiencing human emotions and the condemnation of the devil. The Bible says that Satan is our accuser who condemns us night and day, but here we see that God does not. When we fall, He takes us by the hand to lift us up. His goal is for you to finish the race and obtain the promise. God is your strength, not your accuser.

Simple Faith.

Do not make faith a complicated process. It's a gift from the Lord. Faith is an act of grace – unmerited favor. God showed His favor toward us, not because we deserve it, but because we are the Lord's creation.

If you walk by faith, every promise is an open door. Your heavenly Father wants you to succeed and it's His good pleasure to give you of the kingdom. Let the Spirit speak through the scriptures and seek to understand so you can apply it to your life.

Never entertain the idea that you have learned all the Bible has to say, or that you have arrived. Each principle that you learn becomes the foundation for what God is going to teach you next.

The deeper you grow, the more you'll realize how little you know. But you will also see how much you've gained.

Consider the oak tree. It grows slow and methodical. Compare this to a pine. I live in Georgia, and the most common tree is the Georgia Pine. These trees grow very fast and are tall and thin. When wind storms or freezing weather arrives, they are the first trees to fall. They can't bear the adverse conditions and snap.

An oak tree grows little by little. You will never see a hundred year old Georgia Pine, but ancient oaks are a frequent sight. I've never seen an old oak tree bending over by the wind. They only fall when they are rotten inside, or the foundation isn't strong enough to hold on to their roots.

Our spiritual growth is much like this. Some Christians take off like a rocket, but the first sign of trouble they fall away. Others take care to grow precept upon precept. They lay the foundation of their lives in Christ and then build one brick at a time.

Jesus used the illustration of a house to explain how to build our lives on the word. The one who hears Jesus' word and applies it to their life has the sure foundation. To illustrate this, he told the story of two men building their houses. One built on the sand, and the other on a rock.

One of my first jobs out of high school was construction. I worked on a crew that laid foundations for homes. We had a contract to build a house near a river, and the entire lot was sand. It took only a few hours to dig a four-thousand square foot foundation. It was easy work, but this house was destined for foundational problems. I wouldn't be surprised if it's not standing today.

Another house was to be built in the North Georgia Mountains. This lot had about an inch of dirt before hitting solid rock. Picking eight inches down into that solid rock was a long and painful process. But this house will not quickly pass away.

Jesus' illustration is this very thing. I picture the man on sand quickly finishing. In no time he was sitting on the shade of his porch, watching the man across the street picking through hard rock. Perhaps passersby saw the man wasting his life digging through rock and suggested he find an easier way. After months of digging, he finally was able to build the rest of his house upon that sure foundation.

At first glance, his house appeared no better than the house on sand. It could have been years before either of these men had trouble. The two houses may have looked very similar and the house on sand showed no signs of problems. But then one day a fierce storm came and beat on both of these houses. As the rain pelted the foundations, the sand began to wash away and one house had a great fall. In the morning, the house on the rock stood strong, but the one on sand was wiped away.

Life in faith is very much like this. Two people may appear to be on equal footing in the church. Both attend regularly and both have all outward signs of faith. But one has labored in the word to establish his life in the rock of Christ, while the other took the easy route and did the minimum. Both are good people by all outward appearances.

In every life storms arise. When hardship hits, the foundation of a Christian is revealed. We all have to endure pain and hardships. Some will collapse under the winds of life, while the other stands firm. The person built upon a deep foundation in Christ will experience pain, but their lives will not be moved off their foundation.

This is what simple faith is all about. Living a victorious Christian life isn't complicated. Don't mistake hard work for being complicated. It takes effort to prepare, but the truth of scripture is plain to him who understands. Or as **Proverbs 8:8-9** puts it:

[8] All the words of my mouth *are* with righteousness;
Nothing crooked or perverse *is* in them.
[9] They *are* all plain to him who understands, And right to those who find knowledge.

Nothing in scripture is twisted, or the cause of confusion, but truth is plainly stated and easy to understand – if we find knowledge. And anyone who seeks will find.

My prayer for you is that you apply these things to your life and find the simple faith God has laid out for all who will seek to find it. Do these things and discover the joy of walking through this life in fellowship with your creator. May you discover what it means to be called a friend of God.

Staying close to the Truth.

Good teaching cannot replace diligent Bible study. Great teaching can't replace it either. No matter how good teaching is, it only presents a portion of the gospel. This is why good discipleship teaches people how to study on their own. A godly teacher can present insights that refresh and present a portion of scripture from a perspective we may not have considered. However, it's a mistake to think of that perspective as the only thing to glean from a passage.

Also, a lesson or sermon focuses on a scripture where the teacher is drawing a particular insight. But they can't present the context of the passage in every case. Nor is a lesson able to fully explore all the supporting passages, or the scriptures leading up to the passage being focused upon.

The point we must not miss is that the only way for you to fully understand scripture is to study to show yourself approved, as the Bible commands. Then when you hear a message, you'll see how it fits into the context of the whole Bible and not misunderstand or draw a false conclusion of a scripture.

Errors in doctrine arise when the Christian focuses on a man's teaching. Even if the person has solid doctrine, you are still only getting part of the picture. Groups have a tendency to focus on the man. In time, it becomes a movement. Later still, the movement drifts into error. This can only be avoided by consistently turning our focus back to the scriptures. Glean from good teachers, but don't make a teacher the focus.

Let me give an illustration from my military days. Every soldier is required to qualify with their rifle on the firing range. The target can be up to six-hundred meters away. Before stepping onto the range, we first adjusted our gun sights. A paper target with a grid was placed twenty-five meters away. We'd fire at the target, and depending on where the holes were, we'd adjust our sights up and down, or left and right. We'd keep firing and adjusting until we were hitting dead center. Then we could have confidence that our aim was correct when qualifying on the firing range.

This is much like what the scriptures do in our Christian walk and biblical understanding. The Bible instructs, reproves, corrects, and gives doctrine. When my assumptions or a message I've heard misses the mark, the scriptures correct the error and places my sights back on the center of Christ.

Problems occur when we adjust our sights through a teacher instead of the Bible. Even solid Bible teachers can have misconceptions, or slightly miss the intent of scripture. This does not make them a heretic, but it can affect how we understand. When we use a man as our source of course correction, we miss where he misses and then some. Since we only see the sermons or writings, we cannot see the understanding behind the teaching. So now we only have a limited view of the teacher's understanding, and an even more limited view of scripture.

Later, another teacher will glean from those who he respects, and may add other misconceptions. This is natural since he is filling in the gaps with his own ideas and philosophies, and not the word. Those who depend on this teacher are now two steps removed from the scripture. Even though they are adjusting their sights to the target, it's the wrong target. Each generation becomes farther removed from the standard God has given.

This is why groups drift off course over time, and this is why the Bible instructs us to work out our own salvation. That is work out not work for. We have already been given salvation, and we are to work it out with fear and trembling. This is critical and must be taken seriously, for it affects our future in eternity. We are also commanded to diligently study and show ourselves approved, not depend on man to teach us, and to commit ourselves wholly to the teachings of scripture.

You can know the truth. If you have the Spirit of Christ, you have the promise that the Holy Spirit will guide you into all truth.

But that only happens when we obey the instruction to apply our hearts to the word.

The Open Door is Before You.

The love of God is an open door. Jesus opened the gate that gave us direct access to our Heavenly Father. This is God's will for your life – to know Him and to experience the love of God. Don't lose sight of this one thing, "For God so loved the world that He gave." God doesn't love you because you have been made righteous in Christ. God loved each of us while we were enemies of the cross. As the Bible says, we love God because He first loved us.[180]

God loved you first, and as the Bible also says, it's the goodness of God that leads you to repentance[181]. The more you realize God's great love, the more your heart will be touched by that love. On the cross, Jesus cried out, "It is finished," indicating our debt had been paid and the work of redemption had been complete. At that moment, the veil of the temple was torn from the top down to the bottom.[182]

The veil in the temple kept everyone out of the holiest place of God. It was called the Holy of Holies. Only the high priest could enter in that place once a year. To do so, he had to go through a strict cleansing ritual, and then he would enter with the blood of the sacrifice and sprinkle it on the Mercy Seat on behalf of the people.

When Christ paid the price, sin was removed, thus opening the holiest place to all who enter by Christ. Rather than it being man reaching up to God, God tore the veil from the top toward the bottom, indicating He was reaching down to man. God removed the veil and now each of us has the right and the privilege to walk confidently to the throne of God.

No longer are we outsiders looking in and trying to find out something about God, but we are now adopted as children and joint heirs with Christ. We belong before the throne, just as the children of any king.

---

[180] 1 John 4:19

[181] Romans 2:4

[182] Matthew 27:51

How we walk in simple faith

Love from God came first through the faith God gave to you so you can believe. Now you must abide in that love so you can fully experience the joy of fellowship with the God who created you.

Through faith and obedience we keep ourselves in the love of God by keeping His word by faith. God's love is unchanging, but we are not.

If we aren't experiencing the love of God, it is we who moved. Jesus explained to His disciples how to experience the love of God. He said, "Just as I have kept my Father's commandments and abide in His love, if you keep My commandments you will abide in My love."

The commandments and teachings of scripture are designed to draw us closer to the Lord's presence so we can experience His love fully. Let's conclude with **John 14:23-24**

[23] Jesus answered and said to him, "If anyone loves Me, he will keep My word; and My Father will love him, and We will come to him and make Our home with him.

[24] "He who does not love Me does not keep My words; and the word which you hear is not Mine but the Father's who sent Me.

Notice that this is a relationship founded upon love. The phrase, 'make our home' literally means, 'to cause to abide'. The principle is that when we do the things that conform to God's character (keeping the commands), God creates an abiding relationship with us. We are not merely having a casual relationship or visiting Him, we are abiding, or remaining, with Him. The Lord makes His home with us.

It's God's desire to have a relationship so deep, that He abides within us and pours out His love into every area of our life. In John 16, Jesus foretold of the result of His crucifixion by saying that we won't have to ask Him to intercede to the Father for us, "For the Father Himself loves you because you have loved Me."

Through that loving relationship, each one of us can experience the fullness of joy and walk with a deep intimacy with our God.

How we walk in simple faith   289

Don't allow yourself to be swept away by complicated terms, teachings, or formulas. As Paul said, "I fear that your minds may become corrupted from the simplicity that is in Christ." Let the scriptures speak to you and discover the plainly stated truth. None of us need a spiritual guide, secret knowledge, or to learn a complicated formula. The words of God are plain to those who understand and to those who discover knowledge of the word.[183]

If something presented as truth doesn't pass the simplicity test, we should be very wary of it. When God enlightens our understanding, we see that the thing that once seemed hidden is actually in plain sight. Rather than discovering a hidden truth, we have had our eyes opened to the plain truth.

This simple truth guides you into a faithful relationship with your Creator as you walk in fellowship through this life.
Walk in simple faith.

---

[183] Proverbs 8:9

If you found this book to be helpful, please rate it on Amazon at http://www.amazon.com/Simple-Faith-experience-intimacy-ebook/dp/B005HXRTBS/

The ebook version of Simple Faith is free on the Exchanged Life website at http://www.exchangedlife.com. You can support Exchanged Life books by purchasing the book in ebook or printed version. If you are an Amazon Prime member, you can offer your support by borrowing the book as well.

You may also enjoy I Called Him Dancer, also available in ebook or printed versions.

I Called Him Dancer is about a boy growing up in a broken home. His fragile world is shattered when his mother leaves him with a relative and walks out of his life. After seeing a man dancing with grace and acrobatics, he decides to imitate the man and discovers a natural talent for dance. His life's passion becomes dance and eventually the young man achieves his dream of Broadway. A drug addiction and his inner demons destroy his life and he eventually becomes homeless. His previous dance partner refuses to let go and reaches out to him, but he rejects her. Bitter at God and the world, the dancer embraces a solitary life on the streets. Though he lashes out at God, the Lord has other plans for the fallen dancer.

*** See what readers are saying ***

This book is a page turner from cover to cover, [The author] makes you feel like you actually know the characters in his book. - B. Tillman, OR.

Almost too good to put into words. ...you'll find yourself saying, "Just one more chapter". K. McNabney, IL

This book is a must read. Through this book the

reader will learn about true love and the power it holds. T. Franklin, TX

I loved this book from cover to cover, the author makes you feel like you actually know the characters in his book. T. Webster

Acknowledgments

It is said that five people truly make an impact on the average Christian's faith. I've often thought about this, and have concluded more than five deserve a little acknowledgment.

My parents, Linda and George Snipes. I'm grateful I was raised in a Christian home. Though I had a time of straying, the church life I experienced played a role in my life and prevented me from straying far from my faith.

James Welch, the Sunday school teacher that taught me in my youth. His love and passion for the scriptures has impacted my life and I still find myself drawing from those lessons I learned.

Dave Stout. He was the pastor who performed my wedding ceremony and impacted my early adulthood. His genuine faith and caring personality touched my life during a vulnerable time. The leadership he showed and the church life he inspired is something I still draw from today.

Pastor Dewey Davidson. When God began calling me to the ministry, Dewey reached out to me and brought me into fellowship with other future ministry leaders. It was under Dewey's leadership that I began preaching and serving in ministry.

My grandparents, Mildred and Jack Morrow. My grandfather committed himself to the promise of Psalm 37:25 and served God with only the hope that his grandchildren would not be in need. Also, it was my grandmother who led me to Christ.

Hugh and Deb Wilson. Their ministry to soldiers touched my life deeply. The times we worshipped and broke bread together were some of the fondest memories in my Christian life.

Steve Brown. When God first called me out of one of the darkest times of my life, your radio show became a catalyst that set my future ministry in motion. It was you who gave me the first opportunity to tell my story. We talked live on the air, and that was a big step for me. It also inspired me to write out my experiences, which later led to a writing ministry. Thank you for your faithfulness and encouragement over the years.

Finally, an anonymous manager whose determination to harm me played a powerful role in my life. This person's intention to cause me pain became one of the greatest lessons in the Christian life I've ever experienced. Though the intent was harm, it taught me more about forgiveness and trusting the Lord than any biblical training could have ever done.

To my wife Jennie and my children, Emily, Lucy, Natalie, Sophia, and Abigail. You guys are the inspiration of my life.